The Transatlantic Smiths

The Transatlantic Smiths

by Robert Allerton Parker

Random House

New York

Acknowledgments

The author takes this opportunity to thank the following, who are, unless otherwise indicated, the copyright owners, for permission to make brief direct quotations in the course of this work:

D. Appleton-Century-Crofts, Inc. *Portrait of Edith Wharton.* By Percy Lubbock. Copyright, 1947.

Crown Publishers, Inc. *Journey into the Self, Being the Letters, Papers & Journals of Leo Stein.* Edited by Edmund Fuller. Copyright, 1950, by the Estate of Leo D. Stein.

Doubleday & Company, Inc. *With Walt Whitman in Camden.* Vols. 1 and 2. By Horace Traubel. Copyright, 1903, 1906.

Harcourt, Brace and Company. *Philadelphia Quaker: The Letters of Hannah Whitall Smith.* Edited by her son Logan Pearsall Smith. With a Biographical Preface by Robert Gathorne-Hardy. Copyright, 1950. *The Life of John Maynard Keynes.* By R. F. Harrod. Copyright, 1951. *Intimate Memories.* Vol. 2: *European Experiences.* By Mabel Dodge Luhan. Copyright, 1935. *A Victorian in the Modern World.* By Hutchins Hapgood. Copyright, 1939. *A Writer's Diary.* By Virginia Woolf. Copyright, 1953, 1954, by Leonard Woolf.

Harvard University Press. *The Thought and Character of William James* (shorter version). By Ralph Barton Perry. Copyright, 1937.

Longmans, Green and Company. *Our Partnership*. By Beatrice Webb. Copyright, 1948. *Beatrice Webb's Diaries*. Copyright, 1952.

The Macmillan Company. *Recollections of Logan Pearsall Smith*. By Robert Gathorne-Hardy. Copyright, 1950.

W. W. Norton & Company, Inc. *The Amberley Papers: The Letters and Diaries of Bertrand Russell's Parents*. 2 vols. Edited by Bertrand and Patricia Russell. Copyright, 1937.

The Pantheon Press. *Sketch for a Self-Portrait*. By Bernard Berenson. Copyright, 1949.

Princeton University Press. *Florentine Art Under Fire*. By Frederic Hartt. Copyright, 1949.

The Saturday Review. Review of Logan Pearsall Smith's *All Trivia*. By Don Marquis. Copyright, 1934.

Charles Scribner's Sons. *Persons and Places*. Vol. 2: *The Middle Span*. Vol. 3: *My Host the World*. By George Santayana. Copyright, 1945. *The Letters of George Santayana*. Edited, with an Introduction and Commentary, by Daniel Cory. Copyright, 1955.

Simon and Schuster, Inc. *Rumor and Reflection*. By Bernard Berenson. Copyright, 1955. *Portraits from Memory and Other Essays*. By Bertrand Russell. Copyright, 1951, 1952, 1953, 1956. *Bertrand Russell: The Passionate Skeptic*. By Alan Wood. Copyright, 1958.

Weidenfeld & Nicolson, Ltd., London, England. *Ideas and Places*. By Cyril Connolly. Copyright, 1953.

The Yale University Press. *A Quaker Childhood*. By Helen Thomas Flexner. Copyright, 1940.

Charles H. Craig, for the Presbyterian and Reformed Publishing Company. *Studies in Perfectionism*. 2 vols. By Benjamin Breckinridge Warfield. Copyright, 1931.

Philip C. Duschnes. *The Colophon:* New Series, No. 2. Copyright, 1937.

Charles H. Hapgood. *A Victorian in the Modern World.* Copyright, 1939.

Sir John Rothenstein and the executors of the estate of Sir William Rothenstein. *Men and Memories: Recollections of William Rothenstein.* 3 vols. Copyright, 1931, 1939.

John Russell. *Unforgotten Years.* By Logan Pearsall Smith. Copyright, 1939. *A Portrait of Logan Pearsall Smith, Drawn from His Letters and Diaries.* Copyright, 1951.

Marjorie Wells and the executors of the estate of H. G. Wells. *The New Machiavelli.* Copyright, 1911.

Contents

Introduction

This is the case history of a family of American Quakers who migrated to Europe. It is an attempt to weave isolated strands and fragmentary threads into a coherent and consecutive pattern. The temptation has been strong at times to give this book the subtitle "a family portrait." But without sacrifice of interest, it is impossible to exclude from this portrait in prose the friends and associates of this unpredictable family—such celebrities as Walt Whitman, Henry and William James; the Fabians when they were young: Bernard Shaw, Graham Wallas, Beatrice and Sidney Webb; the detached observer George Santayana, a sort of Greek chorus of the whole expatriate tragicomedy; Geoffrey Scott and John Maynard Keynes. This history of the Smiths begins roughly with the marriage of Hannah Whitall to Robert Pearsall Smith on June 25, 1851, and ends almost precisely a century later with the death of their youngest daughter, Alys, the last survivor of the transatlantic pilgrimage.

The name of Smith is ubiquitous and noncommittal; not

so the branch we are dealing with in this book. They are the birthright Quakers, Robert Pearsall Smith and his wife, Hannah Whitall Smith, of Millville and Haddonfield, New Jersey, and Philadelphia—later of Friday's Hill, Fernhurst, Sussex—and the three of their children who survived them: Mary, who became the wife of Benjamin Francis Conn Costelloe, and later, in 1900, the wife of Bernard Berenson; Alys, her younger sister, who became the first wife of Bertrand Russell; and their brother Logan, celebrated as the author of *Trivia,* who became an arbiter of English style and usage. Mary's two daughters by her first husband were Rachel Conn Costelloe, who became the wife of Oliver Strachey, elder brother of Lytton Strachey; and Karin, who married Adrian Stephen, younger brother of Virginia Woolf.

During the nineteenth century, American exiles in Europe represented a countermovement to the general westward trend. Students of American culture have too long ignored the study as a group of this small but influential elite which settled permanently in Europe—individuals such as Henry James, John Singer Sargent, James A. McNeill Whistler; lesser writers like Henry Harland, Harold Frederic, Stephen Crane; and in our own day such poets as Ezra Pound and T. S. Eliot. It is a temptation to characterize the Smiths and their children as typical expatriates; but the truth is that, like the Jameses, this Philadelphia family was typical only of itself. Put these Smiths into a novel of the type made famous by their friend Henry James, in his last period, and the plot and action would fail to carry conviction or credibility. Their life story abounds in too many irrational coincidences, too many real-life celebrities, too many mysterious silences, too many inexplicable motives, too many ironies accented by the passage of time.

In one respect, however, the Smiths were comparable to other expatriates. They were assured of security and privilege and position by a steady income derived from a thriving American industry. In his *Ambassadors* Henry James never mentions the product produced in the Newsome factories in Woollet, Mass. Seemingly it was against the code of expatriate etiquette to mention the source of one's income. The Smiths were supported by glass—glass bottles and containers and other commercial necessities manufactured in the Whitall-Tatum works. Behind all their European adventures stood the patriarchal figure of Hannah Smith's father, John Mickle Whitall, who established the family business of the Whitall-Tatum Company in southern New Jersey. Whitall-Tatum became the beneficent *deus ex machina* of this real-life drama. Whitall-Tatum is of the *dramatis personae* (a dynamic, organic, symbiotic entity in itself), growing ever more generous, with the technological advances in the emergent industry of glassmaking. (This family business was eventually merged, in the mid-thirties, with the Armstrong Cork Company.)

But Robert Pearsall Smith, who married Hannah Whitall in June 1851, was evidently not (in the jargon of our day) a good "company" man. Having been "caught up into paradise and heard unspeakable words which it is unlawful to utter," he deserted the glass works in sandy Millville, took up evangelism and revivalism, and preached the "Higher Life" and "divine guidance." He crossed the Atlantic to save souls in Britain and on the Continent. In this field he was a precursor of his fellow Pennsylvanian Dr. Frank Buchman—for the earlier Pearsall Smith was also a phenomenal success at Oxford, at Brighton, and in the great country houses of the British aristocracy. Like our own contemporary, Dr. Billy Graham, Pearsall Smith tasted triumph in Germany although he could not speak a word of the language. Any novelist, no matter how skilled, who would transport his hero, the superintendent of a glass factory in Millville, New Jersey, to become the adored hero of a religious house party at Broadlands, the stately country seat of the great Prime Minister Lord Palmerston, might be accused of fantastic exaggeration—but only by critics unfamiliar with the evangelical zeal of the Victorian seventies. Equally incredible is Pearsall Smith's fall, as sudden as it was unexpected, brought on by spiritual *hubris*. And hardly more believable seems the hospitality of the elder Smiths, who entertained at their country house, Friday's Hill, such firebrands as Bernard Shaw, Graham Wallas, Beatrice and Sidney Webb, Israel Zangwill, George Santayana, William James and their own son-in-law-to-be, Bernard Berenson. This "conversation piece" brings to mind the final scene in Max Beerbohm's *Savonarola Brown*, in which all the celebrities of Renaissance Florence pop out upon the stage.

Mary Smith pursued life in sharp counterpoint to the spiritual values of her mother and father. At eighteen, Mary discovered Walt Whitman, she became his "bright particular star," and later publicized him in London. She was closely associated with the Fabians in the London of the eighties and nineties. Though a great success in social and literary circles, she abandoned this life to begin a third, as student and wife of Bernard Berenson, as mistress and hostess of I Tatti, that place of pilgrimage and study for art experts and museum curators, connoisseurs and aesthetes. For there her husband, in this vatican of the fine arts, exerted a world-wide influence. But the good fairy who showered her with extraordinary gifts at her birth in obscure Millville exacted a stiff penalty from Mary Berenson in her last days, when I Tatti was surrounded by the retreating Nazis.

Logan Pearsall Smith lived to become the most famous of all these Quaker Smiths, with a fame belatedly won by the carefully polished prose of his aphoristic *Trivia*. Most famous as well as the best documented: we have his own *Unforgotten Years*, his letters edited by John Russell, *Recollections of Logan Pearsall Smith* by his secretary and companion, Robert Gathorne-Hardy, and many of his letters and papers which are preserved in the Library of Congress. His fame may be due in large part to the excessive and inordinate value attached to the purely literary by an age which condemned the more naïve gullibility of its Victorian ancestor. Logan's life ended in a tragic breakdown, of which the chief victim was his gentle sister and companion, Alys Russell.

To the best of my knowledge, this volume is the first attempt to weave the complete history of the Smith family in a consecutive and integrated fashion. However, this survey is neither exhaustive nor without the possibility of inaccuracies. I have not succeeded, for instance, in tracing letters written from London by Mary Costelloe to Walt Whitman—if they still survive. Evidence concerning Robert Pearsall Smith's evangelical efforts, and the type of Perfectionism which brought him fame, is buried in theological archives both here and in Germany; much of it impossible to unearth. Some of the story is recounted from the subjects' own points of view and embodies dubious value judgments and assumptions.

"Anthropology should begin at home," Bernard Berenson wrote in exile. "I could wish that our anthropologists grew serious and . . . would devote laborious years to the study of all that is naïvely taken for granted, and no less tenaciously than irrationally held, by the average matron, the

average businessman, the average cleric . . . in our own so-
cieties, high and low, low and high." Even the Berenson
scale of values may be so examined.

Although we are here dealing with evangelism, aestheticism and literary taste, my predominant interest in this study
of several generations of one expatriate family has been, in
Mr. Berenson's sense, anthropological and sociological. Although its data is removed in time, its significance for our
own day may become apparent. If there is criticism for lack
of sympathy for the cast of expatriates, it may be well to recall
Santayana's admonition to Logan Pearsall Smith: "You may
say that Henry James has done it once for all; but he, you,
all Americans in print, are too gentle, too affectionate, too
fulsome. The reality requires a satirist, merciless but
just. . . ."

A glance at the Bibliography will indicate to the reader
how voluminous and seemingly scattered have been the
sources of this "family portrait." Much that has found its
way into print consists of repetitious paraphrase of standardized errors and inaccuracies. The author is therefore the
more grateful to those who have contributed personal recollections of various members of the Smith family. While a
complete list cannot be given here, I am especially grateful
for contributions from Richard Aldington, Anne Fremantle,
Julie Medlock and Steffi Kiesler, and for a letter from Igor
Markevitch with its touching tribute to Mrs. Berenson. Richard Whitall, a kinsman, has described the reaction of American relatives to the activities of their kinsfolk in England and
on the Continent. Daniel Rhoads, assistant to the president of
the Armstrong Cork Company, has allowed me to read an
unpublished summary of the early years of the Whitall-

Tatum Company in Millville—a summary which clears up many of the factual mistakes which have been repeated even by those whom one would expect to be better informed. I must acknowledge a special debt to Mr. George V. Speaight, who discovered in the British Museum an otherwise inaccessible copy of the *Pall Mall Gazette,* containing Mary Smith Costelloe's tribute to Walt Whitman, and also a list of her first husband's publications. Nor should I forget a dinner conversation with Lord Russell, who answered without embarrassment and with characteristic frankness my impertinent questions concerning his first wife and his mother-in-law.

Without the resources of the New York Public Library, and those of the Library of Congress, this book could never have been completed. I am also indebted to Vieva Dawley Smith for her patient editorial and secretarial aid, extending over a period of years.

Finally, my debt is great to my wife, Jessica Daves Parker, who has brought professional insight to the task of final revision and condensation of a manuscript which tended to burst the bounds of a single volume.

ROBERT ALLERTON PARKER

New York, October 1958

The Transatlantic Smiths

Anthropology should begin at home.

—Bernard Berenson

*Cælum non animum mutant
qui trans mare currunt.*

—Horace

Chapter 1 · Whitall-Tatum

Hannah Whitall was born on February 7,
1832, the first child of John Mickle Whitall. Hannah's father
was thirty-two years old when she was born, and he already
had behind him a venturesome career at sea. When
John was fourteen years old, his Quaker father was in a bad
way financially, and his three sons were compelled to leave
school to help on the Whitall farm, near Woodbury, in
southern New Jersey. John Whitall rebelled against this
drudgery and, when he was sixteen, went up to Philadelphia
and signed on as an apprentice aboard the vessel *William
Savory*. Between the ages of sixteen and twenty-four, the
young seaman completed eleven voyages to England, India
and China. At twenty he attained the status of second mate,
and three years later he signed on as a chief mate. At the age
of twenty-four he became the captain of the *New Jersey*,
then reputed to be the largest sailing vessel ever to have left
the port of Philadelphia. As a birthright member of the Society
of Friends, John forbade his officers and crew the use of
profane language.

After his marriage to docile, meek Mary Tatum, John gave
up the hardships of a seafaring life and entered the cotton
business in Philadelphia. He was shrewd and he was rigidly
self-disciplined, but he somehow failed to make a success of

3

the cotton venture, and was drawn into the young glass industry by a kinsman named Scattergood.

John Whitall's interest in the glass plant at Glasstown, near Woodbury, was first stirred in 1836, and in 1838 he became controlling director. Later, young Edward Tatum became a member of the firm, and by 1858, when the company name was changed to Whitall-Tatum, there was another plant at nearby Millville, an office and store in Philadelphia, and a warehouse in New York. From the beginning, John Whitall aimed at the creation of a glass dynasty, and for the next hundred years, the development of Whitall-Tatum into a vast industry engaged the energies and acumen of four generations of Whitalls and three generations of Tatums.

Hannah Whitall, her little brother James, and her three sisters were brought up in the strict discipline of the Society of Friends. They were taught from infancy to seek and take the advice of godly parents, for any disobedience to mother or father was a breach of the moral law, and offensive in the Divine sight; they were not expected to answer frowardly or crossly. All the little Whitalls were disciplined in industrious habits; they must never indulge in vain or expensive fashions, never associate with corrupt or frivolous persons or waste precious time in idle conversation or harmful diversion. They were taught that it was wicked to enter picture galleries or museums, or indeed even to look at a statue.

Not until she was almost seventeen did Hannah defy these teachings of the Society of Friends, and venture, with beating heart, upon a perilously wicked excursion into the Academy of Fine Arts in Philadelphia. There, suddenly, she found herself gazing upon a statue of Hero and Leander. Long afterward, she remembered blushing furiously at the nudity of Leander. "I suppose now I'll go straight to Hell, but I cannot help it," she whispered to herself. "If I must go to Hell, I must! But I *will* look at this statue!" She felt herself to be a confirmed sinner, and was surprised to find herself unharmed by the swift judgment of an offended Creator. But despite this early rebellion against Quaker tenets, Hannah was to maintain throughout her long life a prejudice against the fine arts.

From her little-girl days, Hannah dreamed that someday she would become a preacher. She imagined herself, in scoop bonnet and kerchief, standing before the crowded benches in the Friends' Meeting, delivering sermons with an eloquence surpassing that of "all orators since the world began." Sometimes, instead of a preacher, she saw herself as an inventor of machines more miraculous than any ever before invented. But more often she pictured herself as the most superb singer the world had ever heard. Hannah could never understand why she dreamed of becoming a prima donna, since worldly music was forbidden among the Quakers, and especially since she had never heard such music in public or in private. But there beside her mother on the bench, the little girl sat through many almost interminable meetings, outwardly prim and meek, but inwardly swelling and bursting with the imagined glory of a future triumph on the stage —a realm condemned by everyone she knew.

Not only was secular music taboo. Quakers condemned all interest in worldly literature. Romantic poetry and fiction, and indeed art in all its various sensual or sensuous manifestations, were all taboo. Hannah's mother was especially strict about fiction; the Whitall children were forbidden to read even the most innocuous Sunday school stories. The very word "novel" was wicked. But during one "First Day," Hannah surreptitiously borrowed a book from one of her playmates and, providing herself with a plate of apples and some gingerbread, stretched herself on her bed to read and eat at her leisure. The naughty book was an innocuous novel called *The Earl's Daughter,* by Grace Aguilar. This first indulgence in Sunday sin "seemed to give me the nearest approach to perfect bliss I had ever before experienced," Hannah remembered.

At eighteen, Hannah was courted in the decorous Quaker manner by a number of swains. Most persistent was a young man named Robert Pearsall Smith, who worked for the Whitall-Tatum office. Some five years Hannah's senior, with good looks and engaging traits, Robert was demonstrating ability as a salesman. He was already being sent farther and farther afield, even to South America, selling Whitall-Tatum's bottles and vials to apothecaries and patent-medicine manufacturers.

Robert came from a rather more distinguished intellectual and literary background than Hannah. His mother was a member of the Pearsall family, which had helped to carry Quaker principles to Long Island and was prominent in the village of Flushing. Most celebrated among his father's ancestors was James Logan, from County Armagh, Ireland, who came to Pennsylvania in 1699 as William Penn's secretary. Chief Justice of the Supreme Court of Pennsylvania from 1731 to 1739, James Logan also served as acting governor of the colony after the death of Governor Gordon in 1736. In 1726, in the northern outskirts of Philadelphia, he built the great mansion Stenton, whose sedate simplicity, absence of ornament, and honest, straightforward design reflected his staunch Quakerism. James Logan bequeathed some two thousand books to the city of Philadelphia, volumes now treasured as the Loganian Library.

The Smiths, too, were birthright Friends—born into the faith. John Jay Smith, Robert's father, was active in editing, publishing and printing, and for many years was librarian to the Library Company, Philadelphia's public library. He was succeeded as librarian by one of Robert's three brothers, Lloyd Pearsall Smith, who later became the first editor of *Lippincott's Magazine*. Robert's three sisters all married into the aristocracy of orthodox Quakerdom.

In June 1851, Hannah and Robert were married in the simple Quaker ceremony at the Philadelphia Meeting. She was not yet twenty and he was a few months more than twenty-four. From the time of his marriage to John Whitall's eldest daughter, young Smith began to grow up with the family business, for it was old John Whitall's basic conviction that the fortunes of the family and the glass works should be closely woven together. For thirteen years Hannah and Robert lived pleasantly in aristocratic Germantown, which, soon after their marriage, was absorbed by the spreading metropolis of Philadelphia, but remained the stronghold of the Society of Friends. Summers were spent mainly at the Cedars, John Whitall's country place across the river at Haddonfield, New Jersey, which was the gathering place for all the Whitall children and grandchildren.

Robert continued as a successful traveling salesman for the family glass works, until in 1865 he was promoted to resident manager of the South Millville plant, which Whitall-Tatum had acquired a few years before. Neither Robert nor Hannah received the news of this promotion with unmixed pleasure. Their son needed proper schooling, and Millville, where they were to live, was a primitive village with none of the educational possibilities of Germantown. But in the discipline of the Friends, even adults accepted parental decisions without protest.

When the Smiths established their household in Millville,

they had had three children, but their first daughter, Nelly, had not survived her fifth year. Their first son, born in 1854, was Franklin Whitall. On February 14, 1864, a doubly precious daughter, Mary, had arrived to take the place of the little lost Nelly.

On October 25, 1865, another son was born to the Smiths and was named Logan in honor of that most distinguished ancestor of his father, James Logan. While little Mary was growing exactly as Hannah wished, Logan seemed from the beginning a problem child. Before he was six months old, his perplexed mother wrote in a letter: "I whipped him until he was actually black and blue, until I really could not whip him any more, and he never gave up one single inch. However, I hope it was a lesson to him. He is going to be another 'Gorilla' over again for screaming." Before her son was three, Hannah considered him the most perverse little mortal she had ever encountered. Even at that age, Logan seemed to be composed of two individuals, one bent on spiting the other to the utmost of his capacity. Yet even then his response to beautiful things was strikingly evident; nothing escaped the notice of this unusual child: he treasured threads and shreds of bright-colored rags; green leaves and bright flowers delighted him, and he responded with cries of joy to the clouds drenched in sunset light.

Logan continued to be his mother's greatest puzzle. "He certainly was born to be an only child," Hannah wrote, ". . . he is always happiest when he is playing alone, and if he can have undisputed sway in the nursery . . . he is as good as a boy can be. I find I can generally *kiss* him out of his naughty spells, sooner than I can end them in any other way, and I am convinced that there is a secret chord in his nature, that some day will send out very sweet music."

Another daughter, named Alys, was born in 1867; and still

another, Rachel Pearsall, the following year. In November 1868, when her eldest son was fourteen, Hannah Smith wrote happily of the younger children: "I am quite amused as I walk through the suite of rooms in which are deposited the various babies—in the first one Mary and Logan—in the next little Miss Alys, who requires a room all to herself, and in the last Madame Rachel—four little beds—just think of it!"

Hannah felt herself no ordinary Quaker housewife. God had endowed her, she was sure, with the vocation of a pioneer; she could not and did not expect much understanding or sympathy in this role. Breaking through imaginary hedges, fences and stone walls could never be a pleasant path, nor win the approbation of community opinion. At thirty-six, Hannah was quite prepared to be a martyr. She was proud that she had been the first woman in Millville to use a sewing machine—an invention denounced in those days as a new-fangled contraption of the devil. But rather than offend Millville neighbors Hannah hid her sewing machine in the attic, and kept its presence a secret. So earlier had the steam cars been denounced, and Hannah remarked that in her grandmother's day suspenders to hold up men's trousers had likewise been considered a device of the devil.

Robert Smith found it more difficult to adjust himself to life in Millville than Hannah did. Isolated in the sandy flatness of Cumberland County, the village had little stimulation to offer this charming and gregarious young husband. The meager population was made up mostly of glass blowers and their families, who formed a special caste of their own. Settled in that section of New Jersey before the Revolution, they had followed from father to son their strange and unchanging vocation. Robert possessed the secret of winning friends in all classes, without stepping beyond the pale of propriety, but as his adoring wife soon discovered, he was a

man of ups and downs. His outbursts of enthusiasm were
often followed by a sharp descent into the pit of unexplained
depression. In Millville he became most successful in fulfill-
ing the paternalistic social services of the company—for, as
John Whitall used to repeat, foreshadowing the modern business cliché, Whitall-Tatum was just one big family.

In the glass plant, boys came to work at the furnaces at
the age of ten; as soon as they had demonstrated ability, they
were advanced to oversee the ware in the tempering ovens, or
to the foot bench to gather molten glass for blowing. At the
age of sixteen these lads became eligible for apprenticeship,
a five-year term at half-pay. Many of them remained with
the company all their lives. Robert Smith was not confronted
with labor troubles nor with strikes, for in those mid-sixties
there were no labor problems as they are today understood;
there were no unions, no talk against child labor, no retire-
ment fund—only the paternalism of the Quaker managers.

There was hardly a trace of machinery in the making of
glass, and the work was slow and hazardous. At first each
worker toiled alone, completing all his tasks at the furnace,
both blowing and finishing. Then, in 1865, the "glory hole"
was introduced and the blowers worked in teams of three
men, two to blow and one to finish. The "glory hole" was a
furnace constructed in the form of a horseshoe and contained
seven open pots around the curved front and down either
flat side. Oak and pine wood, with rosin and forced draft,
were used to obtain the intense heat to fuse the batch.

Glass workers were a breed apart. The veteran blowers,
especially, possessed secret traditions and a hidden lore of
their own, transmitted by word of mouth from one generation to the next. They were vastly proud of their craft, with
a tendency to breathe their own life into their tools. All the
furnaces at Millville had, for one reason or another, been

given names. One was Hen's Nest; another was Owl's Nest. There was York House, Pigeon's Nest, and Union House.

The glassware was first packed in barrels and boxes, protected by hay or straw; all the shipping was done by water, from the company's dock on the Maurice River. Whitall-Tatum's "fleet" consisted of two sloops, two schooners and a steamboat. When the railroad came to Millville (only two years before the advent of the Smiths) some of the merchandise was trucked to the depot by teams of horses.

A peculiar institution was the company store, where the employees bought all their supplies. "Everyone was paid off here, getting their wages in money if they asked for it," says a history of the early days of Millville. "Every two weeks they ordered the money they wanted. At the end of the year a settlement was made and the rest of their money given to them. The stores were finally closed in 1916, when it was no longer possible to deduct a man's store bill from his wages."

As manager of the Millville plant, Robert Smith lasted only four years, but it was not so much that he lacked the executive ability to co-ordinate the multifarious activities, as that he lost interest in them. His resignation came as the result of a surprising religious experience—the vocation or "call" which converted him into a lay preacher. Released from the restraints of their Quaker upbringing, the Smiths were exposed in Millville to an evangelical wildfire that ran through the towns and villages of southern New Jersey. It was a period and a region subject to the excesses of camp meetings, which aimed to edify and succeeded at least in exciting the population. The Whitall-Tatum blowers exhibited a *mystique* of their own and were intensely preoccupied with salvation. The Methodists had a firm hold upon them.

In 1866, as tutor to their growing son, Frank, the Smiths

engaged a young theological student, and through him they soon found themselves convinced adherents of the Wesleyan doctrine of sanctification by faith.

Some have questioned the influence of Methodist revivalism upon members of the Society of Friends, but Robert and Hannah Smith were not alone in their interest. It has been pointed out by a scrupulous historian of the Society that as early as 1756, Quakerism retreated into a period of quietism, which projected all responsibility onto God, relieving the worshiper of all conscious effort in the world. "Thrashing meetings" fell into disuse, Kenneth Ives writes. Many active, outgoing members left the Society for more aggressive movements—especially Methodism with its red-hot revivalism. Quietism could not satisfy the youthful rebels of the new century; people continued to abandon Quaker quietism for the more exciting, dramatic showmanship of the Methodists. This drew off many of the younger generation from the austere discipline of the Society of Friends.

Perhaps it was loneliness as well as their constant interest in religion that led Hannah and Robert to involve themselves with the Methodist glass blowers. At any rate, many of the senior workers were often invited into the Smith home for religious discussion. As their soggy boots tramped solemnly across her new figured Brussels carpet, Hannah had a moment or two of misgiving, but she welcomed their fervor.

The group in the Smiths' front parlor often discussed "sanctification"—the possibility of complete and permanent salvation from sin—the wiles of Satan in seducing the converted; the dangers of backsliding. In these talks Robert seemed, at moments, to be almost in a trance. A look of ineffable bliss would spread over his handsome, ruddy features as he cried out, "Jesus saves us—*now!*" After the glass blowers and other guests went, Hannah was confronted with the delicate task of bringing her husband down to earth again. Sometimes this excitement, this God-intoxication, lasted for days. The Millville gossips whispered that Robert Smith was "off." They could not understand his divine madness, a madness that would eventually transport him and all his family overseas, to triumphant acclaim from the high and mighty; a madness that would eventually open the door to Hannah's career as a religious writer and spiritual guide.

During 1867, Robert was returning home from a trip one day when he experienced a sudden illumination. "I had been a religious man for ten long and toilsome years, when in the railway carriage, I for the first time saw in the Scripture what the blood of Christ had done for me." He hurried home from the railroad station to break the glad tidings to his wife, and she too, that very day, she assured him, found eternal life in believing.

After that, informal prayer and discussion meetings in the Smiths' home were held more and more often. The master glass blowers and other workmen were invited to testify to their inner experiences of the divine afflatus. Out of these meetings emerged a common conviction of the truth of sanctification by faith, and, in the words of Smith himself, "the wondrous peace and victory and liberty of this newborn spirit . . . the second half of the truth of the Gospels."

Smith's religious experience led to his meeting William Edwin Boardman. A heretical and disturbing character, this itinerant evangelist had first found "rest of heart in Jesus for sanctification" in the remote mining town of Potosi, in southwestern Wisconsin. There he became head of a little "Plan of Union" church. Later he attended a theological seminary in Cincinnati, and he subsequently went on to the Yale Divinity School. For a time he was listed as a supply minister in the minutes of the General Assembly of the Presbyterian

Church. But this restless mystic could not remain long in one community or one denomination. He sailed for California in 1859, for his wife's health; returned in 1862 to enter the service of the United States Christian Commission; and went briefly into business at the end of the Civil War. Now, in his late fifties, finally freed from the humdrum of the regular ministry, Boardman had thrown aside all shackles of conventional theology and denominational ritual and struck out on his own untrammeled way. He was abetted in this new freedom by his wife. The Lord had called upon the Boardmans to give up all worldly possessions, to enter upon a life of full trust in Him for all temporal needs. The Boardmans claimed to be as free as the birds, and as independent of all man-made restrictions. "No more committees! No more organizations! No more denominations!" they cried. Their every step must be directed by the Lord, and the Lord only.

Boardman's first book, published in 1859, was called *The Higher Christian Life*. From this title grew the "Higher Life" movement, in which Robert and Hannah Smith were destined to play leading roles. Vague, inelegant, uncouth, inaccurate in its illustrations, formless, filled with glib fallacies, universally denounced by orthodox theologians, Boardman's book was sold, it was read, and it bore a fruitful crop. During the sixties a hundred thousand copies circulated in the United States and England. In this first book Boardman preached a circumspect, practical doctrine of complete sanctification, which made his teaching acceptable to the Evangelicals. The repentant sinner must not only "enter" by Christ, but "walk" in Christ. Boardman insisted upon the necessity of the "second conversion." Until he received suddenly and consciously a second baptism of the Holy Spirit, the converted subject could not become a complete Christian.

"Forgiveness does not satisfy me!" Boardman cried out.

"I want the dominion of sin destroyed. Purification, not less than pardon, I see required. I became thoroughly awakened to my own wretched bondage to sin!" Reviewing his own religious experience, Boardman stressed the second and deeper work of grace. "It is really more difficult to overcome sin in the heart than to break away from the world at first." The Boardmans traveled about, organizing "conventions for holiness" in Wilmington, Washington, Newark and Philadelphia. Under the Boardman auspices Robert Pearsall Smith made his first public address at a neighboring camp meeting. Here he experienced what he termed "the second blessing." As he afterwards explained, he received, in immediate response to prayer, a baptism of the Holy Spirit—a direct "call" for fuller service and spiritual leadership. During this second religious experience he was less conscious of what his senses presented than of what was suddenly revealed. No creature of the external world was as real as the immediate Presence of the Creator Himself. Having retired to the nearby woods to escape the noise and clamor of the camp meeting, Robert continued to pray alone. He felt so close to God, so inspired by His Spirit, that he seemed elevated to an almost complete identification with the Deity. His exaltation rose to the point of ecstasy as the burden of sin and guilt was lifted, and with his ecstasy came a flood tide of universal benevolence.

In these psychic details, students of religion may recognize the classic pattern of the mystical experience. But the psychiatrist may perceive in these phenomena a paradigm of the manic-depressive constellation, in which the manic state (or euphoria) mounts to a peak and is followed by a precipitous descent into depression. To a full understanding of Smith's fantastic flight as an evangelical world saver, this point must be remembered.

Robert Pearsall Smith returned from that Jersey camp meeting with a sense of destiny and spiritual leadership. Energy and power surged through his being, and he seized every opportunity to spread his glad tidings of complete sanctification. Revivals, religious conventions, protracted meetings, camp meetings were everywhere held in that era of ubiquitous evangelism. The advent of the itinerant revivalist was always an event in community life—an occasion for gathering together, for the eternal drama of repentance, especially for what we know today as audience participation. It has been said that the greatest actors of the nineteenth century were the great preachers, such spellbinders as Charles Grandison Finney, the Beechers and innumerable backwoods thaumaturges who progressed from one frontier community to the next.

His triumphant reception became a heady draught for Robert Smith. The craft of capturing the mass mind may be suspect, but it requires quite special aptitudes. His success in evoking the response of the crowd convinced Smith that at last he had found his true vocation. As the Spirit of the Lord descended upon him, he fell often into his earlier trancelike states. Hypnotizing himself, he also hypnotized his listeners. He must obey this call to spread the light. Nothing could stop him now.

He was stopped only temporarily by a "nervous breakdown." Hannah later wrote: "In the year 1871 or '72, when my husband needed a course of treatment for a nervous breakdown, we took our family to a Hydropathic Sanatorium in New York State. We stayed there for three or four months. . . ."

As an expression of his religious revelation, he resigned entirely from Whitall-Tatum, began to write tracts, and soon began the publication of his own evangelical periodical, which he named *The Christian's Pathway to Power*. His devout father-in-law supported him fully in this decision, both spiritually and financially, and his brother Lloyd helped him with publishing problems. In his endeavor, Robert insisted upon his wife's collaboration. This was the beginning of her long and successful career as a popular religious writer. "I did not want to write at all," Hannah confessed years later, "and only did it at Father's earnest entreaties. He had started a Paper, which I thought was a great mistake, and I declared I would not write a line for it. But he begged so hard that at last I said I would write one article and no more, if he would give up drinking wine at dinner. Then when that article was published, everybody clamoured for another, and Father begged, and I was good-natured and went on, but under a continued protest."

During the summer of 1872, the Smiths suffered a heartbreaking blow—the death of their eighteen-year-old eldest son Franklin, a victim of typhoid. Mrs. Smith wrote to her mother: "Much as I loved him, I never could have given him the peace, and rest, and joy he is in the midst of now. I always cared more for his happiness than for my own, all his life long, and why should I not do so still? Oh, our boy, how CAN we spare him!" She wrote a biography of her son, which was published under the title *The Record of a Happy Life*.

Another sad blow fell the following summer, when a new baby, hopefully expected, died at birth. At forty-one Hannah now looked upon herself as an old woman, with nothing left but "to help and guide and guard" her family of four: "I am in earnest in having a profound reverence for the young, and an intense yearning to give them all the help I can."

But such problems Hannah was compelled, for a time, to face without the aid of her husband. For Robert had made all arrangements to join his friend Boardman in carrying the gospel of the Higher Life to the British Isles, and before September he had gone. It was a decision that was to change the lives of all the Smiths.

Chapter 2 · Broadlands

Mr. and Mrs. Boardman had preceded Robert Pearsall Smith to London. All three were there in the fall of 1873. From 1873 to 1875, those skilled young showmen of the Gospels, Moody and Sankey, were preaching all over Great Britain and Ireland in their sensational revival meetings. The Higher Life movement followed into the field prepared by these master revivalists. While the younger men effected countless conversions, Smith and Boardman followed with their gospel of the "second blessing." First the two crusaders from New Jersey were presented in a series of breakfasts. Week after week, Smith and Boardman met select parties of clergymen, Christian workers and the Evangelicals of London, to explain to them the foundations of the Higher Life gospel.

As early as September, Smith was urging Hannah to join him. No earthly consideration except being with Robert could make the thought of a residence in England, or even a visit there, in the least pleasant to Hannah. To leave family and friends and cross the Atlantic with four small children, who would necessarily in a strange land absorb all of her time, was not a happy prospect. Nevertheless, in the middle of January, Hannah Smith and her brood set out on the long sea voyage to England. Mary had not yet celebrated her tenth birthday; Logan was eight, Alys was six, and little Rachel scarcely five. Robert met them at a station in the London suburbs, where they had a jubilant reunion; then he took them to a furnished house he had rented at Stoke Newington. "He looked so very Englishy that we hardly knew him at first."

Evangelism was a widespread movement over the Western world in the seventies. Its peremptory demand for sincerity, its delight in plain speaking, its austere accent on moral conduct, all found a variety of expressions. Thomas Huxley may be described as an evangelist of Darwinism, and John Ruskin as an evangelist of art—although Ruskin was becoming bored by all gospeling efforts in the directly religious realm. "I have been horribly plagued and misguided by evangelical people all my life," he was complaining in *Fors Clavigera,* "and most of all lately; but my mother was one, and my Scotch aunt; and I have yet so much of the superstition left in me, that I can't help sometimes doing as evangelical people wish—for all I know it comes to nothing." Even the redoubtable Charles Bradlaugh, editor of the *National Reformer,* who was refused his seat in Parliament because he would not take the Bible oath, was in his propagandizing fanaticism a secular evangelical, as was his comrade and co-editor Annie Wood Besant, who was later converted to theosophy and became famous as the high priestess of that cult.

The ferment showed itself at work in the emphasis on personal salvation, the mushrooming of little cults and groups of intimate "comrades." In the more immediate circle of the Higher Life movement, the Smiths found themselves facing curious competitors. Even among the revivalists, preachers and orators they discovered "a Jew who had been converted by studying the Law of Sacrifice, a Negress who had been a slave, and a working printer who taught that sin was a disease." But the Smiths were soon to take their place among more affluent and privileged circles than these.

Robert insisted that Hannah have an equal part in his great work. This she felt she could not do unless the birthright English Friends first heard her and were fully alive to the purport of the Higher Life message. Therefore, a number of Friends were invited to the Stoke Newington house to hear one of Hannah's Bible lessons. ". . . If they do not like me, then I shall know God has not chosen me to help in the great work . . . and shall be perfectly content." This meeting went off quite satisfactorily. She received their approval, and began a series of Bible lessons in Devonshire Place Meeting House. Here Hannah met a group of moneyed English Quakers, among them Mrs. Henry Ford Barclay, who had been born a Gurney, had married a rich Quaker brewer, and lived at Monkhams in Essex.

At the home of Lady Ashburton, one of the famous hostesses of the era, Hannah met the aristocratic Duchess of Sutherland, who invited the Millville Smiths for a weekend at her country place. Another aristocrat, who became a lifelong friend, was the controversial feminist Lady Isabella Somerset, who had two years earlier married Lord Henry Somerset, son of the Eighth Duke of Bedford. A few years later, Lady Isabella broke the unwritten code of Britain's Victorian upper class by publicly exposing her husband's infidelities in a suit for a legal separation. She was known as Lady Henry Somerset until the end of her life.

The Smiths' first evangelical triumph in England was at Broadlands, which had been the country seat of Lord Palmerston, and was now the property of his heir, William Cowper Temple, discreetly termed Lord Palmerston's "stepson." The Honorable William Cowper Temple (later elevated to the

peerage as Baron Mount Temple) was a pious Christian Socialist, a philanthropist, a Sabbatarian, yet a member of the
great world inhabited by his aristocratic relations. He and
his beautiful wife Georgina were annually the hosts at a great
religious meeting known as the Broadlands Conference,
where hundreds of Evangelicals met, listened to sermons and
Bible lessons, prayed and talked among themselves.

If for nothing else, Broadlands would have been celebrated
as the birthplace of the great Lord Palmerston, the Third
Viscount, who succeeded his father to the peerage in 1802.
Lord Palmerston's marriage to Cowper's mother, who was
Emily Lamb, Lord Melbourne's sister, was the culmination
of a thirty-year romance. While still a young girl, Emily
Lamb had married Lord Cowper, a man with an outstanding
reputation for dullness—slow of speech, slow of gait, and nine
years older than his bride. It was not to be expected that she
could resist the ebullient young Palmerston—nicknamed
"Cupid"—already a Cabinet member, and also her popular
dancing partner at Almack's. But it was 1839 before they could
finally be married—twenty-eight years after the birth of William Cowper, who was nominally the son of Viscount Cowper, but who was named Palmerston's heir when the latter
died in 1865, and who added the Palmerston family name,
Temple, to his own at that time.

When Parliament was not in session, the Cowper Temples
entertained at Broadlands regularly. It was of easy access to
London, close to the abbey town of Romsey, from which it
was divided by a long, lichened wall; the house was white-
pillared, placidly and modestly elegant, standing back from
the swirling river that hurried between banks planted with
low cedars and enormous chestnut trees. During the Broadlands Conference, this vast house with its hundred rooms and
limitless gardens was so crowded with devout guests that

many of the less favored were compelled to seek lodgings in the inns of Romsey.

Despite the invading Evangelicals, the great house was still filled with the spirit of Victoria's Prime Minister. On the walls hung portraits of the Temples done by Reynolds. On the heavy sideboard in the great dining room one could still see the racing plate Palmerston had won. When in 1839 the great Pam brought his adored "Em" to Broadlands, little Lady Palmerston had found the great hall, with its Roman antiquities, a bit severe for her taste; later she would stand in a tall window in the upper floor and watch the gentle stream that flowed across the spacious park. Beyond, in the brown and mauve distance, lay the New Forest.

The birth rate among the pious Victorian Evangelicals was high; the nursery wing at Broadlands was crowded with well-brought-up little Britons and their equally numerous nannies and governesses. Little Alys and Rachel Smith were too small to escape the vigilant eyes of their strict English nurses, but Mary led her brother Logan on private tours of inspection, completely oblivious of the strict caste system that prevailed among the household staff. The nursery footman, at the beck and call of the nannies, tried in vain to control the insatiable curiosity of these little Quakers. By their innocence and naïveté they established friendly relations with everyone they saw below stairs, but it would have been impossible for them to know all of the vast staff.

Out of doors, gardeners directed the little Yankees through the vast and intricate creation of the famous "Capability" Brown, the best-known landscape gardener of all England. Visitors to the great gardens, alive with azaleas, camellia trees, and towering rhododendrons, were usually told of "Capability's" remark: "Now there, I make a comma, and there . . . where a more decided turn is proper, I make a colon; at another part, where an interruption is desirable to break the view, a parenthesis; now a full stop, and then I begin another subject."

Before tea, lady guests were led on conducted tours of the gardens, while a small army of housemaids descended upon the deserted drawing rooms to tidy up. The corps of maids toiled long and arduous hours for microscopic wages. In addition to the drawing rooms and the nursery quarters, they had forty or more bedrooms to "do" at this pious *omnium gatherum,* for this annual Broadlands Conference in July meant that every one of the bedrooms was occupied. Some of the more privileged lady guests brought their own personal maids, who had to be accommodated in the servants' quarters, along with the vast army of regular domestics required to sustain the pursuit of the Higher Life.

Despite the density of population in the nurseries and schoolrooms, the delegates found little time to spend with their children. Each day they faced a heavy schedule of religious activities. Morning tea having been served in their bedrooms, at nine they were ready for a hearty breakfast. Prayers were set for ten, followed by a half-hour talk on thoughts suggested by the prayer leader. They met under the beeches at eleven, for consideration of the Higher Life. Luncheon was served at one, after which they reassembled under the beeches or in the Orangerie at two. Afternoon tea was served at five, followed by Hannah's Bible reading in the great drawing room, while in some cool spot of the formal gardens, the people of Romsey were invited to listen to an edifying talk by a visiting celebrity. Mrs. Smith's Bible readings and lessons in the drawing room, before a feminine congregation, were scarcely less impressive than her husband's exhortations.

Dinner was served at eight, after which the entire adult population of the vast house gathered for family prayers. At

ten, each of the guests was presented with a bedroom candle
by the solemn-looking butler and his staff. Then the visitors,
especially the ladies, began visits from room to room. Confidences were exchanged, troubles poured out, perplexities
aired, so that it was often midnight or past before the house
was silent for the night.

Two of the most regular confidantes were Hannah Smith
and Georgina Cowper Temple, who quickly established an
intimate friendship which was to endure all their lives.

At the age of fifty-four or fifty-five, Georgina Cowper still
retained some traces of her early Pre-Raphaelite beauty. At
twenty-eight the beautiful Miss Tollemache had become the
second wife of William Cowper. As the new mistress of
Broadlands she was, like the Athenians of St. Paul's days, "always interested in some new thing"—an evangelist from
North America, or the new phenomenon of spiritualism and
the séances of Mr. Daniel Home, and all that was new in the
spheres of the arts and letters. Carlyle was a guest at Broadlands, as were Rossetti and other Pre-Raphaelites. Georgina
was born to be a confidante. Her sympathetic ears were never
shocked. It was, apparently, to her alone that in 1868 Ruskin
had told the reason for the failure of his marriage to Effie
Grey. Ruskin had a pet Greek name for Georgina. He called
her Phile.

Night after night Hannah and Georgina visited each other's room and exchanged confidences. Palmerston and "Em"
had passed the first night of their marriage, Mrs. Cowper
Temple confided to Hannah in a whisper, in the very bedroom in which the two women sat. That belated union,
Georgina assured the lady from Millville, was a perfect marriage, although of course it held few surprises. It was with
something of a shock that Hannah Smith learned of the ir-
regularity of her host's ancestry.

This Broadlands Conference, at which both Robert and Hannah Smith preached to their fellow guests, was followed by a great Oxford Union meeting called by Smith. This was "for the Promotion of Scriptural Holiness: convening from August 29 to September 7, 1874." Smith presided and governed the Oxford meeting in all its aspects, while his older colleague, Boardman, was more or less relegated to the background. Boardman's activities were mainly in organizing details; he accomplished much valuable work in dealing with individual disciples, and welcomed delegates from foreign countries. Three or four of these Continental emissaries became Smith's disciples and carried the agitation for the Higher Life back across the Channel with them.

One effective speaker on the Oxford platform was the eccentric Frenchman Theodore Monod, a mystagogue and God-seeker whose American training and experience fitted him to address these English-speaking congregations with ease and force. Upon his return to France, Monod diligently expended his energies as Smith's foremost disciple. He wrote *De Quoi il s'agit,* a book about the Higher Life movement, and he also spread the new gospel by holding meetings in Paris, Marseilles and other French cities. Lion Cachet became an ardent apostle of the movement in the Low Countries, but Holland manifested little sympathy with it.

Of all the Continental disciples, the most ardent and loyal was a German pastor named Theodor Jellinghaus. Born in Wuerttemberg, Jellinghaus was an earnest Lutheran who had served as a missionary to India. Returning to Germany, he had been appointed pastor at Raednitz, near Grossen on the Oder. (He remained the leading exponent of Fellowship Christianity until the final years of his long life, when he renounced the entire Perfectionist heresy.) Jellinghaus urged

Smith to come to preach in Germany, and Smith promised to do so the following year.

After the blazing triumph of the Oxford Union meeting, the Smith family returned to America. As part of his plan to carry his campaign to the Continent, Smith went to Cleveland, Ohio, to call upon the leaders of a minor sect of German origin known as the Albrecht Brethren. He detailed to them the progress of the new movement in Germany, mainly under the leadership of Jellinghaus, and announced his intention to go to Berlin before Easter of the following year. "If the Lord will give the people of Berlin into my hands as He did at Oxford"—then he corrected himself at once: "But in the business of my God, I no longer know any *if*— the Lord does it according to His word." The Albrecht Brethren were deeply impressed with his quiet sincerity; he spoke decisively and confidently of his coming triumph.

Leaving his family with Grandpa Whitall, Smith again sailed across the Atlantic the next year, in March 1875, and hurried on to Berlin. Jellinghaus later wrote: ". . . the beloved R. P. Smith was invited to Berlin, and made, by the power of the Holy Spirit, a deep impression on many hundreds of souls in many cities of Germany, such as I suppose no one ever did before in so few weeks." Smith had been invited to Berlin not merely by Jellinghaus and other disciples, but by laymen of the highest standing and authority. Through the intervention of Court Preacher Baur, Kaiser Wilhelm I placed at his disposal the old Garrison Church. Smith was acclaimed as a world missionary—*ein Weltmissionar*—this despite the fact that Smith could speak no German, and therefore addressed his congregation only through an interpreter. He took as his battle cry a single sentence in the German tongue. This was the refrain of a hymn composed for his meetings by Pfarrer of Zurich: *"Jesus erretet mich jetzt!"* ("Jesus saves me now!")

To the more emotional among his German listeners, Smith's appearance took on the aspects of a theophany, an embodiment of God in actual human form. Some spoke awesomely of the Second Coming. One eyewitness has left a vignette of Robert Smith as he stood in the pulpit of the old church on the first day of April, in 1875. "At the hour of the evening service . . . a singular man stood in the pulpit of the Garrison Church in Berlin—Robert Pearsall Smith. He was preaching. But his manner of speaking was wholly different from what men were accustomed to hear. He spoke urgently as if he wished to grasp his hearers and obtain a decision from them at once, in an instant. By his side in the pulpit stood or sat men who interrupted the Assembly, 'Rejoice, rejoice at once!' On Sunday, the fourth of April, he gave voice to the enthusiastic aspiration: 'My brethren, I expect this evening great things from the Lord!' He longed for the return of the Apostolic age. As the disciples of Jesus had been baptized with the Holy Spirit ten days after the Ascension, so he looked for the Baptism of the Spirit on the tenth day. In the meetings everyone who felt inwardly moved to it led in prayer. Even sisters had equal rights before the Lord."

Had the golden Apostolic age of spiritual power and brotherly love returned in Smith? Many hoped so; and perhaps it was because of this hope that the Court Preacher gave Smith his welcome at the first meeting, and many pastors spoke enraptured words as if under the compulsion of a mighty spirit. Only a few stood aloof in doubt and warned against desertion of the firm ground of Reformation doctrine.

The Vereinshaus hall was crowded as it had never been

before; hundreds were turned away for lack of room. Smith addressed ministers of the various denominations, and he also spoke to the laity. To all, he emphasized his nondenominational position. He renounced all ecclesiastical connections, and presented himself as an unattached teacher who would serve all denominations alike. "I belong to no church at all. I wish to serve all churches, to call in all of them the unrepentant to conversion, the converted to sanctification . . . I work for Christ only and His Kingdom."

Smith declined all invitations of denominational hospitality and instead registered in princely fashion at the best hotels. In his brief campaign, he hastened from Berlin to Basel, Switzerland, then to Stuttgart, Frankfort and Heidelberg, then down the Rhine to Bonn, thence to Elberfeld-Barmen— everywhere arousing the greatest enthusiasm and even hysterical excitement. Later, when engraved portraits of Smith were placed on sale, eight thousand were sold in Germany. German Fellowship Christianity (*Die Heiligungsbewegung*) derived its impulse, according to competent authorities, directly from Robert Pearsall Smith. Of course Smith did not create this movement out of nothing: the field had been prepared. The great Luther himself had advocated *Gemeinschaft* (fellowship), admonishing the faithful: "Let those who earnestly wish to be Christians and confess the gospel with hands and lips enroll themselves by name and gather together by themselves somewhere or other in a house, to pray, read, baptize, receive the Sacraments and to perform other Christian duties." These fellowships, working in more or less complete independence of national church organizations, had in certain regions maintained an unbroken existence for centuries. Pearsall Smith's two months' visit quickened these brotherhoods into new life; they supplied the mold into which the Higher Life movement ran. A new zeal for evangelization sprang into bloom, and the new doctrine of immediate sanctification through faith alone was to remain implanted for decades to come, even when Smith himself had sunk into oblivion.

"All Europe is at my feet!" Smith cried out a few weeks later at the great Brighton Meeting organized in his honor. Earlier he had written to his wife urging her to bring the children back to Europe. In his exaltation he confided to her that he had no intention of returning to the dreary and unappreciated chores connected with the Whitall-Tatum Company. He was through with the bottle business forever. Hannah remained discreetly silent about her husband's renunciation of the family business: "I suppose the Lord will care for us, if thee really feels it thy duty," she answered, "but indeed, my darling husband, I cannot consent to live on other people. I am sure it would not be right. I can go and live over at the Barracks [the guest quarters at the Cedars] and economize, or I can go to work to gain our living myself. But I *cannot* sponge, or live on collections or subscriptions. PLEASE do not ask me to do this. I can see plainly that the Lord is calling *thee* to a life of devotion to His service, and I rejoice in it. But I am sure it can be managed without our living on other people."

Smith insisted that her presence was essential for the success of the Brighton Meeting, which was scheduled to be held between May 29 and June 7. Scarcely a week before that date, Hannah landed at Liverpool with her four children and twenty-seven pieces of luggage. Robert met his family at Willesden, near London. ". . . Robert and I just had to rush, without even exchanging a kiss, to hunt up the luggage, and did not dare to take time even to contemplate one another's countenances until it was all safely deposited in a small pyramid on the platform." They went to Monkhams, in Essex, as the guests of the Barclays, and there Hannah addressed a Friends' Meeting. Later she found out that John Bright, the eminent Quaker statesman, and his wife and daughters were among her listeners. She boasted in a letter to her parents that John Bright had said to Mr. Cowper Temple that she "was one of the few people who could preserve a natural conversational manner *on their legs*."

When the Brighton Meeting began, Hannah's own success under the Great Dome was scarcely less spectacular than that of her husband. Mrs. Smith's *The Christian's Secret of a Happy Life* had just been published and had been immediately accepted in evangelical circles. This book was to become her most famous; it paved the way for her long career as an author of religious books and was as popular in England as in America. Hannah insisted that she would "say her say in her own way" and would never be tamed, "for I shall not alter a line to please anybody. Every line I write is a *pure favour* to the world, and I ask no favours from anybody."

The English edition was already familiar to many of her listeners at Brighton, where every afternoon at three she gave a Bible reading, ostensibly to the ladies only, but in reality to ever gathering crowds. In the words of J. B. Figgis, one of the Smiths' sponsors, "Anything more impressive or delightful . . . than this series of addresses we can never remember hearing . . . such was the enthusiasm that each afternoon people crowded together to listen to . . . Mrs. Pearsall Smith, with interest so keen that the Great Dome could not hold the numbers that came; and after the earliest days the readings had to be repeated an hour later in the Corn Exchange."

In her quiet, persuasive way, Mrs. Smith preached a sort of passive Christianity. "We cannot create life, but we can let life live. We can lay hold of it by an entire surrender to

Christ, who is our life. The spiritual life grows only by surrender and faith," the gentle lady from Millville told her
Brighton listeners. They were as much impressed by her simple dignity as by her quaint transatlantic accent. She warned
them against the common mistake of thinking that although
we cannot create life by unaided efforts, we are to make it
grow. Life, she insisted, is a mighty, dynamic force that asks
only for a chance to grow. "The lily grows by the power of
its inward life principle, and according to the laws of a lily's
life. No amount of . . . stretching or straining, nor any
pulling up by others, would help its growth. It is all folly,
and worse than folly, for Christians to make such mighty efforts to grow. If they would only let the Christlike within
them grow, unhindered by their interference, they need
have no fear of the result. We need not trouble ourselves
about it any more than the fig-tree troubles itself about its
fruit." The more orthodox among the critics of Hannah's
doctrines pointed out that they were merely a variation or
a debasement of the quietism of Madame Guyon, the French
mystic of the seventeenth century. Some even gibed that this
missionary from across the Atlantic was translating the American slogan of "Get rich quick!" into "Get *saved* quick!" But
such denigrations apparently never entered the minds of her
rapt listeners under the Great Dome.

Every evening Robert admonished his listeners not to in-
vent limitations on the power of God, or to postpone the
completion of their salvation. All must press on to the final
destination of their soul's pilgrimage. "Remember that soul-
health is very different from maturity," he preached, voicing
his own variation of the basic tenets of American Perfectionism. "The sour apples in April are perfect. In October they
are matured or 'perfected.' At the best we are but ripening
. . . Little children are 'perfect' in all their immaturity. Do

not confound an unattainable absolute, or Divine Holiness, with an obtainable victory over known sin."

The Brighton Meeting was brought to an apparently triumphant close on June 7; but even before the thousands who attended had dispersed, rumors were circulating about the questionable behavior of the American prophet. It was whispered that Pearsall Smith was teaching privately to some of his feminine followers an extravagant esoteric doctrine of mystical betrothal with Jesus. It was a story long familiar to all historians of the Christian heresies. "Salute one another with an holy kiss," St. Paul had counseled the Romans; and out of this early Christian doctrine of the Agape had developed the doctrine of the *agapetae* or *virgines subintroductae*. Numerous sects had in the past embraced the theory of spiritual wives, so intimately connected with the doctrine of Perfectionism; in most instances, it was pointed out, spiritual wives had soon become carnal mistresses.

No one ever knew just how far Pearsall Smith had gone in his consolations of adoring females, because there was no impartial record of the Brighton incident, but among the unregenerate of the resort town, the gossip was magnified and distorted, and for weeks after the meeting rumors of a disquieting kind were taken up and guardedly touched upon in the religious press.

Although Smith's defenders denounced these veiled accusations as "a stream of most rancorous and malignant calumnies" to which no one with any respect for the Ninth Commandment should pay attention, Higher Life meetings planned for other popular centers in Britain were nevertheless canceled, and Pearsall Smith was advised that as far as England was concerned his public career as a world evangelist was now at an end. The Smiths sought temporary escape from rumors and "calumny," by taking a brief holiday in

Switzerland, but they found no peace there. "The flat sandy roads of New Jersey," Hannah wrote home to her parents, "look beautiful and lovely to my mental vision, and I feel as if all my life long I had treated them with the most cruel injustice in not appreciating their charming flatness. Never again shall I sigh for mountains or valleys in the country of my habitation."

The departure of the Smith family for America as soon as they returned from Switzerland did nothing to allay the repercussions of the Brighton Meeting. The scandal re-echoed, even resounded, across the Atlantic and into certain religious weeklies, and was the occasion for revived denominational discussions of the ever recurrent antinomian heresy, the heresy of believers who place themselves above the Law.

Before the end of 1875, the British sponsors of the Brighton Meeting were compelled to issue a defense and an explanation. Eight of these Evangelicals signed a statement making it clear that the American's withdrawal from public agitation was not at his own instance nor entirely on account of illness. These gentlemen did not seem to realize that one excuse is more valid than two, as witness their public statement: "Rumors of an exceedingly painful character with regard to a prominent teacher, which had for some time been in private circulation, having now had currency given to them in your and other papers, we consider it right, in the interests of truth, and in justice to the person in question, to make the following statement:—Some weeks after the Brighton Convention, it came to our knowledge that the individual referred to had, on some occasions in personal conversation, inculcated doctrines which were most unscriptural and dangerous. We also found there had been conduct which, although we were convinced that it was free from evil intention, was yet such as to render action necessary on our part.

We therefore requested him to abstain at once from all public work, and when the circumstances were represented to
him in their true light, he entirely acquiesced in the propriety of this course, and recognized with deep sorrow the
unscriptural and dangerous character of the teaching and conduct in question. In addition to the above, a return of the
distressing attacks of the brain, from which he had previously
suffered, rendered the immediate cessation from work an
absolute necessity." The committee suggested that a fall from
a horse in 1861 had led to a brain concussion and the conse-
quent distressing symptoms of nervous disorder.

Even Pearsall Smith's most ardent evangelical admirers
finally admitted that he had lapsed into antinomian error
with his positive and unqualified belief—and public asser-
tion—that those who are "in Christ" are no longer subject
to the letter of the law as the rule of their conduct, that
they are lifted to a higher sphere of life, and thus walk in a
freedom unknown to those who are strangers to the exalted
adventure of the new and better life.

Hannah Smith gave a courageous exhibition of unflinch-
ing loyalty, but her eyes were opened to the traps set by
Satan for those who were righteous overmuch. She claimed
she had warned Robert against the fallacy, but he had
plunged ahead.

At the same time, Mrs. Smith consoled herself with the
conviction that her husband's dereliction was caused by his
brain concussion fourteen years before, which she felt had
been the reason for his nervous disorder in 1871. This was
a more comforting thought than that of erotic ebullience and
sexual prowess. She sedulously cultivated the myth of Robert's precarious health, and years later wrote to J. B. Figgis:
"Mr. Smith's health is very poor, and he is obliged to live
a very quiet and domestic life. He thinks he cannot live long,

but, of course, this is something we know nothing about.
Some physicians say that he has a very serious heart trouble.
I believe myself that the springs of his life were sapped in
1875, and that existence can never be anything but weari-
ness and suffering to him again this world."

Although Smith was so quickly lost to his European disciples and cast back into the outer darkness of the New Jersey glass business, his influence in Europe had been great.
The movement he initiated has persisted even to our own
day, more than three quarters of a century later. It is a fact
that the new type of Fellowship Christianity known as Moral
Rearmament received its first impetus, as did the Higher Life
movement, in Oxford, and that both these movements were
originated by leaders from Pennsylvania. And although the
Keswick Movement in England and the *Heiligungsbewegung*
or Fellowship Movement in Germany extended far beyond
the essential teachings of Robert and Hannah Smith, the in-
itiating inspiration was undoubtedly theirs. While Smith himself was seeking refuge in America, in the transactions of the
Whitall-Tatum Company, solemn German theologians continued writing serious tomes and articles about the Higher
Life and their lost leader.

Chapter 3 · "Bright Particular Star"

Back across the Atlantic once more, the Smiths returned in 1875, not to Millville, where Robert's post had been filled by a Whitall relative, but to a place Grandpa Whitall found for his prodigal son-in-law in the Philadelphia office of Whitall-Tatum. The family took refuge at the Cedars for five months, then established a permanent residence in the heart of Germantown, at 1307 Arch Street.

As Hannah wrote, a blight seemed to have fallen on her beloved husband. A more generous, tender-hearted and sensitive man had never lived, she insisted; he would never have treated his worst enemy as he had been treated by those who professed to be his dearest friends. In the depths of his depression, Pearsall Smith shut himself off from his evangelical associates. The winds of gossip and scandal that had blown across the ocean, in theological circles at least, had almost wrecked their lives.

Robert Smith's staunchest American defender was one Dr. Charles Cullis, of Boston, who had begun his career as a homeopathic physician but soon became the leader of his own faith-cure movement. In 1876, while Robert was in the pit of depression, Dr. Cullis took it upon himself to reinstate his friend in the eyes of evangelism and the world. To this end he organized what he wittily—but privately—termed a "scamp" meeting, a convention for the promotion of holiness, which could more rightly have been called a convention for the promotion of Robert Pearsall Smith.

Utterly indifferent to this project, the Smiths made no preparation for the meeting; they neither studied, nor prayed, nor meditated in advance. No religious meeting could have been undertaken in a worse frame of mind than the disillusioned Smiths brought to this one, although they did their part with perfunctory efficiency. They were completely lacking in interest and enthusiasm—to them the work was like a treadmill, the sessions a bore. Yet, surprisingly, its results were successful. Souls were saved; backsliders were restored to faith; confessed Christians were "sanctified"; and all attending seemed to receive infinite blessing. Dr. Cullis, the organizer, proclaimed it the best meeting ever held in his vicinity.

The meeting was successful for Pearsall Smith, too; he was treated with all the old deference and respect. This gave the Smiths a new insight into the techniques of itinerant revivalists. "We are done!" Hannah cried, content now to return to Germantown and devote her life to the happiness of her children; and Smith rose out of his depression, free at last of fanaticism. From then on, he became a professed backslider and man of the world. Hannah, too, confessed that her orthodoxy had fled to the winds. "I am Broad, Broader, Broadest!" she proclaimed, capitalizing those B's to emphasize her new-found liberty and breadth of mind. This indifference brought her a sphinx-like calm and peace of mind. Tempests in sectarian teapots appeared faraway, puerile, petty. "Be not righteous overmuch!" took on new meaning. In discarding the narrow and uncharitable prejudices of sectarian orthodoxies, however, Hannah still retained her Christian faith, but it was to find expression in simpler ways. She admitted that the "poetry of mysticism" was not for her. "I have got to plod on in the prose of commonplace life always."

Ever since the Smiths' return from England, Hannah had devoted herself with particular concern to the education of her children. They should have every advantage; in addition to regular school studies there were governesses and tutors in foreign languages, and special lessons in swimming, horseback riding and music.

A defender of the younger generation against the strictures of their elders, Hannah came to grips with this problem in an argument with her own mother. "I told her plain out that she must not interfere in my children's lives and I advised her not to criticize my management of them . . . She cried, and it was very hard for me and for her too, but it worked like a charm and was far happier for her as well as the rest of us ever afterwards . . . I think Mother really loved me better after that than before."

At the beginning of 1880, after an illness of a few days, Hannah's mother Mary Tatum Whitall, died. On the day of the funeral, little Ray, aged eleven, was stricken with scarlet fever, sank into a delirium, and then, suddenly, was gone. It was God's choice, Hannah Smith told herself. But "I never did care very much how *I* fared myself, if only my children were happy. . . ." The children were three in number now—Mary, Logan and Alys—the three who were later to be the weavers of the curious transatlantic web.

During the summer of 1880, the Smiths toured the West as far as the Pacific coast. On this journey Hannah visited one of Brigham Young's widows at Salt Lake City, a meeting which broadened her understanding and tolerance of all varieties of religious heresies. During these years just after her husband's fall from grace, she never missed an opportunity

to investigate the eccentric cults and sects which were pro-
liferating in the United States. Besides her Salt Lake City
call, she visited her friends the Oliphants, members of the
colony established by Thomas Lake Harris north of San Fran-
cisco. These and many similar experiences were the material
for her book *Religious Fanaticism,* which was published after
her death.

In 1881, the Smiths joined a large party of tourists in the
Rocky Mountains and spent several weeks in Yellowstone
Park. In 1882, there was an expedition to Yosemite Valley,
and the following summer to Maine, with a side excursion
to a revivalist gathering at Martha's Vineyard. Hannah was
becoming a detached observer of life rather than a participant in evangelical fanaticism.

Hannah's daughter Mary, however, had no intention of
either being a detached observer or "plodding in the commonplace prose of life." She determined to work for a college degree, and she chose Smith College, in Northampton,
Massachusetts, which was just completing the first decade of
its existence, and which claimed an opportunity for scholas-
tic training equal to that of any men's university. Mary's decision was seconded by her mother. "Girls have a *right* to a
college education," Mrs. Smith said. "They ought to be made
to get it, even . . . at the point of a bayonet!"

Later, in 1883, Mary decided to study at Harvard, which
she was enabled to do through the organization that had
been formed two years before as the Society for Collegiate
Instruction of Women—later Radcliffe College. She persuaded her parents to allow her to take this daring step;
their only proviso was that Logan should go too.

Life for teen-age Logan was mostly an effort to keep in
step with his brilliant and fast-moving elder sister. After his

years at the William Penn Charter School, next door to that citadel of orthodox Philadelphia Friends, the Meeting House, Logan had enrolled at Haverford College, in the outskirts of the city. Quaker Haverford was a miniature university with a student body of less than seventy-five, but it boasted a campus laid out in the English manner and a devotion to the English game of cricket. One of Logan's fellow students was the Maine-born outsider Rufus Jones, who was later to become the leading exponent of Quaker mysticism, but Logan was still much more interested in his home and his pets, especially an oversized St. Bernard that his mother described as monstrous and a houseful. Nevertheless, he was happy to transfer to Harvard and go up to Cambridge with his big sister.

Armed with letters to William James, who was a friend of their parents, the two set out, and through the Jameses' kindness found lodgings in the comfortable home of two elderly maiden ladies.

Both young Smiths met the leading figures of the academic elite at Cambridge, although a prejudice against women students in some of the advanced courses made things a little difficult for Mary. However, one professor who had courteously received her into his class fell in love with this articulate young lady from Germantown.

A German governess had conferred on the girl the diminutive of Mariechen, and to her relatives and close friends she was Mariechen for the rest of her life, but suddenly there was nothing diminutive about Mariechen. She was no longer a *jeune fille en fleur,* but rather a russet-blond goddess, a Bruennhilde, as she would later be called. Long before her twentieth birthday, she bloomed into full maturity. Tall, completely Anglo-Saxon, and attractive, Mary became the central figure in her social groups. This gentle goddess was acutely observant and possessed a phenomenal gift for memorizing the poems of the fashionable stars—Keats and Shelley, Tennyson and Browning. Helen Thomas, one of Mary's Baltimore cousins—who later became Helen Flexner —presents a glimpse of Mary expounding her Emersonian philosophy of life to a gathering of ladies in the Thomases' parlor. Her subject was "The Duty of Self-Development." Mary's radiant beauty and "a kind of vital force emanating from her" bowled over her younger cousin—even her green velvet dress seemed alive. The light from a window struck the dress, which took on the shimmery color of leaves, and the yellow rose at her waist shone like her hair. "A slight lisp broke her speech with momentary pauses." Mary shocked some of her relatives by insisting that it was the duty of every human to develop his own gifts, that each person must seek and find his own vocation. Duty to society and to oneself lay in finding something one could do with pleasure and then pursuing it wholeheartedly. Congenial activity alone, she insisted, was successful activity. Indirectly she suggested the futility of self-sacrifice, of submitting to unattractive toil. At the conclusion of her address the older matrons failed to applaud. Such ideas of enlightened egoism sounded a bit too radical to be voiced in a Quaker parlor in Baltimore in that autumn of 1884.

With her "advanced notions," Mary promptly became an activating spirit among her young cousins, the Thomas children and other Whitall connections. Because Mary possessed the quite unquakerish gift of attracting beaux, one unsolved question among her gossiping cousins was whether she deliberately and consciously made young men fall in love with her. Edith Carpenter, who later married one of the Thomas boys, committed the error of remarking at a family dinner party: ". . . she does lead men on to fall in love with her. An atmosphere of adoration seems necessary for her happiness . . . Mary finds a new love affair stimulating. She is very much like Goethe in temperament."

Mary's mother, seated opposite Miss Carpenter at the long dining table, grew pale with anger. Despite her Quaker upbringing, Hannah possessed the fury of a tigress in defense of her daughter. "How dare you say such a thing?" Hannah's voice rang out, silencing all conversation. "You call yourself Mary's friend, and you compare her to Goethe, the most notoriously immoral man who ever lived!" Alys mildly intervened, but her mother lashed out: "Mary is an angel of goodness. She cannot help it if men fall in love with her, but she uses her power over them only for their own good, to lead them to higher things, and you dare to tell me she is like Goethe. Take that back, Edith, and apologize, or I will never speak to you again!"

"I never meant to say anything against her!" Tears streamed down the poor girl's face. "Mary is my dearest friend. I apologize!"

Those prim Quaker matrons and cousins who listened to the radiant Mary as she voiced her radical theories in her Aunt Mary Thomas's front parlor in Baltimore may have decided that the young woman had absorbed too many of her heresies from such New England heretics as Emerson and Thoreau—whom they knew only by name. But the ladies would have been truly shocked had they realized that Mary had struck up a friendship with the disreputable poet Walt Whitman. A lady lecturer at Smith had aroused her interest; she obtained a copy of *Leaves of Grass,* absorbed it at a sitting, and was promptly converted to Walt's glorification of himself. During the Christmas holidays of 1882, she decided to make a pilgrimage to Whitman, who was then living in the home of his brother George in Camden, across the Delaware from Philadelphia.

Logan's report of this pilgrimage, published in his *Unforgotten Years* many decades later, is an extremely "retouched" account. We rely on him for color and on other sources for the basic facts. The story begins when Mariechen came home for the Christmas holidays in 1882 and informed her parents that a great American poet, perhaps the greatest—though most Americans were not at all aware of his greatness—was living in poverty and neglect "not far from our neighborhood." It was her purpose to go without delay and offer him her praise and admiration. Her father, Robert, forbade the visit. He vaguely knew the poet's name, which was by no means a name of good repute in Philadelphia; no daughter of his, he declared, should, while she lived under his roof, be allowed to take so unseemly a step.

Robert Smith's refusal had no effect on Mary—she thought of going, she said, on the following Thursday. Her father then decided that the best thing under the circumstances was for him, as well as Logan, to accompany her, and thus lend an air of propriety to the visit. So on Thursday afternoon, off they started from Germantown, behind a fine pair of horses.

The Smiths went through Fairmount Park and across Philadelphia, took the ferry across the river, drove half a mile through flat, low-lying Camden with its modest middle-class houses, and dashed up before the little cottage where Walt was living with his brother's family. An elderly woman answered the doorbell and ushered them into a little parlor. She shouted upstairs, "Walt, here's carriage folk come to see you!" Mary informed him that their name was Smith, that she had read his *Leaves of Grass* and had come to express her admiration for that work. Her tribute was received with great complacency; all were invited to follow him upstairs to his den, where they sat down on what chairs could be hastily provided, and were soon engaged in lively talk.

According to Logan: "My father, who at first held himself aloof in the most disapproving manner, soon, to the surprise of my sister and myself, began to join in this friendly conversation and we were still more surprised, when we got up to take our departure, to hear our impulsive parent invite the object of his grave disapprobation to drive back with us to Germantown and spend the night. 'No, Mr. Smith, I think I won't come,' the poet answered; but when he had hobbled to the window and seen, waiting in the street outside, my father's equipage, he said that he thought he might as well come after all and, hastily putting a nightshirt and a few other objects in a little bag, he hobbled downstairs and we all drove off together.

". . . Walt Whitman remained with us a month . . . and he would often afterwards return."

In 1883, when Mary's friendship with Whitman began, the literary denigration and defamation of the enigmatic poet had not yet begun. Acclaimed on both sides of the Atlantic as a liberator, an iconoclast, a true heresiarch, he sat in his study in Camden as a gray-bearded prophet, the very incarnation of the "good gray poet" portrayed by his Washington friend and disciple William D. O'Connor. Walt was then sixty-three. Twenty-eight years had passed since the publication of the first edition of *Leaves of Grass*—years during which that slim volume with its ninety-five pages of untitled and untrimmed poetry had grown and been published time after time. During those years the Whitman cult had taken root and shot forth trunk and branches, and scattered seed around the globe. The history of this book is one of the miracles of communication from person to person; few publications in the Western world have had so widespread and so continuous an effect.

Shrewdly skilled in provoking gifts from near and distant sources, Whitman planted rumors of his financial insecurity and even destitution. But his devout admirers needed little urging to send him checks and money. Respectable ladies invited him to sire their hoped-for children. He was called the greatest poet of his century, but he was something more than a poet—he was a shaman. His genius was prophetic: God had sent him the gift of speaking in strange tongues, the gift of proclaiming the priority of the human person, body and soul. Walt's "I," so often used, was in essence the divine First Person, the "I" of the god Krishna in the Bhagavad-Gita. It is not surprising that now pilgrims from all over the world were seeking him out, as pilgrims seek out the holy men, the *rishi*, in Asia. These devotees unconsciously felt the need of direct personal communication with this *guru*, or yogi, who had liberated them from the restrictions and prohibitions of their puritanical era. And who could begrudge such heartfelt tribute? Did he not deserve this recognition, he who had stood so staunchly by his insights?

Walt was used to adoring visitors. He enjoyed them and welcomed them, even eccentrics and cranks who came to quarrel. But he had never had the good fortune to receive one who so embodied the very spirit of eager, communicative youth as this eighteen-year-old girl who bore the simple name of Mary Smith.

The visit of the three Smiths to Camden was the beginning of a warm, intimate friendship with the old man, which lasted until his death in 1892. Whitman became one of the most frequent and welcome of the Smiths' numerous house guests. Logan and Alys shared Mary's affection for the eccentric poet, while their father, in retreat from his evangelistic debacle, enjoyed Walt's outspoken crackerbox radicalism. "They always treated me with peculiar consideration," Walt told his friend Horace Traubel, "—made their home so much mine, its servants so much at my beck and call. . . . The house could not have been more mine if I had owned it—the overflowing table which contained everything but a tipple—you know the Smiths were opposed to all tippling! Yes—everything but a tipple, which, by the way, some of us would slip out and get around the corner."

Still suspicious of all poets and artists, Hannah could never quite approve of old Walt; the two of them never "hitched." "She is very evangelical," Walt remarked. "She takes her doctrine, if she don't take her whisky, very straight: the sort of get under my feet religion, which gives hell out to the crowd and saves heaven for the few. Well—I didn't agree very well with Hannah—still, there was no demonstration. Pearsall himself, though once a missionary or something or other of that useless sort, is an agnostic—a man more or less of the world—fond of horses, good living, believing in goods— yet seeing more, too, than that."

Whenever Walt made one of his prolonged visits to the Smith home in Arch Street, lively controversies flared up about literature, poetry and the philosophical ideas of the day. Smith vehemently denounced the books of Thomas Carlyle; Walt vigorously defended the sage of Chelsea. During 1882, Oscar Wilde had made his appearance on the lecture platform in Philadelphia, and the presence of the aesthete in knee breeches and eccentric attire was talked about for weeks afterwards. Some condemned his poetry and philosophy as dead and artificial. With her dim view of all literary men, and particularly of secular poets, Hannah declared that Oscar Wilde was a "sell." She said that he looked like two radishes set up on their ends. She granted that once in a while he said a fine thing about art—"just about what I would say about religion. But his manner is so poor and his style so excessively 'Rose Matilda' that I believe everyone is disgusted." Logan admitted that he had not been able to get one idea from him; Logan was not yet seventeen.

"Pearsall, too, has his contradictions," Whitman ruefully commented to Traubel. "For all his radicalism, he likes the English life—likes to be near the big fellows there—likes to be served—obsequiously served—to get among people who don't consider themselves as good as he is—or a good deal better. But that whole serving business is a stench. It is offensive to me. I believe that people who serve you without love get even with you behind your back."

Of all the Smiths of Germantown, Walt's favorite was Mary, who seemed to respond to all he stood for far more warmly than the rest of them.

About a year after his meeting with the Smiths, Walt at last acquired his house on Mickle Street in Camden, his "shanty," he always called this tiny frame house, with its narrow front door, and its five prim windows overlooking a mean little street. Gifts from admirers helped to make up the purchase price, which was less than two thousand dollars, and he persuaded the tenants of the house to remain rent-free, in exchange for cooking and keeping house for him. The three young Smiths helped Walt settle into the first home that he had ever been able to call his own. They brought a comfortable chair, sheets and pillowcases, towels, afghans and antimacassars. But they could not reform the disorderly habits of this carefree invalid of sixty-four. As a contemporary noted, Walt exhibited a "generally higgledy-piggledy attitude toward domestic comfort," preferring the comfortable disorder of his Mickle Street "study" to the Smiths' well-kept guest rooms in Germantown.

His housekeeper took great pride in keeping Whitman's surroundings shipshape, as far as might be. Anyone who saw him in his little sitting room or parlor looking on the street would form a very erroneous idea of the poet's personal tastes. The real man was reflected in the den upstairs. This was a spacious, square, uncarpeted room, with broken blinds and ample sunlight. In one corner, a bed; diagonally opposite, a large writing table of rough wood; between them, against the wall and between the windows, a collection of trunks, never more than half unpacked since he came from Washington, in which lay bundles of old letters, souvenirs of his mother, and a flood of manuscripts. By the table and the window, with the sunlight on his head, Walt sat and wrote in his vast rocking chair, the gift of the Smiths. The long afghan which covered it, and, when needful, was wrapped about his knees, was made for him one Christmas by a group of college girls. At the back of Walt's writing table, piled high against the wall, stood an odd medley of books— his favorites, Walter Scott and Omar Khayyám, Homer and Shakespeare, plus presentation copies of books from literary friends, and a large assortment of undistinguished novels, the last two classes being usually dealt with by the process which he called sampling, which consisted in reading a few pages here and there without the least desire or effort to read the whole. Free space on the table was littered with his work. Walt liked to write on torn scraps of paper or the backs of envelopes; these, when he found a sequence, he pinned or gummed together. Until then the sibylline leaves fell in a shower not only over the table but on every part of the floor. On the table, also, Mary used to notice sundry pictures, stray bunches of flowers in broken glasses, current correspondence, his shoes, his white knitted gloves, or his well-known "wide-awake" hat. More often than not a shoeblacking box stood in the middle of the room—on which sometimes was the pair of shoes which the poet had half finished blacking. In a corner beside his washstand, a door led to a side room which served the double purpose of library and woodshed, with an etching of Blake's on the wall and others lying about.

Old Walt passed an uneventful but cheery life, eagerly awaiting post time, always grateful for any remembrance or check from absent friends, known and unknown. In summer he took in his letters from his good friend the postman through the open window of the parlor. There he sat most of the day in hot weather, often in his shirt sleeves, cooling himself with a great palm-leaf fan. He had great delight in frequent gifts of flowers brought by the milkman as he came in from the country, or the butcher or the telegraph boy as they passed his "shanty." Ragamuffins loved to come and play under his window, in the light of his indulgent smile. When he had been better able to get around, Walt's chief recreation was to walk over to the Camden ferry and cross and recross the river, chatting with sailors, watching the human tide. After his second stroke of paralysis he had become less and less able to walk, but at last friends subscribed to provide him with a quiet horse and a low carriage in which he could take a daily airing. This was his luxury. He had never drawn large receipts from his books; and once when he received fifty dollars for a short poem in *Harper's* he remarked to Mary that it was worthwhile to be a poet. He added a bit to his microscopic income by occasional lectures and other services, and was able on the whole to provide the necessaries of his unexacting and simple life, which found its chief delight in nature rather than civilization.

In full retreat from the "miserable sinner" Christianity and the sanctimonious hypocrisy which he was convinced had wrecked his career, Robert Pearsall Smith came to share his elder daughter's devotion to good old Walt. Smith decided that he must pay some public tribute to his friend. In 1887 he decided upon a great reception for Whitman in New York. He engaged a suite of parlors at the Westminster Hotel in Irving Place—"at what must have been a great expense," Walt later commented. The poet protested against the whole project, "making this splurge in the face of my protest: arranging everything, however, with a certain grace and generosity that touched me. The reception, as you know, was a thing of which I didn't approve. First and last I opposed it—tried to beg off. Smith has two admirable daughters—I have a real affection for them for their unusual qualities. . . . Well I ought to like the Smiths, even if they ought to like me!"

The reception, on April 14, 1887, was an even greater success than Pearsall Smith had anticipated. An endless succession of distinguished guests paid their respects to Walt, enthroned like a king receiving his subjects. Crowds of people, curiosity seekers among the rest, passed through the reception rooms. By midnight, the guest of honor was quite worn out; but at that moment appeared the eminent John Fiske, the eloquent disciple of Herbert Spencer and popularizer of the doctrines and dogmas of evolution. Fiske was anxious to question Walt on his ideas about the immortality of the soul. "I diverted Fiske to Pearsall Smith, saying 'Here's a fellow who knows all about things' . . . For all I know they're still at the spot whacking away at each other!"

When in 1888 Pearsall Smith paid a special call upon Walt to announce that the Smiths, one and all, were going to make their permanent home in England, he said that wherever they lived two rooms would always be held in readiness for

Walt and his male nurse. But it was too late now for the poet to leave his beloved native land—Walt was immobile, but comfortable.

Mary took deep pleasure in Walt's large heart and kindly ways, his cheery content and restfulness, his ready welcome for all, and especially for English visitors who brought him word of "those old fellows over the sea."

As she matured and gained self-assurance, Mary became more advanced and radical than her father—"almost an anarchist," said Walt. She reminded him of one of the outstanding heroines of his youth, Frances Wright; she had Fanny's ardor, impetuosity, inner fire. In his earlier years, he had often heard the lectures of the firebrand Fanny. Filtered through the Scottish burr of her native Dundee, her indignation against social injustice had seemed all the more convincing and memorable. Mary Smith also reminded Walt of his staunch English adorer Mrs. Gilchrist. In fact, all of the aging poet's images of the feminine ideal coalesced finally in the remembered presence of Mary Smith, whom he liked to think of as his "bright particular star." The very mention of her name brought praise to his lips. ". . . Quite a great woman in her way," he was to say in later years. "Though going so whole-heartedly, so devotedly, into public work she does so abrogating nothing of her wifeliness, sisterliness, motherliness, womanliness: all these remain not less, rather more richly demonstrated than before. Mary is much like Mrs. Gilchrist—much that style of woman."

Speaking of Mary to Horace Traubel, Whitman mentioned his surprise "at the extent to which she has thrown herself into public life there [in England]—almost swallowed the whole camel." But then he added: "That should not be puzzling either; it is just like Mary: just what might have been expected of her impetuosity, ardor, which is of a high order."

Breaking "an iron rule of my life, not to give letters of introduction," Whitman gave Mary and Alys letters to both Tennyson and Lord Houghton, when the sisters went to England in 1885. It is not probable that they met the latter, since Monckton Milnes died at Vichy on August 11, 1885, but they made a pilgrimage to the Isle of Wight, where they met Tennyson, and reported that meeting to their old friend in Camden. Walt was delighted. "Tennyson (the sly old rascal)," he told Traubel, "is a lady's man—is fond of the girls . . . rather prefers them. They say he particularly affects children—is often seen with one on his knee!"

After she went to England to live, Mary never saw Walt again. One of his last notes to the family (June 20, 1890) contained this characteristic message: "My last poem rejected and sent back by *The Century*. I have now been r'buffed by all the magazines here but you know I am used to that— Love to Mary and Logan and Alys and all and God bless you all—Walt Whit."

At Whitman's death in 1892, Mary found a certain consolation in the importance attached to this passing by the English press. She herself had done much to increase interest in him, and her efforts had borne fruit. For as Harold Frederic, correspondent of the *New York Times,* wrote: "Americans, happening to be in England during this week, must have been greatly surprised to see the amount of space the English papers devoted to Walt Whitman. It is no exaggeration to say that his death created twice the amount of interest that Lowell's evoked." The special irony of this was that James Russell Lowell, poet and Ambassador to England, had long been an adverse critic of Walt Whitman's genius.

Chapter 4 · Frank Costelloe

One of the guest lecturers Mary Smith heard and met at Harvard was a young Anglo-Irish barrister named Benjamin Francis Conn Costelloe (Costelloe with the accent on the "*Cos*"). Although not a scientist he had come to the fifty-fourth annual convention of the British Association for the Advancement of Science which met in Montreal, late in August of 1884. Later, like many of the visiting notables, he came south to visit the States, and was invited to lecture at Harvard. And there he met Mary Smith.

The meeting between the tall, red-haired Quaker-bred girl and the slight, dark Irishman ten years her senior was the first link in one of those curious chains of events that change the course of many lives. Because of it, the Smith family would return to England, never again to be really at home in America. Alys would marry the brilliant Bertrand Russell; Logan would make his place, minor but marked, in English letters. And Mary herself, glowing, brilliant, beloved, embarked on the long, strange journey of her life, the journey which ended, so long after, in an Italian villa made famous as the home of Bernard Berenson.

Frank Costelloe was a graduate of Balliol and one of the favorite pupils of its distinguished Master, Benjamin Jowett, the translator of Plato. Costelloe's interests were not confined to Plato, Hegel and the law: he was a burning advocate of

54

Home Rule for Ireland, of housing reform in Great Britain. And he was an outspoken, dedicated Roman Catholic. His Catholicism might have given pause to most Quaker-bred young ladies, but Mary, in full rebellion against the conventions of her grandparents and her parents, fell headlong in love.

When Costelloe visited the Smiths in Philadelphia, Mary drove her new friend over to Camden to meet Whitman. Although the young Irishman was inches shorter than Mary, Walt was always to recall him as a man of commanding stature. To be truly a great actor, Walt always claimed, a man must have a panther concealed within him. The actor Junius Booth, Edwin's father, "had the panther," Whitman asserted; this gave him vitality and "pounce." And Costelloe, barrister from London's Chancery Lane, also "had the tiger" —an inner drive and spring to match Mary's. Through the years, Walt was to take a paternal pride in Frank's achievements.

After Costelloe went back to England, letters kept flying across the Atlantic all through the winter of 1884–85. At the beginning of the summer of 1885, the Thomas cousins learned to their surprise that all of the Smith family were planning to return to Europe. They suspected that Mary was the instigator of this plan, for she was more and more coming to be the bellwether of the Smith flock.

Robert and Hannah were most reticent about their elder daughter's secret engagement. They claimed that their impending voyage was rather to renew and to revive friendships they had made ten years earlier—to revisit Lady Mount Temple, the Barclays of Monkhams, Lady Henry Somerset. There was, indeed, little to hold them in America now. After the death of Hannah's father, the Cedars had been sold, so there was no longer a gathering place for the old and young

of the Whitall clan. To replace the Cedars, the Smiths had
joined their Baltimore cousins in planning a joint summer
home. The Thomases had bought a site for it, almost equi-
distant between Baltimore and Philadelphia in the Blue
Ridge mountains, and now they were compelled, not without some resentment, to undertake the full expense of this
house because of the withdrawal of the Smiths' co-operation.
"A sudden catastrophe had sent all the Pearsall Smiths sailing away to England," says Helen Thomas Flexner. "Some-
time during the winter Mary had fallen in love with a strange
Irishman lecturing for a few weeks at Harvard and had announced to her parents her intention of marrying him and
settling in London. At her mother's entreaty she had con-
sented not to engage herself formally until she had seen her
lover again and met his people. However, everyone now
knew that Mary's mind was made up. The rapid fire of letters . . . exchanged across the Atlantic had settled the matter. Brilliant, entrancing letters they were reported to be. In
my imagination they figured as probably the most wonderful
love letters ever written."

Everything happened as Mary planned. The return to
England, in June 1885, and the welcome they received after
a ten-year exile, put the elder Smiths in a benign and receptive mood. Broadlands received them once more; elsewhere
they were welcome guests. It was therefore not difficult for
Mary to persuade her parents that it would be a waste of
time and money to expect a busy young barrister like Frank
Costelloe to cross the Atlantic once again, merely to satisfy
the outmoded conventions of stuffy Germantown.

Mary and Frank were married in Oxford, with a reception
in the great hall of Balliol. Benjamin Jowett, Master of Balliol, Regius professor of Greek, translator of Plato and Aristotle, vice-chancellor of the University, made a felicitous address of congratulation to the bride and groom.

After the wedding Robert and his daughter Alys once more crossed the Atlantic, for it was time for Alys to resume her college course at Cousin Carey Thomas's recently inaugurated Bryn Mawr. Logan, now a tall, timid youth of twenty, was awarded a year's travel on the Continent with his cousin Harry Thomas, and with his mother as chaperon for part of the time. Logan was scheduled to begin his apprenticeship, "learning the family business," with the Whitall-Tatum Company the following year, but his imagination had been captivated by the life and ideas of Europe, especially the sights and sounds of Oxford, the ritual and the dignity of the great hall of Balliol.

When the Costelloes returned to London after the honeymoon, Frank at once found a house which they felt fulfilled their needs perfectly. It was at 41 Grosvenor Road (now Millbank), on the Westminster Embankment, and it contained ten rooms, some of them quite small. Mary was carried away by the beauty and ever changing interest of the view from the little front balcony, which faced the Thames. Across the river the sun rose behind Lambeth Palace, and on clear days, looking eastward, Mary could see the dome of St. Paul's and the distant spires of the City churches. The sun gleamed on the oily surface of the river which flowed just beyond the Embankment. Barges with red or yellow sails passed; under the Vauxhall and Lambeth bridges timber rafts and coal steamers drifted by. When the tide ebbed, mud banks appeared and the water lapped the anchored river craft. At times the river was lost in fog and mist, white, yellow or black, and seemed as limitless in its expanse as faraway Delaware Bay.

Arm in arm Mary and Frank strolled past the Battersea Bridge (which had already been "glamourized" by Whistler), past the Royal Hospital and the physic garden till they came to the upper reaches of old Chelsea. Or, turning to the left, they soon came upon the Houses of Parliament and the Abbey. Frank pointed out the dwelling place of the British Civil Service, the stately Inns of Court with their quaint gardens. Sometimes the newlyweds ventured of an evening into the crowded Strand, eastward into Fleet Street as far as St. Paul's, or penetrated that narrow and winding maze of streets in the Jewish Ghetto quarters, which sprawled out from Bishopsgate to Bow and from Bethnal Green eastward toward the London docks. Sometimes they lost their way in the darkness of narrow streets, were brought face to face with alien, frightened eyes, sensed the smoldering symptoms of exiled misery in the crowds of Jewish refugees from Russia and Poland—all driven from home by the persecution of their tsarist oppressors and the secret police. Here these exiles, "children of the Ghetto," were creating new industries. To eke out a bare living the majority were employed in the sweating trades of the East End, where girls and young women toiled endless hours to make ten or twelve shillings. London's East End was the hotbed of revolutionary legend and the propaganda center from which subversive and anarchistic ideas spread to many countries. A handful of intellectuals had founded a paper named the *Arbeiter Freund* (Worker's Friend), and soon to be published was *Freedom* (1886).

Among the guests the Costelloes received at 41 Grosvenor Road, the majority were ardent Ibsenites and outspoken feminists, both English and American. Mary was one of several energetic young American women who were then undertaking, to borrow only the title of a book by Henry James, the Siege of London. These compatriots of hers were not, any more than she had been, mere heiresses in search of titled husbands; many of them were actresses, writers and artists seeking the stamp of English approval. Mary's English friends were people of similar interests. Among them were two maiden ladies, Kate Bradley and her niece Edith Cooper, who had decided that by uniting their talents they might produce one full-sized poet. To this synthetic poet they gave the name of "Michael Field." Michael Field seemed to be accepted as a perfectly legitimate creation in London's *fin de siècle* literary circles. In Michael Field's diary, later published, we read under the date of May 25, 1892: "As we are looking . . . Oscar [Wilde] comes up. He shakes hands with Mrs. Costelloe." Mary's ardent bridegroom took a touching pride in introducing his wife to his friends, and the "beautiful Mrs. Costelloe" was admired in a variety of social circles.

But in the midst of all these activities, Mary found time to write long, newsy, gossipy letters to her darling old Walt—letters full of "frivol." Their friendship was a precious thing to both of them, and Mary was resolved that it should not be destroyed by distance. She appointed herself a sort of volunteer publicity agent for Whitman in London, and met the members of the "Whitman circle" at Toynbee Hall in Whitechapel. In June 1885, Mary and Frank were present at the ceremonies opening Toynbee Hall, a pioneer university settlement named in honor of Frank's friend Arnold Toynbee, a former tutor at Balliol, who had died in 1883, at the age of thirty-one. Young Toynbee had worn himself out devoting himself to the disinherited masses of the East End.

Mary wrote to Walt of the aims and ideals of the dedicated founders of Toynbee Hall, and told him about the group of Whitman admirers who were beginning to hold regular meetings there to discuss his ideas, and to whom she had given a talk. This letter brought a reply from Camden, dated July 20, 1885: ". . . The account of Toynbee Hall and chat deeply interesting to me . . . These libations, ecstatic life-pourings as it were of precious wine or rose-water on vast desert sands or great polluted rivers—taking chances of returns or no returns. What were they (or are they) but the theory and practice of the beautiful God Christ? or of all divine personality?"

The English had discovered Whitman—as later they would discover their own Thomas Traherne—in a second-hand book stall. One William Bell Scott, a saturnine painter and poet of the Pre-Raphaelite periphery, stumbled on a copy of *Leaves of Grass* which had been shipped across the Atlantic in a jobber's pack of "remainders." Scott took it home, and read it with mounting excitement. Bursting with the ecstasy of his discovery, Scott sent the volume as a gift to his friend William Michael Rossetti, who received it warmly. Little Algernon Swinburne shared this first English enthusiasm; later, under the influence of his guardian Watts-Dunton, he retracted in his venomous, insulting essay entitled "Whitmania," printed in the *Fortnightly* in 1887, in which he likened Whitman's Muse to "a drunken applewoman sprawling in the gutter." But others remained loyal, and many English travelers visited Walt, among them Monckton Milnes, Edmund Gosse, Oscar Wilde—even Henry Irving, when he appeared in Philadelphia. In London the Whitman cult had been kept flourishing by such idealists as Edward Carpenter, Havelock Ellis, John Addington Symonds, Ernest Rhys, the Gilchrists and lesser-known provincial converts. Thus Mary's proselytizing was well received.

Hannah returned to London from the Continent to help settle Mariechen and Frank in their new house: "Busy, busy, busy is the word that best describes my life . . . busy with house-fixing, busy with people, busy with meetings, busy with a thousand interests of every kind. Too busy in this busy

London to get one tenth part of the things done that I want
to do."

Later, thanks to the guidance of Frank Costelloe, the elder
Smiths settled into a similar house, at 44 Grosvenor Road.
But to Hannah, this "hard little house: with its ten rooms—
some of them dark and narrow"—made her feel at times like
a poor lame turtle weighed down by an enormous shell, as
though she could hardly twist her poor head around to see it
properly, let alone keep it in order as it should be kept.

Hannah had left Logan and his cousin absorbing German
culture. She had found that she could respond neither to
German music nor to the Old Masters in the picture galleries
through which Logan and Harry dragged her. "I do not like
them," she expostulated. "I am sure if any modern painter
were to paint such poor pictures now, he would be hooted
out of the profession." Rubens's pictures at Antwerp disgusted her. "They were great masses of coarse flesh . . . the
anatomy was repulsive." To Hannah, the Old Masters were
wonderful only because they were painted so long ago; in
Dresden she confessed that she did like the Sistine Madonna
of Raphael, either. Logan was a staunch defender of the Old
Masters; but Harry's mother, Hannah's sister Mary, marched
through the great galleries with her skirts drawn closely
around her in fine contempt, and Hannah herself wrote
home: "I really would like to know what *is* the bottom truth
about all this fuss that is made over the Old Masters. Is it just
a fashion, such as makes even ugly ways of dressing look
beautiful when once we have been convinced it is 'the thing'?
Or is it a real fact that any painting which looks so inferior,
can really be, in some occult way, so infinitely superior? I
confess I cannot help believing in the first hypothesis. But
Logan says I am like a child who thinks Mother Goose's

rhymes far superior poetry to Shakespeare; and of course this is possible, for I know I have no education in art. But still—when the thing is right there before my eyes how *can* I believe I am so deceived?"

At Toynbee Hall, where Mary Costelloe was invited to talk on Whitman, she could listen as well to lectures by such distinguished liberals as Leslie Stephen, Frederic Harrison and Sir Alfred Lyall. Occasionally a young man named Bernard Shaw enlivened the debates; and a self-dedicated young woman named Beatrice Potter used the settlement as a base for her social research.

Through the Whitman group, Mary met the editors of the *Pall Mall Gazette* and persuaded them to promote a fund to be contributed by English admirers of the Camden prophet. The chronic indigence of Walt Whitman was considered a disgrace to all Americans with any taste for literature, "which means five people out of six in fifty million," according to the estimate of the *Gazette*. The paper pictured the poet neglected, seated alone in a narrow room with uncarpeted floor and little furniture, dragging himself up and down stairs with the help of an old stick. "This 'good gray poet' certainly seems one of the easiest persons in the world to provide for," the *Gazette* complained. "His remaining days cannot be many; but the years during which his 'poems' will be talked about as among the most curious literary phenomena of our time will be as many as will witness the survival of our language itself—surely the contrast of these two facts is enough to cause Walt Whitman to be placed beyond the reach of mere physical distress arising from poverty. It would be a pleasure to send him fifty pounds for a Christmas present. Who will enable us to do it?"

The following day, the *Gazette* was compelled to counteract rumors that Whitman was starving, and quoted an extract from the *New York Evening Post* describing Walt's state of modest comfort. "Donations to the Christmas present are nevertheless welcome." Contributions were received from seventeen Whitman admirers, making a grand total of eighty-one pounds, six shilling, sixpence. On December 23, 1886, the newspaper published Mary's unsigned article entitled "Walt Whitman at Camden." Its authorship was "by one who has been there." Written by a young woman who was not yet twenty-three, this article, with its vivid, direct expression and its concrete detail, reveals a defined journalistic sense.

In March 1887, Mary's first daughter arrived and in memory of Mary's sister was named Rachel Conn Costelloe. As soon as she was able, Mary sent her happy news to Walt Whitman, who returned his "fondest love to little Rachel."

Two years later, Mary's second daughter, Karin, was born (the Karin who was later to be sister-in-law to Virginia Woolf). Walt Whitman told Horace Traubel: ". . . there came a message from Hannah Smith, Mary Costelloe's mother, telling of the birth of Mary's second child . . . on the tenth of March . . . They come and they go. The procession is endless."

As a rising young barrister with headquarters in Chancery Lane, Frank Costelloe knew London well. In the wide circle of "advanced" friends to whom he introduced Mary, some were now calling themselves Fabians. Though predominantly secular in character, the Fabian Society grew out of a group which called itself the Fellowship of the New Life. The first meeting of the New Life group had been held on the evening of October 24, 1883, at the rooms of Edward Reynolds Pease at 17 Osnaburgh Street, Regent's Park. In the group were Havelock Ellis; Percival Chubb (who later migrated to the United States, where he was fairly well known as a preacher and teacher) ; Mrs. Hinton, widow of James Hinton; Frank Podmore, the spiritualist; and Miss Owen, granddaughter of Robert Owen of New Lanark. On November 7, Hubert Bland turned up and began to advocate socialism. By January 4, 1884, the Fellowship of the New Life gathered for the fifth of its meetings at Pease's rooms and decided to change the name to the Fabian Society. Under the leadership of Bland, the Socialists infiltrated and successfully captured the little group of idealists. George Bernard Shaw, then an irrepressible juvenile of twenty-eight, did not attend Fabian meetings until the May sixth after the "Fabian" christening. At that time this exile from Dublin was living with, and off, his mother and sisters a few doors away, at 36 Osnaburgh Street, where he was trying to write novels. To the innocuous minutes of that May sixth meeting was later added a note in Shaw's characteristic handwriting: "This meeting was made memorable by the first appearance of Bernard Shaw." Shaw afterward described the character of the Fabian Society as a silly business. "They had one elderly retired workman. They had two psychical researchers . . . There were anarchists . . . There were young ladies on the look-out for husbands, who left when they succeeded . . . There were atheists and Anglo-Catholics."

Witty, iconoclastic, always eager to attract attention, Shaw liked to indulge in clownish exaggeration. In contrast, Costelloe was serious, earnest and industrious in his intellectual pursuits, had won an M.A. degree from Balliol. In addition to his interest in social problems, Costelloe was a devout lay propagandist for the Catholic faith, and an authority on the Irish problem. As a lay lecturer, he was asked by the Catholic Truth Society to deliver lectures to non-Catholic audiences.

Two of these, delivered at the South Place Institute in London, were entitled: *The Church Catholic* and *The Mass.* Later published as tracts by the Catholic Truth Society, they reveal with what care and erudition young Costelloe fulfilled his task. Mary was proud of her husband's knowledge and fervor, but she must have known that his exposition of the significance of ritual and sacrament was over the heads of his scattered listeners—and even over her own. The busy young barrister found time to publish a paper for the Irish Franchise Committee on Irish affairs and another on taxation; to prepare a paper for the Manchester Society on the housing problem. Later he undertook a translation, in collaboration with J. H. Muirhead, of Zeller's *Philosophy of the Greeks,* which under the title *Aristotle and the Earlier Peripatetics* was published with a dedication to the Master of Balliol in 1895. Its many learned notes indicate Costelloe's exceptional scholarship in Greek.

Sidney Webb soon joined the Fabian Society and became one of the triumvirate—the others were Shaw and Sydney Olivier—which dictated its policy. Like many other mushroom radical organizations, the Fabian Society was chiefly composed of enthusiastic youngsters—and oldsters who never could or never would grow up. They gabbled incessantly of the coming revolution and placed all their hopes on the sudden tumultuous uprising of the workers of the world. Before this millenial outburst landlords and capitalists were to go down like ninepins, leaving society to reorganize itself into a new Utopia. The date for this social revolution was fixed by the more ardent for 1889, just one hundred years after the beginning of the French Revolution. It was against this catastrophic and chiliastic myth that Webb, Shaw and Olivier developed their policy of gradualism.

Chapter 5 · Friday's Hill

For their country home in England, Hannah and Robert decided upon a house where they could be as hospitable as their natures and habits of life demanded. The Costelloes helped them find capacious, comfortable Friday's Hill House, in Fernhurst, near Haslemere, just south of London. Haslemere was once described as London's suburban Alps; it was a colony of intellectuals, artists and musicians. It was in that neighborhood that Arnold Dolmetsch initiated his school for the study of ancient instruments, with his own children as his first pupils. Nearby lived Lord Tennyson; the philosophical editor and polemist Frederic Harrison, founder and editor of the *Positivist;* and Rollo Russell, a younger son of the illustrious Prime Minister, Lord John Russell. Friday's Hill was within driving distance of Broadlands and Hannah's close friend Georgina Cowper Temple.

The Smiths took Friday's Hill in 1889 and it remained their home for the next sixteen years. There they entertained American visitors and their own and their children's English and American friends. In the early years, the Costelloes often rented a cottage nearby and brought their weekend guests over on Sundays. The Smiths established friendly relations with most of their distinguished neighbors; they renewed acquaintance with Tennyson, and came to know Israel Zangwill, whose most famous novel, *The*

Children of the Ghetto, was to bring him international re-
nown in 1892, and others of the great of that day who came
to lunch, relax and talk at Friday's Hill. A glimpse at the
guest book would reveal the names of many who were already famous, as well as many who later became so.

A vivid account of life at Friday's Hill is found in the
memoirs of the artist Sir William Rothenstein. In 1894, as
a young man of twenty-two, Will Rothenstein made his first
visit there. He recalls: "Mrs. Costelloe was then living close
to the Pearsall Smiths, where I spent the greater part of the
summer of 1894, painting a portrait of her sister . . . Friday's Hill was a hospitable house, which saw much, and some
oddly varied company. Old Mrs. Smith was a Quaker of strict
and narrow principles, rigidly held. Her children, while re-
specting her faith, talked freely before her, and encouraged
their friends to do likewise; and as they brought to the house
anyone they thought interesting, whatever his or her views
might be, there were lively discussions.

"It was my first country-house visit, and the ways of a
large household were new and attractive. Mrs. Costelloe
took me under her wing. I was devoted to her two young
children, Ray and Karin; their mother was writing a story
book for them, for which I made the drawings. Meanwhile
I worked regularly on my portrait.

"There were pleasant visits to neighboring houses, to the
Frederic Harrisons', to the Rollo Russells', to the Tennysons',
and to Mrs. Rogerson's, where I would meet my *National
Observer* friends. George Street, George Stevens, and Charles
Whibley were constant visitors. Lady Henry Somerset and
Miss [Frances] Willard paid a visit and overawed me by the
ethical and social ideals they preached. I was a very moderate drinker, but not an abstainer; and I knew that my life
would not bear the scrutiny of Miss Willard's searching eyes.

But I had Logan and Mrs. Costelloe, thank Heaven! to support me. Logan was all for adventures, of the spirit at least. A Puritan himself, he enjoyed the indiscretions of others, and his broad intellectual sympathies were at the service of all his friends. Among these was Zangwill, who visited Friday's Hill just after I left. I heard from Logan:

" 'Zangwill was here—it was the last of our parties for the summer. Zangwill's novel "The Master" is finished—everybody is writing about artists—you people are in great demand as models.' "

Fresh from Bryn Mawr in 1890, Alys found herself a bit abashed by the advanced young thinkers who nearly every Sunday lounged about the sunny terrace of Friday's Hill. All were, to put it mildly, articulate, while Alys found herself a non-talking member. She had bloomed into a tall, willowy woman of twenty-three, with regular features, vivid complexion, bright blue eyes, and soft, curly nut-brown hair. She smiled a great deal and laughed often; she was warm-hearted and sympathetically intelligent; but she had not developed any gift of easy intimacy; and she was completely devoid of any gift for flirtation. Not at all like her audacious sister Mary.

The Costelloes' guests had endless discussions on the terrace. These visitors were not the type usually invited to large country houses; although some of them were later to become international figures, they were at that time mostly unimportant civil servants, journalists, lecturers, writers or, like Frank himself, struggling young barristers. Their discussions, mostly of social problems, went on from morning till night. Alys found herself dazzled by the bold ideas these visitors put forward, and by the brilliance with which they defended their shocking heresies. Even during the long afternoon walks up Blackdown Hill, the discussions still went on among smaller groups. All returned for tea and more talk on the terrace until the cold Sunday supper took them indoors. One evening Frank Costelloe monopolized the conversation all through the cold beef and pudding; it was not until he stopped inadvertently to bite into an apple that Sidney Webb was able to barge in and hold forth until the party broke up. Even if she had had an idea to express, Alys would have found it almost impossible to interrupt the garrulous guests.

A young man named Graham Wallas especially interested Alys. Wallas was one of the early members of the Fabian Society. Six feet tall, slouching in his slovenly, unpressed clothes, he seemed utterly unself-conscious, without the slightest personal vanity or ambition. The son of a poor clergyman, Mr. Wallas had at first earned his living as an usher and schoolmaster. Without his Fabian convictions, he might have lounged through life; with them he became a lecturer and the author of *Human Nature in Politics,* which was to be recognized as a landmark in this field of study. With his gentle face, his clothes hanging on his emaciated figure, Wallas was for a time, to Alys, the most attractive member of the group.

All were more or less disinterested and selfless, but Wallas, especially, gave the young woman from Bryn Mawr a sense of unworldly integrity and outspoken truthfulness. In his honest features and open smile she found something almost angelic. As a young man just beginning, he had lost an excellent post in a school over a question of religious conformity, and had then taken up university-extension teaching. A superb lecturer, Graham knew how to inspire his students in suggesting subjects for research. He was the absolute prototype of the absent-minded professor. Someone told Alys that a timid student had found him wandering into his classroom without a necktie. When this omission was pointed out to him, he had replied: "Oh, would you mind going and getting me one?"

During the following years, Alys became Wallas's devoted friend. She even visited his dreary lodgings in Bloomsbury, and later, when he was away lecturing in the States, she persuaded his landlady to let her furbish up his rooms with new curtains and cushions and a rug. But when Wallas returned, he hardly noticed these efforts at interior decoration.

Then there was Mr. Shaw, the Dubliner with flaming red hair and beard, cold, steely blue eyes; always provoking or contradicting. Mr. Shaw usually wore khaki-colored "health" clothes made of Jaeger flannel. His trousers, those of a golfer or cyclist, stopped at the knee, and had been cut by some special tailor. Alys was confused by the witticisms and paradoxes of this outstanding star on the terrace at Friday's Hill.

Once Alys induced Sidney Webb to accompany her on a buggy ride through the Fernhurst valley and across the rolling Sussex hills to Lyndhurst. Sidney ignored the scenery, and declared that the only difference between London and the country was that London compelled you to wash your hands oftener. Alys brought up the subject of poetry, but Sidney continued his own lecture on economics. She found that it was true, as some of the young women guests had told her, that if you went out with Mr. Webb, he simply poured forth information.

Through Webb, Alys came to know the brilliant Beatrice Potter. Miss Potter was spending the weekend with the Frederic Harrisons, and one Sunday Sidney brought her over to meet the Smiths and the Costelloes. This was the beginnings of a lifetime friendship between Alys and Beatrice. Beatrice, ten years older than Alys, discovered in her an eager and impressionable disciple, and Alys rapidly came to idealize Beatrice. She seemed to possess nobler ideals than anyone Alys had ever known. In the years to come, Alys made few decisions without asking herself: "Would Beatrice approve?"

In her thirties, Beatrice Potter was indeed a commanding personality. Handsome, alive, erect and queenly, she was beautiful to look at. She could hold her own in any discussion, for she was an eager and persuasive talker. But she preferred exposition to argument.

Because Beatrice loved to talk, Alys found it easy to draw her out about her past life. Beatrice was the daughter of a railroad magnate, next to youngest of the nine famous Potter sisters, most of whom had made very good marriages. Her conversation always seemed to come back to her friendship with the Liberal leader Joseph Chamberlain. Beatrice had admired Chamberlain very much, and he her, but when Alys asked Miss Potter why she had not married him, the visitor only replied quickly, "Impossible!" On another occasion, Beatrice said that when nothing had come of her friendship with Chamberlain, some of the ladies of London's best society had dropped her—their invitations had quite faded away.

No one could have been more forthright than Beatrice in recounting to Alys the story of her family's rise to fortune. The industrial revolution was a real chapter in her own family history. When cotton became king, her grandfather had floated to fortune from farmyard and weaver's cottage. Politics had taken him into the House of Commons. Her father, Richard Potter, was intended for the life of a country gentleman, but a turn of the industrial wheel sent him into business. When the financial crisis of 1848 swept away his modest fortune, his family arranged a partnership for him in a firm of timber merchants at Gloucester. Then came a directorship in the Great Western Railway. Other directorships followed, and he became president of the Grand Trunk Railway of Canada, which led to other undertakings characterized as Big Business. But he was a cultivated man with a wide circle of friends eminent in science and literature; one of these was Herbert Spencer, who encouraged Beatrice, when she was fifteen years old, to undertake a translation of *Faust*.

Richard Potter maintained country seats in Gloucestershire, Westmoreland and Wales. For Beatrice as a girl there were London seasons of dancing, flirting and dressing up, and occasional long tours on the Continent. At twenty-four, Beatrice had become the head of her father's household, administered his income, acted as his secretary and counselor. Her father even suggested that she be given formal status as his business associate, but Beatrice confided to Alys that her life at home was becoming painfully distasteful. She yearned for serious work, but in what field? For a time she had served as secretary to Herbert Spencer, thorny and old; but at twenty-five she felt that she had outgrown this cranky opponent of state socialism, decided that she must observe poverty at first-hand, and so had become a social worker. She undertook the management of a block of working-class buildings and was for a term a visitor for the Charity Organization Society, which was then at the height of its reputation. But she felt condemned to endless groping, and at last decided to become an investigator of all social institutions. At twenty-eight, Miss Potter had published a book on *The Economic Theory of Karl Marx,* and another on the rise and growth of English economics, which she described as her salute and farewell to deductive economics. Beatrice had been greatly influenced by her cousin by marriage, Charles Booth, who, when planning his inquiry into the *Life and Labour of the People of London,* assigned to Miss Potter an investigation of dock labor in the Tower hamlets. From that she had gone on to studying the clothing industry sweatshops in East London.

And now Miss Potter's eyes were captured by Sidney Webb, frankly of the lower middle class, the son of small shopkeepers. With his big head, bulging eyes, bushy mustache and square-cut short beard, his small but rotund body, his tapering arms and legs, diminutive hands and feet, Sidney was a man of unique appearance. His mother had set up a retail shop in a street of shops in central London, which became the home of the family and the principal source of its income, while Beatrice came of a family firmly established in that class which, as she admitted to her American friend, "habitually gave orders, but . . . seldom, if ever, executed the orders of other people." However, although Beatrice definitely and consciously renounced the luxuries and creature comforts of great wealth, Alys was to discover that her new friend had not overcome the habit of giving orders and "managing" other people. Miss Potter felt herself to be very competent, and she could not suffer fools gladly; in fact, she was a mistress in the art of snubbing, even to the borderline of bad manners. In addition, she felt that personal indulgence was perfectly unimportant, and this extended to matters of dress. With her new outlook, Beatrice Potter disdained any concession to fashion; deliberate dowdiness became the pose.

Like the Quakers, the Fabian group condemned all the minor arts and music. Logan's lively interest in literary style and *le mot juste* seemed to the Fabians a totally frivolous preoccupation. They were friendly with Logan, but they regarded him as a lightweight. Alys soon came to realize that all of them—with the exception of Mr. Shaw—were a little lacking in humor. Beatrice, it was evident, could never understand the Dubliner's elaborate jokes and contrived witticisms.

Much as she appreciated him as a Fabian Socialist, Beatrice never seemed to enjoy the coruscating brilliance of Mr. Shaw. He had for years worked at the routine of the Fabian Society with as much loyalty and persistence as Graham Wallas or Sidney; but, Beatrice confided to Alys, while he was agile, graceful and even virile, Mr. Shaw was also lacking in weight. A woman should be careful not to idolize him; for Shaw, according to Miss Potter, was a born philanderer, a Don Juan of the intellect, a professional blasphemer who refused to be hampered by either passion or conviction, and who had too often got himself tied up into knots which he had to cut before freeing himself for another adventure. Basically, according to Beatrice at this period, vanity was the bane of Shaw's nature. Beatrice was never to understand Shaw completely, close as their personal and professional friendship became. To her, his conceit was monstrous and he never seemed aware of the pain he could inflict by jeering words and laughing contempt. She could even confide to her diary: "A world made up of Bernard Shaws would be a world in moral dissolution." When it came to choosing a husband, she would seek one with whom she would live and work in an equal partnership.

One day in London, Alys wandered into the National Gallery, and there in a deserted corner, she stumbled upon Beatrice and Sidney engrossed in a whispered conversation. Alys was embarrassed by her inadvertent intrusion into their privacy, but the truth flashed into her mind: Beatrice and Sidney were going to be married. Later, Beatrice confessed that her premonition was correct; but of course, she said, they would have to wait. Alys timidly asked why they should wait, but Beatrice did not answer; however, on New Year's Day, 1891, her father died, and within a week's time her engagement was made known. "But we were in no hurry to get married," Beatrice wrote. When Herbert Spencer learned that his ex-secretary was to marry a Socialist, the old fire-eater cut her name as his literary executor out of his will. Sidney was taken on a round of visits to meet all the well-to-do elder sisters. Sister Kate Courtney wrote in her diary: "We met him [Webb] again at Theresa's [Cripps] with Daniel [Meinertzhagen], W. Cripps and Lallie [Holt] who was in great form in her most genial mood. Yes, I *think* we may like this new brother-in-law whom we certainly should not have chosen. . . ."

In London, rumors circulated that Miss Potter had rejected some of the most eligible suitors in the country (including both Balfour and Chamberlain), in her preference for this insignificant civil service clerk who shared her desire to replace an irresponsible and inefficient plutocracy by a new, trained, disinterested and representative leadership. They were married July 23, 1892, and spent the first part of their honeymoon investigating the ramshackle trade unions of Dublin. Social conditions in the Irish capital turned out to be appalling, a fact which convinced the newlyweds of their omniscience. The Webbs then went to a Trades Union Congress in Glasgow, collecting union documents and interviewing trade union secretaries. They had a weekend with R. B. Haldane and a Sunday on Loch Awe with Auberon Herbert. Beatrice recalled the gaunt figure of her Scottish friend, "wrapped in an old shawl, with vague blue eyes, soft high voice, flowing white beard, waving one hand at us, while pushing his sailing boat away from the shore; giving his final blessing: 'You will do a lot of mischief and be very happy in doing it.' "

But neither the Webbs nor any of the talkers on the terrace at Friday's Hill were aware of the fame of their hostess, Hannah Whitall Smith. For Hannah had become a transatlantic best seller, though her vast audience did not include her children's more advanced friends, or even her own. Her books would today be classified as "inspirational." Theologians might riddle her logic and point out the obvious contradictions and inconsistencies of her teaching, but to thousands of innocent readers her works had become a source of consolation and illumination. Not only in the United States, but throughout the British Empire, the number of her readers kept increasing. Many made pilgrimages to Friday's Hill to express their admiration. *The Christian's Secret of a Happy Life,* which sold more than a hundred thousand copies in England, was followed by other books of which the titles give some indication of their character. *Every-Day Religion* was followed by *Soul Rest: or The Joy of Obedience; Child Culture:* or *The Science of Motherhood; Christ Enough; Old Testament Types and Teachings; Living in the Sunshine; Difficulties of Life;* and *God Is Love.* She also translated and published her own version of *The Practice of the Presence of God,* by Brother Lawrence. She was later to publish *My Spiritual Autobiography.* From Hannah's indefatigable pen streamed an endless series of booklets and tracts, most of them published by the Fleming H. Revell Company. Great batches of letters from China, Japan and Germany were forwarded by her publishers, but the bulk of her mail came from those states of the Union where the evangelical sects predominated.

Mrs. Smith was a most persuasive figure on the platform and in the pulpit. She was a close ally of Frances Willard, the outstanding temperance reformer of that day. Miss Willard's deepest interest lay in the Woman's Christian Temperance Union, and at the age of forty-eight she became president of its international organization, with the aim of uniting all women in one organization for the prohibition of alcohol as a beverage. Hannah and Frances became lifelong co-workers in the W.C.T.U., and Mrs. Smith served as a liaison officer between the American and the English organization, the Woman's Temperance Association.

Hannah's old friend Lady Henry Somerset, a career reformer and champion of women's rights, founded and led the British W.T.A. She was an eloquent speaker and often managed, it is said, to overcome the prejudices of those who were predisposed against her. After hearing her, the mayor of a town in the north of England is reported to have closed the meeting with this remark: "I am bound to confess that, although I have always disapproved of ladies appearing in public, I have examined her Ladyship closely and observed nothing *ondacent,* either in word or in gesture."

During the nineties Hannah persuaded Lady Henry to go with her to the United States, to meet Miss Willard and to attend a W.C.T.U. convention in Boston. The two women found themselves the lions of the occasion; delegates absorbed every moment of their time. Lady Henry was beset on every hand. "It is a battle to get her out of every meeting," Hannah wrote. "I have to pull both her and Frances out by main force . . . the women are lovely, but there are a great many of them, and it is very tiring. Sixty pulpits were filled by our women on Sunday and I preached three times. Lady Henry's Sermon was a great success. The crowds were something fearful. She sent me ahead . . . and came later herself, and she was nearly torn to pieces getting through the crowd. She has a perfect ovation everywhere. Of course, she is so lovely that all hearts are captured . . . I have to guard her as a hen guards its chickens from the hawks, or she would be simply crushed with kisses, and handshakes, and birthday-books, and every other form of admiration possible."

Lady Henry was received at the White House by Mrs. Harrison. In Hannah's eyes the wife of President Harrison was not a lady and neither acted nor looked like one. "She was dressed in an old done-up black silk made in the fashion of about ten years ago, and apparently pieced out with all sorts of odds and ends of silk." Mrs. Harrison first addressed the British aristocrat as "Miss" Somerset, then as "Miss Lady."

Later Hannah took Lady Henry to the President's public reception. There they mingled with workingmen in stained and frayed coats, with workingwomen in shabby waterproofs and carrying brown-paper parcels, examining with undisguised curiosity all the rooms to which they were admitted, or lounging on White House sofas and easy chairs. It seemed incredible to English eyes, but Lady Henry delighted in it, and Hannah felt proud of a country where such a thing could be. In a letter to Mary, Hannah wrote that she trembled in her boots for fear that Lady Henry and her dear Frances Willard would not like each other. But the two reformers came to an immediate understanding, united perhaps by their common aversions to alcohol and sinful men.

Whenever Mrs. Smith was questioned by fanatical prohibitionists about what kind of bottles the Whitall-Tatum Company made, she dismissed the whole matter by claiming that never in its long history had the family company ever indulged in the manufacture of containers for any alcoholic beverage. This may, indeed, have been true at the time; but these scruples of Whitall-Tatum were not always to be maintained.

On their return to England, Lady Henry enlisted Hannah's help in various reform activities in London. Together they visited the Salvation Army shelters, but Hannah expressed grave doubts of the wisdom of such shelters, believing that such efforts only encouraged shiftlessness and tended to pauperize the recipient. The night she went there, it seemed hopeless to try to reach "such a sodden set of drunkards." Lady Henry was evidently a birthright Quaker herself, for in a note to her American friend she wrote: "It was such a joy to see thee. I wish I could tell how much thee is to my life. I always turn to thee as a sort of rest and often just think about thy face when I get troubled. I am not very good at saying all I feel, but deep down I do feel it all so much."

Miss Willard also expressed her admiration by writing a brief but fulsome biography of Hannah. Rereading this tribute years later, Hannah commented, in a letter to Mary, "It surprised me very much to find what a nice person I was! . . .Whether true or not, it is what Frances thought of me, and to look like that sort of person in her eyes I feel to be a decided feather in my cap. Thee has no idea how set up I am in my own opinion!"

To Hannah, the talkers on the terrace at Friday's Hill were not unlike the Evangelicals she had addressed at Broadlands years before. These young revolutionists and reformers could not be expected to see things as she had seen them; the spiritual food that satisfied her own generation could never satisfy them. But this did not trouble Hannah. "We did not see things as the generation before us did. We *could* not, as each one of us individually knows, and we must let

this make us tolerant of the generation that is to follow us."
She felt that she and Robert could now listen with indulgent
acceptance to what she called the "clash-ma-clavers." Hannah, now in her mid-sixties, chuckled inwardly to think
that some day these youngsters in their turn would have to
listen to the "clash-ma-clavers" of generations coming after
them with such indulgence as they could summon. She could
not agree with all the ideas they voiced, but she was
thoroughly convinced that it would be folly for the older
generation to think that they could make the younger con-
form to old modes of thought. In her naïveté, Mrs. Smith was
certain that these young people were all good and right-
minded and that she need feel no anxiety. "God loves them as
He does us," she reassured herself, "and cares for them as ten-
derly. He will lead them by the right way into His fold, perhaps by the *South* gate, while our entrance was by the *North*
gate, but none the less safely into its green pastures and beside its still waters."

Hannah now missed few opportunities to preach and lecture. The old days of the Quaker garb and the sugar-scoop
bonnet were gone forever; her "black plush" was remade
into a "princesse" with a train. With her friend Lady
Mount Temple, she attended the Women's Jubilee Meeting
at a large hall in Lambeth which was called "The Old Vic."
"Dear Lady Mount Temple, with her gentle, patrician voice,
was like the rustling of a violet in a thunderstorm. *I* managed to make them hear, and I made a right loyal speech,
spite of my radical Americanism. I was surprised to find
how much I had to say on the subject when once I began. I
find my *feet* very inspiring." Her life was taken up with so
many meetings, in fact, that she once said that the epitaph
on her tombstone might appropriately read: "Died of
too Many Meetings." In one day she might address the

British Woman's Temperance Association meeting in the
morning; a Moral Reform Union meeting in the afternoon,
followed by a conference of Women Guardians; and in the
evening attend the Jerusalem Medical Mission. She was in
continual demand in the provinces to give her famous Bible
readings. With her unsated appetite for public appearances,
she even acted as chairman at a women's trades union meeting, and surprised herself by making a speech in favor of such
unions, which she explained as an illustration of the growth
and spread of ideas.

Logan Smith was seldom an active participant in the talk
on the terrace at Friday's Hill. He preferred to absorb culture on the Continent.

When Logan's Grand Tour came to an end, he had reluctantly gone home to begin his career in the family business,
but for a young man with Logan's literary and artistic nature, Frank Costelloe felt that this was a grave error. Logan
should go to Oxford, Frank Costelloe thought, and he
promised to do all he could to facilitate his admission to
Balliol. Sadly Logan returned to America to "learn the business from the ground up," beginning in the New York ware-
houses of Whitall-Tatum. He lived in a rented room at 258
West Fifty-ninth Street; he had to be at his job promptly at
eight-thirty every morning; there was only half an hour for
lunch; and the long hours of afternoon toil seemed interminable to this young aesthete, who had just enjoyed a tour
of the Continent and had even met in a Dresden *pension*
the great Matthew Arnold. "Tell Father that I don't want
to become a partner yet," the unhappy Logan wailed to his
mother. The counsel of his brother-in-law kept re-echoing
in his mind. Oxford would not only mean the completion of
his education, but would release him from the gibes and

practical jokes of his warehouse coworkers, rough fellows who looked upon the boss's son as a congenital "sissy." At times their uncouth manners became more than Logan could bear.

At this juncture of his depression, during a visit to Philadelphia, he called upon his redoubtable cousin Carey Thomas. With her consuming passion for higher education, Cousin Carey decided the problem for Logan. Of course he must go to Oxford. All he needed, according to Cousin Carey, was an allowance of five hundred a year.

This problem Logan took up with his parents. If he were to leave Whitall-Tatum, he would be compelled to relinquish his personal share in that burgeoning business. It was possible for him, however, to turn over his share, inherited from his grandfather, and live on the interest of the principal thereby obtained. This Logan decided to do; or perhaps it would be more accurate to say that his mother persuaded him to this course, for not only was Hannah a passionate advocate of higher education, she was becoming more and more Anglophile in her outlook. On the other hand, Robert had at last realized the tremendous possibilities of the Whitall-Tatum business, with all its technological advances, and hoped Logan might wish to share this future. But Logan, in his revolt, shrewdly touched on his father's grievances against Whitall-Tatum because of their failure to recognize or to reward Robert's ability in determining policy.

Logan had grown into a tall, gentle-featured and gentle-natured young man. Endowed with the basic good looks of his father, he also had some of his personality. Behind his winning, open smile lay concealed a deep-seated melancholy. From childhood, Logan had often been the butt of the practical jokes of his sisters. He was not gifted with the dash and determination of Mariechen. His undefined inner conflict prevented him from reaching clear-cut decisions of any kind; nor had he given any evidence of verbal felicity in his written words. When Logan Pearsall Smith was twenty, he could write from Dresden: ". . . I have however come here to hear *Siegfried* as it is very well given here. . . ." Later, writing to his sister about Balliol, he reported that "The inside is as nice as the outside." A dozen years later this sentence would have shamed him with a craftsman's anger. How did so imperfect a natural gift become so changed and so disciplined?

Logan found a strong and cunning ally in his mother. He would rather be a poor professor with just enough to live on moderately, Logan told Hannah, than the most successful businessman alive. Hannah persuaded Robert that this was the only right choice for Logan, especially as he would always receive a moderate competence from the family business. So, after a year in New York, Logan rejoined his parents in England, and began to study under a private tutor to prepare himself for Oxford.

Little attention was paid at Friday's Hill to old Mr. Smith. The younger guests were apparently unaware of their host's spectacular rise and fall, and he added little to their endless intellectual chatter. If he spoke at all, it was rather of the glass factories in New Jersey, or of his friendship with Whitman. As he grew older he was bored by the endless conversations and arguments on the terrace. To him, the discussions of these new evangels of Fabian Socialism were like the endless theological squabbles he had known all too well in earlier days. His friendship with Walt Whitman had liberated him from all concern with another life, whether it be in the old Heaven or in the future. Robert Pearsall Smith had become a complete backslider.

Chapter 6 · Enter B.B.

Young Bernhard Berenson made his first appearance at Friday's Hill in 1890. "Today we have a great genius staying with us," Hannah wrote to her niece Carey. "He has been in Italy studying art for two years and he knows everything about it. . . . I believe he is really an authority on Art. And to hear him dethroning one idol after another, with all our party listening open-mouthed, is something delicious." This "great genius" was at that time twenty-five years old. According to Hannah: "He utterly abhors Blake and Rossetti and Burne-Jones and all modern painters." Hannah's unexpected ecstasy may have been a reflection of Mary's enthusiasm for their audacious young visitor. Even at that age he spoke with authority—there was nothing juvenile in his words. In appearance and manner this fastidious young connoisseur seemed unaware of the vicissitudes of ordinary human life. He might be disliked but he could not be ignored. "Berenson charmed Oxford for a time," the poet Lionel Johnson had written, "and vanished; leaving behind a memory of exotic epigrams and, so to speak, cynical music . . . He is something too misanthropic; but always adorable."

Adorable indeed the ladies of Friday's Hill found this protégé of Boston's Mrs. "Jack" Gardner—whom B.B. was later to characterize as "Boston's pre-cinema star." Along with other benefactors, Mrs. Gardner had gathered a little purse (some said it was seven hundred per annum) to permit this Harvard prodigy to pursue his study of art in Florence, and incidentally to collect Old Masters for his benefactress, whose Fenway Court—now the Gardner Museum—in Boston, became a monument to young Berenson's connoisseurship.

At Harvard, Berenson's first interest had been in European literature, especially the great Russians of the nineteenth century. At twenty-one he was one of the editors of the *Harvard Monthly;* he wrote an essay on Gogol's *Revisor,* and a review of a book by the young Anglo-Florentine woman who wrote under the name of Vernon Lee. To the youthful readers of the *Andover Review,* Berenson opened the world of Leo Tolstoy, and in 1888 the *Review* published his survey of contemporary Jewish fiction. Berenson had also reviewed the formidable Lotze's *Outline of Aesthetics.* He was something of a poet in those years, for the *Harvard Monthly* published a poem of his, entitled "The Mood of an Autumn Day."

The Smith ladies were fascinated by Bernhard (that Germanic *h* was not to be dropped until the First World War). He looked to them other-worldly, as if he had stepped out of the folklore pages of his birthplace, Lithuania, which was better known after the eighteenth-century partitions of Poland as the Jewish Pale of the Russian Empire—the nerve center of the Jewish Dispersion.

Albert Berenssohn, father of Bernhard, had emigrated to Boston in 1875. He was compelled to scratch out a living for his growing family in the humblest toil, but social barriers seemed nonexistent for his delicate first-born *Wunderkind.* The boy picked up Boston English in no time at all, was admitted to the exclusive Latin School, and eventually, with the help of benefactors, was sent to Harvard. Bernhard was an egregious figure among the undergraduates. (If Mary did not actually make his acquaintance before her departure from Cambridge, surely she must have noticed this small and fastidious youth, made conspicuous by a sort of peasant haircut—locks parted severely in the middle and cropped in a russet coif—above his blazing eyes of Baltic blue.) However, young Berenson never courted the attentions of his fellow students; he sought rather the friendship of instructors and members of the faculty. He enrolled in courses in the history of art under Charles Eliot Norton, proud friend and disciple of John Ruskin—indeed almost an idolater of that erratic prophet. Norton worshiped both Greek and Christian art, loved refined English life and spoke a rarefied English. He took a paternal interest in his little foreign-born pupil. However, "Berenson has more ambition than ability," Norton once remarked to Barrett Wendell, who was tactless enough to repeat this to Berenson—and Berenson never forgot nor forgave this slight. But in those early years his interests were not exclusively focused upon art as interpreted by Charles Eliot Norton. He also studied Sanskrit under Charles Rockwell Lanman, who produced what some consider the best Sanskrit reader in English. (In some classes Logan Smith had been enrolled with both Santayana and Berenson, but the three did not become acquainted with one another until later.)

While still an undergraduate, young Berenson became what may be described as a page at the court of the controversial Mrs. Gardner. Following the fashion of the 1890's, "Mrs. Jack" collected real or alleged works of the Old Masters, and also of some modern painters, among them her beloved Sargent. She collected to collect; and her collections could have only one end, a public museum. This inevitability worked a subtle change in her bearing and in her aims. She became an agent for her own museum—it was rumored that sometimes she walked about on public days and acted as *cicerone*.

This was the unusual background of the young man who, at Friday's Hill, was talking to the fascinated Mary Costelloe about his favorite subject. A great revolution was taking place among Continental art experts, said Berenson, and its leader was Giovanni Morelli. Morelli, an Italian senator and patriot, had taken up the study of art only as an avocation. A native of Verona, where he was born in 1816, *il senatore* had been trained as a scientist, and was now bringing his training in quantitative analysis to the study of disputed masterpieces. A large percentage of the Old Masters in most of the galleries of Europe, Morelli discovered, were erroneously catalogued; the errors were inherited mainly from the days of the private collections. Morelli, so young Berenson told Mary, published searching studies on the Italian pictures in the Borghese, the Doria Galleries, and Dresden and Munich. (At first Morelli used the pseudonym of "Ivan Lermolieff," announcing himself as "a visitor from the steppes.") Among the Teutonic connoisseurs and curators his revaluations generated a scandal. His enemies accused Morelli of acting as a surgical dissector, carving up ancient masterpieces so that in the end they were nothing more than lifeless corpses. Others compared his work to the technique of Bertillon, tracker of criminals and famous chief of the identity department of the Paris Prefecture of Police.

Mary could see how much young Berenson had learned from Morelli the diagnostician, the morphologist, operating in his special field. Each of the artists of the Italian Renaissance, it appeared, had his own special way of looking at the external world, his own idiosyncrasies in transmuting outer forms to the two dimensions of his canvas—but also, in addition, his own little personal obsessions, his unconscious formulas for drawing ears, eyes, hands, or mouths, all clues which might reveal the identity of even the least characteristic works of the masters. But all that was merely the beginning of this delicate art of attribution; in the end, intuition must play its important role.

Once Mary and Berenson met at the National Gallery, and Berenson dazzled Mary with his knowledge of the Italian masterpieces exhibited there. The two visited Hampton Court, where Berenson again pointed out obvious errors in the labels under some of the Italian paintings. He told her of his Florentine nest, up some hundred and thirty steps from the Lungarno, high in the Villa Acciaiuoli, a big castle-like palace built at the end of the fourteenth century, and now used for various purposes, including apartments for exiles and art students. Berenson's study faced the Santa Trinità bridge and his desk was set in a deep embrasure. From his window Berenson could look out at the crowds streaming across the glistening river, see San Miniato glowing in the fire of sunset. There he wrote articles for the New York *Nation,* essays on the new connoisseurship, a monograph on Lorenzo Lotto, his book on the painters of Venice. To Mary's enchanted ears Berenson described the attractions of Fiesole, and the hamlet of Maiano, where the brilliant Violet Paget, whose pseudonym was Vernon Lee, was living, and where all the country folk possessed "good looks, good manners and good music"; where noble pines, myrtle and cyclamen grew. Maiano offered everything for romantic exiles, and not least, villas of celestial cheapness. And nearby was the white village of Settignano, where Michelangelo was born.

All too soon young Berenson was gone from the life at

Friday's Hill. Mariechen often quoted to her mother the many sharp and bitter comments Bernhard had made upon life and art. But their enthusiasm for Berenson was not shared by Frank Costelloe, who failed to appreciate the spell this Harvard aesthete cast upon his wife. So it was with a violent protest, later in the same year, that he received Mary's announcement that she was going to Florence to study art "under the tutelage of Mr. Berenson."

It is impossible to determine just when the Costelloes decided to sever their marital ties. Records indicate that Mary spent longer and longer periods on the Continent. Mention is made of a visit to the museums of Spain, in Berenson's company, but with "Michael Field" accompanying Mrs. Costelloe, possibly as a sort of twin chaperon. In 1894, under the pseudonym of Mary Logan, Mary Costelloe published a little guide to the pictures at Hampton Court, attempting to correct the erroneous attributions of some of the paintings in that collection. She usually spent the summer months at Friday's Hill, writing children's stories for her two daughters, or acting as hostess to the radical intellectuals who came for the summer Sundays on the terrace. There is no evidence as to the exact time of any definite break with Frank Costelloe. In 1895, however, Mary was living in a *pensione* at Fiesole.

In 1894, Mary had shared Berenson's pride in the publication of his first book, *Venetian Painters of the Renaissance*. This was issued in brown cloth as a small octavo volume which could be carried in the pocket. The text was brief, and with it was published a list of paintings of the Venetian school and the galleries and private collections in which they could be found. A copy of Bernhard's virgin work was sent to his Harvard teacher, Charles Eliot Norton.

In 1896, *Venetian Painters* was succeeded by *Florentine*

Painters of the Renaissance; in 1897 followed *Central Italian Painters of the Renaissance,* and years later *North Italian Painters of the Renaissance.* The first book, *Venetian Painters,* less an exposition of Berenson's theories than the other three, is able, but is a historical record only. In his works on the Florentines and the Central and North Italian Renaissance artists, Berenson's concern with art itself, the core of his life's interest, begins to take shape. Presumably because of the admirable but unsigned canvases which were seen in all collections, Berenson decided to create the "artistic personality" of the fictitious "Amico di Sandro," a personality pieced together out of pictures erroneously ascribed to known Florentine painters of the late fifteenth century. He called this fictitious painter "Friend of Sandro," meaning Botticelli's friend. Amico di Sandro made his debut in the pages of the *Gazette des Beaux Arts* in 1899, and later appeared in *The Drawings of the Florentine Painters.* And having rescued the followers of Botticelli from pale anonymity, B.B. went on to create a second fictitious painter, "Alunno di Domenico," or the disciple of Ghirlandaio; this disciple was presented in 1903 in the first number of the *Burlington Magazine.* It was only after B.B. had become associated with Duveen that the creation of these two imaginary artists provoked critical controversy.

During these productive years of the nineties, Mary's great gift of forthright expression and direct communication made her an invaluable aide, perhaps even a collaborator, especially in the editing of B.B.'s manuscripts.

In 1897, Mary and B.B. published a little privately printed catalogue entitled *The Golden Urn,* in which they listed what they considered the best-authenticated masterpieces of Renaissance art in the galleries of Europe. However, Berenson's authority was challenged from the very beginning of his career by enemies who ranked him with fortunetellers, astrologers and other deliberate charlatans. It was repeated among the more credulous that Berenson had invented a trick by which one could infallibly discover the painter of any Italian picture. In self-defense, he refused to see clients unless he could be assured that they brought with them no Great Masters for him to authenticate.

Earlier, in Munich, during the summer of 1893, Berenson and Mary had met a young Harvard graduate, who presented a letter of introduction written by his brother, Norman Hapgood. They were a bit abashed by the appearance of Hutchins Hapgood, for into the Glyptothek strode a young American—he was then about twenty-four years old—wearing knickerbockers and a flannel shirt, carrying a weather-beaten felt hat and a game bag containing a change of linen, an extra shirt and a pair of socks. "Hutch" had sent his wardrobe on to Berlin, where he was going to study philosophy. But the three of them struck up a friendship immediately, and this gregarious, ebullient young man remained with Mary and B.B. for two months. The three attended the Wagner festival in Munich, and were soon giving each other nicknames out of the Wagner operas. Mary became Bruennhilde; Hapgood, because of his deep voice, Fafnir; and the small, wiry Bernhard, Mime. After Munich, they walked through the beautiful Dolomites, and then descended into the plains of Venetia. "Many a time we three walked through the streets of some beautiful old town," Hapgood was to recount in his indiscreet autobiography published nearly half a century later, "Berenson with feverish eagerness in the lead, sprinting ahead so fast with his short and lean legs that Mary and I . . . found it not too easy to follow him. . . . This experience repeated itself scores of times throughout those lovely little towns north of Venice. And Berenson's excitement was not merely that of discovery, or the thought of future work based on these discoveries, but was due also to his almost indecent love of beauty; because perhaps it was not quite natural. It was not so much the love of beauty of a man who had been born in it, but of one who had a ravenous desire for it because he hadn't had it." Hapgood was apparently unaware that his companions were not yet married, nor that Mary had left a husband and two little daughters in England. He goes on to explain: "His wife was the one person in the world, apparently, whom he desired most to educate. He eagerly communicated to her all his impressions and notes of authorship . . ." This was not a cool mental or moral obligation with Berenson; it was superheated propaganda, not of ideas, but of aesthetic and scientific facts.

Such was the beginning of an unusual friendship—the Berensons with their almost sacredotal reverence for art, and the rebellious Hutchins Hapgood, obsessed with justice for the despised and rejected of humanity, seeking beauty in the lives of thieves and anarchists. In B.B., Hapgood admired "that restless energy and endless curiosity and mental desire"; while in Mary, whom he described as a splendid blonde, he found a concealed spirit of rebellion and the underlying radicalism which had also attracted Walt Whitman.

Like nature, the will to believe abhors a vacuum. With the collapse of the old evangelical certitude—a collapse hastened by the wave of Darwinism—the more privileged and sophisticated classes were unconsciously seeking a new religion. Some found it in the worship of science, some turned to "rationalism," others to social reform or even revolution —seeking salvation in either anarchism, or communism, or socialism. These fanatical and warring sects became merely surrogate evangelisms. As Richard Aldington has pointed out, Carlyle, Arnold, Huxley and Ruskin were all preachers.

Aestheticism became one of these new cults. The origins of aestheticism, or art appreciation, were not exclusively British, but Continental. But the dogma of salvation through art appreciation was made more compelling for a small but earnest elite by the sulphuric eloquence of John Ruskin.

It would be erroneous to conclude that the so-called "aesthetic movement," the religion of beauty, was limited to the era which was brought to a close when Oscar Wilde stood in the dock at the Old Bailey. This worship of art as an expression of the divine in human craftsmanship was evident on the Continent and recognized as a variety of religious experience. As early as 1868, the youthful William James was awakened to the dangers inherent in this *Religionsersatz*. Writing from Dresden in June of that year, the observant young philosopher diagnosed the symptoms: "Take, for instance, the word *Kunst* or Art. It has a magical effect on Germans which we are quite incapable of conceiving. They write poems about it, couple it with religion and virtue as one of the sacred things in human life—lose, in short, their critical power when thinking of it, just as we do when thinking of morality, for instance. But (except, perhaps, in music) they produce no works of art good for anything, nor do I believe that as a rule those who are most struck by the divinity of *Kunst* in the abstract, have the power of discriminative appreciation thereof in the concrete. The tender emotion carries their sagacity and judgment off its legs. They believe that the mission of art is to represent or create in anticipation a regenerate world, and over every so-called work of art, however contemptible, they are apt to cast the halo which belongs to the generic idea, and to accept it without criticizing. . . ."

In England, the gospel of aestheticism had been initiated

as a cult among certain classes of society by the publication in 1843 of the first volume of John Ruskin's *Modern Painters*. This youthful advocate of the worship of beauty was only twenty-four years old at the time this book created a sensation by the brilliance of its style, and the unpredictability of its views.

If not the only true begetter of the gospel of art in Great Britain, Ruskin had been its most eloquent prophet. He became the fanatical messiah of what we may term spectatorism, a pioneer of the art pilgrimage to shrines on the Continent, the priest of "appreciation." A youth of neurotic sensibility, with an intense love of nature, and above all a gift for words that had been nurtured by enforced reading and rereading of the English Bible, he exhibited all the vagaries and contradictions of a capricious taste in the arts. His were the unco-ordinated and misdirected curiosities of a spoiled child.

Among the emancipated and affluent younger generation of the new-rich trading and industrial classes, Ruskin's shrill preachments found willing ears. Shrinking from the squalor and blight of the industrial revolution, young sophisticates became happy converts to his new cult of beauty. It penetrated the gullible mind as a new revelation of divinity.

Ruskin's gospel effected a sort of mass conversion; one of his biographers estimated that, due to Ruskin's fanatical campaign, the number of art schools in Britain increased from nineteen in 1841 to sixty in 1856. Ruskin's influence crossed the Atlantic mainly because of the unquestioning devotion of his disciple and friend Charles Eliot Norton. The true Ruskinian cachet of Norton's teaching was described as "lectures on modern morals illustrated by the arts of the ancients."

But Ruskin could not succeed in silencing the impudent James McNeill Whistler. In that painter-showman's celebrated "Ten O'Clock" pronouncement, there is one passage unquestionably aimed at Ruskin:

Then the Preacher appointed
He stands in high places—harangues and holds forth.
Sage of the Universities—learned in many matters, and of
    much experience in all, save his subject.
Exhorting—denouncing—directing.
Filled with wrath and earnestness.
Bringing powers of persuasion, and polish of language, to
    prove—nothing.
Torn with much teaching—having naught to impart.
Impressive—important—shallow.
Crying out, and cutting himself—while the gods hear not.
Gentle priest of the Philistine withal, again he ambles pleas-
    antly from all points, and through many volumes, escaping
    scientific assertion—babbles of green fields.

Ruskin's excesses, contradictions and absurdities were more or less balanced by three Oxford aesthetes—the Brasenose don, Walter Pater; the interpreter of the Italian Renaissance, John Addington Symonds; and the flamboyant Dubliner, Oscar Wilde. These three were reigning supreme when Frank Costelloe brought Mary Smith back to London as his bride in the mid-eighties; they provided the predominant aesthetic climate in which Mary found herself. Pater in particular became the new divinity among the advanced aesthetes.

"The religion which Ruskin tried to make an incendiary torch," wrote a recent interpreter, "was for Pater a calm

candle in a tranquilly lovely sanctuary." The devotee of Pater
was to seek only his own aesthetic salvation, serenely indifferent to the bettering of the human condition. The Italian
Renaissance, which in Ruskin's credo stood for moral wick-
edness and bad taste, was Pater's ideal. To Mary, *Marius
the Epicurean* was the great oracle, and the instrument for
her "conversion." It advocated discrimination and fastidious-
ness, the refinement of receptivity, in the eyes of the specta-
tor. It became her *vade mecum;* and she, like others of the
small cult, read and reread it, and underlined one paragraph
in order to memorize it:

"To keep the eye clear by a sort of exquisite personal
alacrity and cleanliness, extending even to his dwelling-
place; to discriminate, ever more and more fastidiously, select form and color in things from what was less select; to
meditate much on beautiful visible objects, on objects, more
especially, connected with the period of youth—on children
at play in the morning, the trees in early spring, on young
animals, on the fashions and amusements of young men; to
keep ever by him if it were but a single choice flower, a
graceful animal or sea-shell, as a token and representative of
the whole kingdom of such things; to avoid jealously, in his
way through the world, everything repugnant to sight; and
should any circumstance tempt him to a general converse
in the range of such objects, to disentangle himself from the
circumstance at any cost of place, money, or opportunity; such
were in brief outline the duties recognized, the rights demanded, in this new formula of life." Marius was "to add
nothing, not so much as a transient sigh, to the great total of
man's unhappiness," but to charge Marius with hedonism,
"would not properly be applicable at all. Not pleasure but
fulness of life, and insight as conducing to that fulness—en-

ergy, variety, choice of experience . . ." these were the goals
of the good Epicurean.

Mary could repeat whole passages from *Marius* almost
verbatim, and Berenson shared her glowing admiration. He
enjoyed a kind of hedonism of the eye: "We must look and
look and look . . ." he used to insist. "If we do not succeed in loving what through the ages has been loved, it is useless to lie ourselves into believing that we do. A good rough
test is whether we feel it is reconciling us with life. No
artifact is a work of art if it does not help to humanize us."

In the cult of aestheticism, knowledge was indeed necessary, and the development of the critical faculty. But these
were considered only the first steps toward initiation into
the sacred arcanum, the secrets of which could never be explained nor analyzed. The *ecstasy* of art could never be communicated to the unregenerate—appreciation could come
only by mystical, never by rational criticism. Oscar Wilde
attempted to popularize, even to vulgarize this worship; and
so successfully, indeed, that he was satirized as the poet-
aesthete Bunthorne in Gilbert and Sullivan's *Patience,* which
was produced at the Savoy in 1881—an indication of the London public's familiarity with the growth of the cult of art.

Mary Costelloe must have experienced what was termed
the "aesthetic moment"—that sense of union, not with God
as the religious mystic experiences it, but with the divinity
in the work of art; that fusion of subjective and objective,
when the work of art is no longer outside the observer, but
becomes one with the initiated; that "aesthetic moment"
which is comparable to the mystic vision or ecstasy of a
Saint Theresa. For only upon some such experience can we
interpret Mary's defiance of social convention during the last
ten years of the century. Walt Whitman had characterized

her as "almost an anarchist," as "radical" as Fanny Wright. And now, with an unconscious fanaticism, as determined as, though less spectacular than, her father's when he set himself up as a world evangelist, she consecrated her life to the rescuing of art from the powers of darkness.

Chapter 7 · Paradise of Expatriates

The sudden death of Frank Costelloe late in 1899 was not without certain providential compensations for Mary, Alys and Hannah. Hannah and Alys had remained on friendly terms with Costelloe, working in his campaign when in 1899 he became the Liberal candidate in East St. Pancras for the London County Council; Hannah appeared on campaign platforms as the candidate's mother-in-law. But when the defeated Costelloe died, the reading of his will disclosed a provision that his two daughters, Ray and Karin, must be brought up on the small income he bequeathed them, by the Roman Catholic lady he named as their guardian. Hannah, with legal advice, promptly got her darling granddaughters appointed wards in Chancery, covenanting that if they were brought up in her care they should be educated as Roman Catholics. (What would her Quaker father have thought, Hannah sometimes asked herself, of this agreement?)

Following this legal victory, Hannah felt, and said, that this new responsibility gave her a new lease on life—made her feel that she was really needed for nine or ten more years. In the next ten years both Ray and Karin would come of age and be free of interference from any guardian. Thus it came about that the real parenthood was shifted from absent Mary to her own mother, and the girls were brought up with Hannah's increasingly "Broad, Broader, Broadest" ideas of education. Aunty Loo (as they called Alys) and Logan were secondary aides in this liberal upbringing.

Costelloe's untimely death—he was in his middle forties —also made it possible for Mary and Berenson to marry. Since many of the Anglo-Florentines assumed that they were already man and wife, their marriage took place in circumstances of the utmost discretion.

On the road between Settignano and Maiano, some five miles east of Florence, Mary and Bernhard discovered the ancient estate known as I Tatti. I Tatti, which since 1606 had been handed down from one generation of the Alessandri family to the next, had, in 1854, come into the possession of a picturesque Anglo-Florentine named John Temple-Leader, by repute a baron. The *contadini*, who worked its farms and olive groves, lived in the little nearby hamlet of Ponte a Mensola. As soon as B.B. and Mary were married, they made an offer for I Tatti, which was accepted. They called in a young English architect named Cecil Pinsent to supervise the landscaping and replanting of pines, poplars and cypresses. They envisaged additional rooms, and terraces sloping down to the Arno, but they could not foresee that it would become a task of decades to bring the estate to the perfection which B.B. demanded. The Berensons added a grandiose library and a music room dedicated to Bach, and with the aid of Mary's income from Whitall-Tatum, I Tatti was eventually developed into a small, autonomous community. Its land system was that of the *mezzadria,* under the charge of a *fattore* or steward (they remembered that Malvolio in *Twelfth Night* was such a *fattore*). This arrangement was pleasant, in that it relieved the Berensons of the day-by-day details of Tuscan agriculture.

Visiting Florence with his wife and children in 1823, Leigh Hunt had discovered two hundred English families living in the city and its suburbs. "We seem to possess," Hunt wrote, "Italy and England together." The English had been coming ever since, as had the Germans, the Scandinavians and the Americans. They invaded the hills of Fiesole, Maiano, Arcetri and all about. They occupied those villas of "celestial cheapness." On a small income, or remittance, these romantic exiles could idle their lives away with the utmost comfort in a town saturated with romance and history. If they had an income of a few hundred pounds a year they could afford a comfortably large villa, two or three servants, good food and, often, a carriage and pair. In the neighborhood lay the Valley of Ladies, out of Boccaccio. Next door one might discover the house of Machiavelli or, not far away at Arcetri, Galileo's. This paradise of aesthetic exiles had kept growing, until now, at the end of the nineteenth century, Florence was the most cosmopolitan and the most international community in Italy—indeed, on the whole continent of Europe.

Among the Florentine English of an older generation were Henry Labouchère and Mrs. Janet Ross. "Labby," then past seventy, had retired to his Tuscan villa, where he lived on a grand scale and served princely dinners to his guests. Mrs. Ross was famous chiefly as an old friend of George Meredith. She had first met the novelist when she was Janet Duff-Gordon, a little girl of eight. She had served as a model for one of the famous Meredith heroines—but no one was quite sure which one. This grim old lady loved or hated at sight, and she was to cause Mary Berenson some disturbing moments; but who could not admire and respect Janet Ross's courage, wit and wide experience of the world? She had not lost her beauty, and her villa provided the perfect setting for her proud and distinguished manner. Every villa had its own history, and Janet Ross's was supposed to be where Boccaccio had placed his company of fine ladies and gallant gentlemen who figure in the *Decameron*.

Then there was Maud Cruttwell, working on her big book about Pollaiuolo. Maud was one of the little group of feminine art experts who specialized in the Old Masters of the Renaissance, but her authority in the field of Mantegna was disputed by rivals. A red-faced Englishwoman, Miss Cruttwell affected mannish tweeds during the day, black satin at night, and smoked long, dark cigars, which stained her teeth brown. When she spoke of Pollaiuolo her voice became emotional almost to hysterics. Maud and her rival experts were all vastly learned in Florentine Renaissance; but among all these erudite ladies, Mary Berenson learned most from Vernon Lee—Violet Paget—a gifted Englishwoman who had lived in Italy and elsewhere on the Continent for most of her life, and knew little or nothing of England. Eight years older than Mary, Violet had begun her literary career at the age of fifteen, when she began to collect material about Italy's eighteenth century. At eighteen, she dedicated to Henry James her first novel, *Miss Brown*. Some years later, before she was twenty-five, she published her *Studies of the Eighteenth Century in Italy*. Her inquisitive mind kept on growing and maturing, absorbing, selecting and philosophizing. "She slashed right and left, she broke into the open with a swinging cut—she thumped out with a judgment, a maxim, a paradox, on a croak or chuckle of her crusted laughter. It all took time, but it was worth while to wait for her," wrote Percy Lubbock in his book dedicated to quite another sort of woman, Edith Wharton. "While she talked on with her pungent and guttural deliberation, a scene unrolled, brilliantly peopled and displayed—a drama was evolved out of all the admonitions, curious and lovely, grand and grotesque, of the genius of this place and this hour. Who will say, listening to Vernon Lee, that a thing of beauty is ever finished or an hour of time accomplished? She knew better; she talked on, planting her weight, as of an elemental earth-force, on any levity or futility of her companions, releasing them with a stroke of her grimly riotous wit—still she talked. Most surprising, most interesting, most exasperating of women, in her power and her humour, her tenacity and her perversity —Vernon Lee holds her ground, to the eyes of memory, in the twinkling ilex-shade of that old garden, as she held it in gnarled and seasoned determination to the end, when her hour was achieved at length. What a figure! It was impossible to control or to civilize Vernon Lee."

A curious American expatriate who became the more or less permanent neighbor of the Berensons was Charles Loeser, whose father had founded a big and successful dry-goods store in Brooklyn. A classmate of Berenson's at Harvard, Charles settled in the Viale dei Colli beyond San Miniato in a villa which he was continually restoring—building and unbuilding for years. "Carlo"—he preferred this name to Charles—collected paintings, bronzes, faïence, drawings, furniture, most of them of Tuscan origin. Late in life he acquired a wife, a German Jewish pianist. He permitted her occasionally to perform in public or private concerts. Later he began to take an interest in contemporary art, especially in the canvases of Cézanne. His Cézannes, however, were shown only to guests who expressed a special wish to see them. Santayana, who had been a friend of Loeser at Harvard, was a frequent guest at his house. ". . . Pictures and books! That strikes the keynote of our companionship," wrote Santayana. "He spoke French well and German presumably better. . . . He seemed to have seen everything and to speak every language. Berenson had the same advantage . . . but somehow I felt more secure under the sign of Loeser. I felt that he loved the Italian Renaissance and was not, as it were, merely displaying it. . . . Loeser was my first Maecenas of this kind, and one of the most satisfactory. His invitations were specific, for particular occasions. He maintained that he had two original works of Michelangelo. . . ."

"Carlo" Loeser fancied he was living a real *quattrocento* life when he ordered his *pasta* in the small underground *trattorie* that snuggled beneath Florence's narrow streets. He ducked under low archways where onions were strung from the ceiling and old tables shone from countless greasy wipings, leading his visiting guests to his favorite little *trattoria*. Entering as though he owned the place, seating his party and then making his way out to the dim kitchen, Loeser picked out his *pollo* and gave minute directions about the *fritto misto* and the *fiasco di vino*, listening delightedly all the while to his own voice, his eyes darting here and there, yet fixed immutably inward upon the picture of himself— "*Fiorentino davvero.*"

"Carlo" never stopped talking *trecento, quattrocento, cinquecento,* and discussing values (Berenson's "tactile values"), lines, dimensions or nuances in knowing phrases.

Like Loeser and Berenson, Leo Stein had studied at Harvard. In 1900 he turned up in Florence and sought out his old friend B.B., who invited Leo to lunch to meet his friend "Mrs. C." Stein was a bit shocked by her appearance. To him, Mary was a large, ruddy blonde of at least forty (she was actually thirty-six) with no outstanding intelligence. Her conversation seemed only a carbon copy of Berenson's. Leo wrote his sister Gertrude that he had blown the Americanism trumpet "as though it was the whole of Sousa's band," and

Mary had told him his Americanism was just a bluff. Obviously Mary did not put herself out for the little man from East Oakland, as she had for the ebullient Hutch Hapgood. Leo was much more impressed by his host, and with his museum-like house, which was filled with antiques, pictures and a superb art library.

Through Berenson's kindness, Leo found himself immersed in the little clique of art experts, mostly British, who were busy writing books on the masters of the Renaissance. He was shocked at the looks and manners of some of them, including Maud Cruttwell. In fact, Leo found most of Berenson's guests busy feuding, trying to destroy each other's reputation for integrity and honesty.

Later, Leo Stein came to Florence again, this time with Gertrude, his older brother Michael and the latter's wife, Sarah. The Steins were the children of German Jewish immigrants to America who had first built up a clothing business in Baltimore. Later they moved to California, where with satisfying business acumen, the oldest son, Michael, became rich enough to endow his younger brother and sister with modest allowances which permitted them to follow their aesthetic pilgrimages in Europe. Leo and Gertrude, at the time they first came to I Tatti, were already fanatical missionaries of "modern" art, a new heresy which produced frequent clashes with Berenson, apostle of the classical tradition. Despite this antagonism in art values, Leo and B.B. were to remain lifelong friends. Leo and Gertrude were typical of the "modern" *avant-garde,* shrewd collectors and possessed of a sixth sense as pioneers of the modern movement. Gertrude claimed to be one of the favorite pupils of William James (who can count them all—those "favorite" pupils of William James?), and she was beginning to attempt in words what she thought the modernists were doing with paint. She found a receptive audience in Edwin and Mabel Dodge in the nearby Villa Curonia.

Conspicuous among the American invaders—always frowned upon by the earlier settlers—was Mabel Dodge. Born Mabel Ganson, heiress, of Buffalo, New York, and endowed with an insatiable appetite for life, she arrived in Florence with Edwin Dodge, her second husband. In her intimate memoirs Mabel Dodge Luhan gives an acid and malicious account of life among the Florentine connoisseurs. Florence in that era, as she describes it, was a place where it was more important to acquire and possess works of art, especially of Italian origin, than to cast a vote for a president. The supreme values of life were centered on the acquisition of relics of the great art epochs. The Steins often stayed with her at the Villa Curonia; there Gertrude Stein composed her historic *Portrait of Mabel Dodge at the Villa Curonia,* which was promptly printed in a small private edition by the Tipografia Galileiana in Florence and distributed by the delighted hostess to her guests and friends. This portrait in prose began with the words: "The days are wonderful and the nights are wonderful and the life is pleasant." The *Portrait of Mabel Dodge* becomes even more vivid in the following paragraph: "A bottle that has all the time to stand open is not so clearly shown when there is green colour there. This is not the only way to change it. A little raw potato and then all that softer does happen to show that there has been enough. It changes the expression."

Of the Steins and their devotion to modern art, B.B. wrote later: "Among the indigent and most unappreciated of the painters whom the Steins took up and treated with almost maternal solicitude was Picasso. Lest I forget it I record now, as it comes back to my memory; meeting this most protean and acrobatic of painters, the most ready to take any jump, to put on any motley or mask, to twist himself into any shape and always with dazzling dexterity—meeting him after he had become the sovereign idol of the public that writes, that 'turtle-cat,' that buys, he condescended to recall that he had known me at the Steins' and added, 'Ah, those Steins, how they did exploit me!' "

For Mary's forty-second birthday, Hannah sent her daughter a telescope cigarette holder with this admonition: "Thee need not advertise that it is a present from the author of the *Christian's Secret of a Happy Life!* But I think it may save thee from a little of the poison of thy cigarettes, of which I have a few fears." In her letters to her mother Mrs. Berenson often complained of the boresome guests who were already making pilgrimages to pay their respects to B.B., and Hannah commented, "I sympathize with thee from the bottom of my heart over your guests, for I know it well from many experiences of incompetent Missionaries with their still more incompetent wives, who were foisted on me by poor Father's unthinking hospitality, and all their burdens rolled over off his shoulders on to mine. But Mother Smith showed me the way out at last, and that was never to take them *into our own house,* to upset everything and make everybody uncomfortable, but to arrange for them to go into lodgings near by, where I could see them as often as necessary, but from where I could escape to the peace and quiet of my own home.

"It is really kinder to the people themselves too; whereas, while they are in thy house, they will simply lie back and depend altogether on thee. At present thee is pauperising those poor dear people, and it is thy duty to force them to work for their own living. I think thee ought to find them lodgings and tell them thee cannot get a villa for them, nor a servant, nor oversee their affairs, as thee makes it a rule not to do things like that for other people. (Make the rule quick, now, as thee reads this letter) ." But with the passage of the years, this problem became more and more complicated for Mary. The stream of pilgrims to Berenson's door kept on increasing.

Meanwhile, Mary's daughters, Ray and Karin, were growing up. The two girls were frequent visitors to I Tatti, and by extensive tours to the museums and galleries of Italy their mother sought to instill in them a love of art. They were with her during the spring of 1906—Ray a resolute and assured young feminist of nineteen, who had finished her first novel, and her sister a more quiet and shy seventeen. With the secret strategy of the born matchmaker, Mary earlier in the year wrote to Alys suggesting that she invite two young men to be guests of the Berensons during the Easter holidays. Alys gave these invitations to Geoffrey Scott, then twenty-one and an undergraduate at New College, Oxford, and to a twenty-three-year-old member of the emerging Bloomsbury group named John Maynard Keynes. Unconscious rivals because Scott was an Oxford aesthete and Keynes a Cambridge economist, the two young men spent some time at Siena, then proceeded to I Tatti. There they found a party of young ladies chaperoned by Mrs. Berenson. Describing this house party, Keynes wrote to his friend Lytton Strachey: "I've no news unless I describe our way of life. I seem to have fallen in love with Ray a little bit. . . . The comfort here is of course incredible; the cypresses and sun and moon and the amazing gardens and villas in which we picnic every day high above Florence have reduced me to a lump of Italian idleness. We go to bed later and later and gradually find methods of working five meals into the day. Last night it was nearly five before we retired. Oh Scott is very amusing and he makes me angry by plotting at the greatest inconvenience to himself never to leave me and Ray alone. Everybody tries to bring it about occasionally, but, no, he forbids."

But, as often happens in real life as well as drawing-room comedies, the twenty-three-year-old Keynes, one of the most beguiling graduates ever to leave Cambridge, was more smitten with his hostess than he was with her rebellious daughter. For of Mary Berenson he wrote to his friend Lytton: ". . . she roars with laughter the whole time, allows you to laugh at her, and never worries one. And when she journalised about the pictures, Scott was always there to make the appropriate remark. The Costelloe females, Ray and Karin, do not talk much. But they did very well. Scott is dreadfully Oxford—a sort of aesthetic person; and of course his point of view always seems to me a little shocking; but we are quite happy together—I have never seen the aesthetic point of view so close. I find I object to it on high moral grounds—though I hardly know why. It seems to trifle deliberately with sacred reality. But isn't this rather cant?"

Mary drove all her young guests through Tuscany on a sight-seeing tour. Keynes found her a delightful hostess to travel with in a motor car—indeed, he admired her "incredible competence" in every field; and he added, with an unconscious anticipation of his future theories, "She was full of Italian and money and which hotel was best and what food they could cook best. We must have cost her pints of gold—for everything down to entrance fees to galleries was paid." Keynes's first visit to I Tatti sealed a friendship which lasted for life. He and his hostess immediately became "Mary" and "Maynard" to each other, and whenever the Berensons visited England, Mary and Maynard renewed their gay intimacy.

The following year Mary persuaded Will Rothenstein, her old friend from Friday's Hill days, to come to I Tatti and paint a portrait of her husband. Rothenstein attempted to capture the cold blue of Berenson's eyes along with the Vandyke beard and innate authority which emanated from the slight, delicately boned head. But Rothenstein was not yet the master of portraiture which was later to win him a knighthood. "We want to hear," queried "Michael Field," "if you have made Bernhard a Professor or a Faun—if the blue that has left his eyes visited your brush, and will make us remember what was so fugitive."

Geoffrey Scott returned that year, also, to study with Berenson. Rothenstein described him as pale and dark-eyed, looking like a Botticelli portrait, more Italian than English in appearance. He had come to I Tatti for a week, but remained several months, an inspiring and entertaining guest. Rothenstein wrote that he had met no one, not himself a painter, who appreciated painting more than Scott, and that both Scott and Berenson were wonderful talkers. Berenson's astonishing intellect delighted in the play of ideas; he could illuminate remote regions not only of art, but of literature, philosophy, politics, history, ethics and psychology. And of course there was gossip, for as Rothenstein says, there were armed camps and fierce rivalries in Florence then, as in past times; but the fighting was far less bloody, concerned as it was with attributions rather than ducal thrones. Berenson, Loeser, Vernon Lee, and Maud Cruttwell all had their mercenaries—and their artillery.

But there was another Englishman who had come to Florence in those days who soon wore out his welcome at the Berensons' villa. His name was Gordon Craig, and he was known to be the love child of Ellen Terry, the fruit of her idyll with the erratic architect Edward William Godwin. As a boy of thirteen, "Teddy" Craig had made his first stage appearance in Chicago with his mother, playing the role of a gardener's boy in *Eugene Aram*. Later he appeared in minor parts with Sir Henry Irving's Lyceum Company, and at twenty-two was playing Hamlet in provincial companies. But his real interest had turned to stage design; and now, in Florence, he was trying to raise money to establish a school of the theater arts. Craig persistently canvassed the rich expatriates for support in his grandiose and visionary schemes, and hoped that the Berensons might help him. But while he had impressed many people, Craig failed to impress the connoisseur of past glories. Craig had visions of the future, while Berenson's eyes were turned to the past. Moreover, Berenson's sympathy was alienated by the carefree habits of this undisciplined genius. Craig neglected to mend the hole in his pocket through which all contributions disappeared with alarming rapidity. But Rothenstein turned to Craig with relief from what seemed to him the oppressing atmosphere in which the scholar-aesthetes lived. After a time, their massive Italian furniture began to pall, and the eyes of the young artist were surfeited with their endless collections of canvases and primitive panels, of bronzes, wood carvings, and Venetian stuffs which he was expected to praise and appraise. These aesthetes moved among priceless and princely objects which, for all their beauty, seemed to Will Rothenstein as misplaced "as an enamelled and bewigged mistress in the house of a young man." The very vastness of the salons was weighted down with intrigues, past and present. He turned to the company of Teddy Craig, with his dreams of creating a theater of the future. Rothenstein would sometimes come upon Craig at some small underground *trattoria*, or rummaging among the books at some hidden antiquarian shop, or swaggering through Florence in his broad-brimmed hat, a greatcoat swinging from his shoulders. Craig had found a perfect treasure of a house and in his workroom had set up an exquisite model theater, fitted with lights, where he played with great mysterious shadows upon his miniature stage. He had just staged a production of Ibsen's *Rosmersholm* at the Pergola Theatre, with Eleonora Duse in the role of Rebecca West. Now he was planning to rent the Arena Goldoni as a workshop, studio and school. But to Berenson, Craig was merely one more of the irresponsible adventurers from England who had inevitably gravitated to Florence and who formed the least attractive part of the social and artistic life in which he and Mary were involved.

But we must now turn the clock back to the eighteen nineties and return to Friday's Hill, to take up the love story of Mary's little sister Alys.

Chapter 8 · Alys and Bertie (1894–1921)

One of the more interesting of many neighbors at Friday's Hill was the Honorable Rollo Russell. In 1883, Russell had acquired a country home in Haslemere and renamed it Dunrozel, after Rozel in Normandy, reputed to be the original seat of the Russell family. In 1885 he brought to it a bride, the former Miss Alice Godfrey. Soon after the birth of a son, she died; and six years later Rollo Russell married Miss Gertrude Joachim, a niece of Joseph Joachim, the eminent Hungarian violinist. Rollo Russell, like others of his family, was a man of unique interests; he specialized in meteorology, became a leading spirit in the Smoke Abatement Society of London, studied the problems of the relation between diet and physical strength, published a now forgotten work on *Psalms of the West*. His mother, the Dowager Countess Russell, and his sister, Lady Agatha, came down to Dunrozel every summer from Pembroke Lodge in Richmond Park.

Among all the Friday's Hill neighbors, Alys Smith was most attracted to one of Rollo's nephews, the Honorable Bertrand Arthur William Russell—a formidable name abbreviated by his friends and relatives to the diminutive "Bertie." At Trinity College, Cambridge, Bertie was recognized as a prodigy in philosophy and mathematics. He was a slight, dark-haired youth, with the prominent forehead, prominent nose, flashing eye, long upper lip and retreating chin of his illustrious grandfather, Lord John Russell. His hands were alert and expressive, his movements quick. In manner and dress the young man was carefully correct, conventionally courteous, punctiliously polite. He expressed himself precisely, with clear enunciation, and there was a pinch of irony in everything he said. He detested all religious and social conventions, proclaimed himself an open enemy of sentimentality; he believed only in rigorous logic and scientific method. Alys enjoyed his mocking talk, although some of it was too abstrusely intellectual for her comprehension.

Unlike her sister Mary, of whose excursions with young Berenson she severely disapproved, Alys seemed destined to play a secondary role wherever she was. In the presence of Bertie Russell, Alys sometimes felt like a barbarian from overseas. Neither scholarly nor philosophical in her temperament, she was inclined to carry out the suggestions of some beloved leader, whether her lion-hearted mother, her cousin Carey, autocrat of Bryn Mawr, or her closest English friend, Beatrice Potter Webb. Alys, an enthusiastic follower of humanitarian and libertarian movements, had in her the makings of the typical "joiner." Her naïve enthusiasm and optimism counterbalanced young Russell's realistic and rationalistic pessimism.

Only gradually did she learn of Russell's tragic background. He was an orphan—both his parents had died before he was four years old. As revealed in *The Amberley Papers,* Bertie's parents vaguely resemble the heroic characters of a George Meredith novel. Lady Amberley, *née* Stanley, was a radiant and articulate young woman, ambitious to promote her youthful husband's political career. Both were radicals and rationalists, friends and disciples of John Stuart Mill. But almost at the outset of his political career, young

Amberley ran into trouble. His honesty led him into association with the Neo-Malthusians, a minority group which advocated what has become known as birth control. Its campaign was largely directed by various members of the Drysdale family, one of whom, Dr. George Drysdale, an impetuous, outspoken young physician, anonymously published a book entitled *The Elements of Social Science*. It was an unqualified challenge to the conspiracy of silence which blanketed all the sexual conventions of the period, and naturally it created a scandal in Victorian England. Even those seriously aware of the dangers of overpopulation were shocked, and young Viscount Amberley was "smeared" by his political adversaries as being an adherent of George Drysdale's extreme views. According to his political enemies, Amberley's association with Drysdale meant nothing less than the advocacy of abortion. His campaign for election to Parliament collapsed disastrously; eventually, after a visit to America, he retired from public life, and concentrated on a work analyzing religious beliefs.

How scandalous the liberal ideas of this young couple seemed to their high-born contemporaries is indicated by a letter Kate Amberley wrote to her mother, Lady Stanley: "Yesterday we all went to see a servants' cricket match and to have tea at the White Lodge with the Tecks: there was no one there besides us but the Duchess of Cambridge who received me by saying 'I know you, you are the daughter-in-law but now I hear you only like dirty people and dirty Americans. All London is full of it; all the clubs are talking of it. I must look at your petticoats to see if they are dirty.' " This Duchess of Cambridge, the grandmother of the future Queen Mary, was living up to her reputation as a coarse-grained old harridan, and in the house of her daughter, the Duchess of Teck, she did not hesitate to insult young Lady Amberley.

In 1873, before Bertie was one year old, the first of several cruel disasters fell upon his parents. Amberley had an epileptic seizure, perhaps several—it is not certain that the diagnosis was correct. The attack introduced an element of deep gloom and doom into the Amberleys' lives. John Stuart Mill's death at Avignon, May 8, 1873, came to both as a heavy blow, the loss of a most valued friend and preceptor.

Before Bertrand had attained the age of three, his older sister Rachel died of diphtheria. Lady Amberley was the next victim, perishing shortly afterward of the same disease. After his young wife's death, Amberley lost interest in life. Deprived of his friend Mill, who had been the agnostic's equivalent of godfather to Bertrand, and realizing that he himself was doomed, Amberley selected as guardians of his two sons two free-thinking friends. The first of these was Thomas James Sanderson, who later called himself Cobden-Sanderson, a disciple of William Morris and founder of the Doves Press. The second was Douglas A. Spalding, an eccentric naturalist who served as tutor to Bertie's older brother Francis.

Douglas Spalding was indeed an eccentric for any day; for the Victorian seventies he seemed rather more so; among other unconventional acts, he turned hens and chicks loose in the library and birds in the bedrooms at Ravenscroft—experiments which disgusted the Amberleys' guests. Spalding was hated by the Amberleys' relations, justly or unjustly. A pioneer in animal behavior, he did valuable work on instinct in chickens and young birds; his one essay on the psychology of animals vastly impressed William James, who, in his famous volume *Psychology*, paid a tribute to the young naturalist. Spalding's life and work were also cut short by premature death.

Lord John and Lady Russell vigorously contested the provision of their son's will which appointed Sanderson and Spalding as guardians of the Amberley sons. The case was carried to the Court of Chancery, which overruled the provision of the will, and the two boys became wards of their Russell grandparents. As they grew older, Francis and Bertie were taught by a succession of German nurses, Swiss and German governesses, and finally English tutors. Frank, seven years older than Bertie, had, before his father's death, already demonstrated that he was to become an incorrigible problem child.

The library at Pembroke Lodge became little Bertrand's schoolroom. He was allowed complete freedom to read the heavy tomes there assembled by his grandfather. At the age of eleven he discovered Euclid; discovered, too, that Euclid begins with axioms which must be accepted without proof; this disappointed the boy at first, but once this difficulty was overcome, Bertie delighted in the Greek geometer. "By the time I was fifteen I had arrived at a theory very similar to that of the Cartesians . . . But since I accepted consciousness as an indubitable datum, I could not accept materialism, though I had a certain hankering after it on account of its intellectual simplicity and its rejection of 'nonsense.' "

One of Bertrand's earliest memories was of finding himself the center of attention in the servants' hall, upon his first arrival at Pembroke Lodge. An even fainter memory was of being presented to the elderly Empress-Queen in the drawing room. Despite all the loving attention enveloping him, Bertie grew up as a lonely little orphan, solitary, shy and priggish but endowed with a sunny and happy disposition.

After the death of Lord John in 1878, at eighty-six, his wife had been comforted by the message of sympathy sent to her by Queen Victoria: "I trust that your grandsons will grow up all that you could wish." But Frank, the incorrigible, was to drag the title inherited from his eminent grandfather into the mire of scandal. First he seduced Emma Billings, one of the two daughters of a nursemaid at Pembroke Lodge, and was sued for breach of promise. Then he was trapped by the amorous wiles of the scandalous Lady Scott, the daughter of a country parson, who started her career by eloping to Paris with a young baronet, Sir Claude Scott, from whom she was finally divorced. This middle-aged and unscrupulous woman set out to captivate young Earl Russell for herself and her daughter. Determined to establish her daughter, Mabel Edith, as the future Countess Russell, she succeeded in bringing off this coup in 1890. Thus the mistress became the mother-in-law, without relinquishing her hold over the insolent, impudent young lord who had not yet "come into his money." It was a plot that might have made a play by the author of *The Second Mrs. Tanqueray,* or a Trollope novel, except for the erotic details that could only be whispered. But the victory of the mother-daughter team was short-lived, for presently Frank was off to Reno in America for a Nevada divorce—a pioneer in this far pilgrimage. An Irish girl, Mollie Cooke of County Galway, went with him and they were married after the divorce. On their return to England the first Countess Russell promptly had the Earl arrested for bigamy—the Reno divorce was held invalid in Britain.

The gutter press made the most of all the sordid details. The young aristocrat's erotic habits were the gossip of the clubs and the servants' quarters. The Dowager Countess issued orders that the Irish girl was not to be admitted to Pembroke Lodge, for in addition to the crushing humiliation of the scandal, Frank had been rude and quarrelsome and disrespectful to his grandmother.

After the death of his grandfather, Bertie's childhood was dominated by his formidable grandmother. A Victorian puritan of the strictest kind, the Countess despised comfort, regarded all bodily pleasures as sinful. One of the minor results of this stringency was that Bertie was forced to take cold baths every morning the year round and to practice the piano every morning before fires were lit. At eighteen Bertrand went to Cambridge, which was for the lonely youth a world "of infinite delight." The great influence there was his friendship with Alfred North Whitehead, who examined him for entrance scholarships and introduced him to some scholars who became his lifelong friends. Whitehead was amazingly kind to the shy youth from Pembroke Lodge, and the friendship then established was to lead to their collaboration upon the *Principia Mathematica* a decade or so later.

During the summer of 1890—certainly not later than 1891 —Bertrand Russell became aware of the existence of the amusing American Quaker family at Friday's Hill. He could not have been much more than eighteen years old; Alys was nearly five years his senior. Fresh from Trinity, young Russell was discovering the universe. His mind glowed and sparkled and spluttered with a seemingly inexhaustible fountain of paradoxes and denials and perceptions. Later these were to be quoted as "Bertieisms." Although those virtuosi of conversation, Sidney Webb and Bernard Shaw, or the more genial Graham Wallas, held forth on the terrace of Friday's Hill, the boyish neighbor could nevertheless draw Alys away and engage her attention. In the flowering, calm beauty of her twenties, Alys became the perfect listener for Bertrand Russell, a comforting loveliness set against the rigors of Bertrand's early life.

After 1892, the Dowager Countess discontinued her summer visits to Dunrozel, perhaps as a way of emphasizing her disapproval of Bertie's intimacy with the Americans at Friday's Hill. She considered the transatlantic Smiths interlopers; they might be received courteously and condescendingly for tea, as were all acceptable neighbors at Fernhurst and Haslemere, but marriage with this barbarian "glass princess" from the wilds of America could only be considered an outrageous misalliance. Moreover, was Alys not five years older than Bertie? Both the Stanleys and the Russells had experienced the dangers of ill-considered marriages, and Bertie's engagement created a definite breach with his grandmother, whose heart was already sore from the scandalous behavior of her problem grandson, the Second Earl. To make matters worse, the Smiths received the disgraced Frank as an honored guest at Friday's Hill. Ostracized by his own caste and class, he became a radical in politics, and was reputed to be the first Fabian in the House of Lords.

The elder Russells and their powerful connections managed an appointment for Bertie in the British Embassy in Paris; later he was transferred to Berlin for several months. But this opposition only intensified his love for Alys Smith. With no ambitions for a diplomatic career, Bertie resigned from his minor post and rushed back to London and Alys. They were married on December 13, 1894, at the Friends' Meeting House in St. Martin's Lane. In the presence of the congregation, Alys and Bertie made their affirmations of love and undying loyalty. Bertie's grandmother did not honor the occasion with her presence, nor did his aunt, Lady Agatha.

The young Russells almost immediately went to Germany for a year, to gather material for a book on social legislation in that country, then considered the leader in "advanced humanitarianism." The book was published, Alys contributing a chapter on the status of women in the Reich.

In 1896, following this year's honeymoon in Germany and the publication of their book, Bertie and Alys set out for a visit to the States. Their first pilgrimage was to see the Mickle Street cottage of Walt Whitman. Alys then took her husband to visit the ever expanding Whitall-Tatum works at Millville, where they met her cousin, Bond Thomas, manager of the great factory, and her uncle, James Whitall, and were a bit terrified by the roar of the mechanized furnaces.

Then the Russells were guests at Carey Thomas's deanery at Bryn Mawr, where both were scheduled to deliver lectures. Alys chose as her subject "The Payment of Motherhood," the implications of which came unwelcome to Quaker ears, especially those of the Bryn Mawr trustees. The Russells, perhaps maliciously, shocked the conventions of Bryn Mawr, and their hostess was hard put to it to explain and justify the radicalism of her youthful cousin and cousin-in-law. In December 1896, Alys's mother wrote her: "You can say things in England that cannot be understood in America and it is always well to keep this in mind. When I was young it was considered indecent to have a baby, and I was made to feel as if I was a prostitute when I had my first baby!"

George Santayana had given Alys and Bertie letters of introduction to friends in Cambridge, Massachusetts. "Haven't the Russells turned up yet?" Santayana asks in a letter to Carlotta Lowell. "I should have been glad to have you meet, they are such nice people. He is mathematical and she humanitarian, but both are human at the same time."

Back in England, Alys and Bertie settled down not far from Friday's Hill in a workman's cottage, to which they added a fairly large study. Bertie's income was sufficient for the simple routine they established; his daytime hours were devoted to mathematics and philosophy, and in the evenings the two of them read history aloud.

It was through the raffish Earl that Bertrand and Alys came to know Santayana, and they lost no time in carrying their new acquaintance off to Friday's Hill, where the Harvard graduate and Cambridge instructor was welcomed as a fellow American expatriate; nothing, in Santayana's mind, could have been further from the truth. He looked upon himself as a perpetual exile from his native Spain, from which he had been transplanted at the age of eight. He had gone to the Boston Latin School and to Harvard, but he liked to think of himself as a Catalonian, a Catholic by birth, a contemplative, with a preference for the timeless and unchanging things of the spirit; he professed himself rooted in the oldest and purest tradition of Latinity. Santayana and Russell were bound to clash sooner or later. Russell suspected that there was something not quite human in Santayana, and Santayana discovered a mixture of folly and willfulness in Bertie's genius.

Russell soon detected a certain element of primness in this newcomer to Friday's Hill. Even for a stroll along the country lanes, the Spaniard wore patent-leather buttoned boots. His lustrous, dark and observant eyes must have expressed a certain contempt in the midst of this innocent family of American Quakers, especially for their tacit assumption that he was an expatriate and a member of the *avant-garde* intelligentsia they were accustomed to entertain. Contrarily, in Hannah he discovered, beneath her Quaker manners and address, and her profession of "broadness," the basic Puritanism which had been so distasteful to him in New England. And it also came as something of a shock to him to see his friend the Earl, when he came one day for luncheon, treated as a close member of the American Smith clan, and to hear Alys and Hannah call him "Frank," a form of address which Santayana had never heard from any of Russell's other friends, or even his assorted wives.

Yet this philosopher Santayana was destined for the rest of

his life to be an intimate of various members of the Smith family—however alien they seemed to him at first.

Never could a young English aristocrat have chosen a more incongruous mother-in-law than Russell found in Hannah Whitall Smith, although Hannah in her sixties carried her love of the English aristocracy to the point of Anglomania. "I frankly confessed," the old lady admitted to her friends in the United States, "that if I *lived* in England, I should want to belong to the aristocracy. My independent spirit would revolt, I fear, at the idea of having anyone Lord and Lady it over me. I always tell the aristocracy this, and they enjoy it greatly." And later: ". . . there certainly is a charm about the English upper classes that is indescribable, and I confess that I do enjoy them exceedingly. For one thing they are far more like Americans than the classes below them . . . And it delights me to see how they appreciate us. To be an American seems to be a certain passport in their favor. . . ."

Hannah remained the "mush-spoon," as she called herself, still tireless in stirring things up. Even at the time of Alys's marriage she had not lost what her children called her "steam-roller" manner—her alarming and explosive outbursts of moral indignation. But she firmly believed herself to be tolerant of everything and everybody—still crying out her familiar "Broad, Broader, Broadest." With her close friends Lady Mount Temple and Lady Henry Somerset, Hannah entered into a routine of secular delights and social services—a sort of transplanted, transatlantic Mrs. Jellyby. Mary and Alys were not blind to the unconsciously comic aspects of her new position. "As for Mother," wrote Mary, "she's past praying for. What with the Ascot Races, the Henley Regatta, the Royal Academy reception and the naval review, she has become so demoralized as to be a regular subscriber to *The Court Journal*—and, in confidence be it said, I am sure that her highest, if most carefully concealed ambition is to see her name some day among the list of the 'Elite'— 'The Duchesse de Whitall-Smith in her black velvet and the family diamonds—' "

At sixty-four, Hannah attended the official opening of Lady Henry Somerset's Inebriate Farm Home at Duxhurst, at which Princess Mary, the Duchess of Teck, gave her royal blessing. Hannah's comment: "For those of us who will endure any moment of dreariness and boredom for the sake of catching glimpses of a Royal person . . . such functions are not so bad. I never saw one before, and I never want to see one again. I can imagine all future ones, without having to stand in the broiling sun for hours, and then see nothing but a fat old lady, who looked like any other fat old lady, putting some mortar on a stone with a silver trowel!'"

As with the passing of the years Hannah became more British and more liberal in her sympathies, she could not help participating in political controversy—though she remained an American. "I confess my Quaker testimony against war has become very unstable of late," she wrote in an open letter to her friends overseas at the time of the Greek crisis in 1897. "There seems to be no way this matter can be settled but by a war that will exterminate Turkey; and I wish from the bottom of my heart that America would step in and support the Greeks, and give the wicked 'concert of Europe' an object lesson in what a free nation is willing to do to help another nation to be free! I can assure you I have actually wished I was a man and young enough to go over to Greece to help them fight; and I almost wondered at some of the meetings, where I have been stirred to the very depths, that I did not come out with a helmet on my head! I never had the slightest idea before of what an overpowering enthusiasm for freedom is like, and I do not wonder now that people have died to secure it."

Such belated enthusiasms and emotional outbursts were not impressive to the cool young mathematician and skeptic who happened to be Hannah's son-in-law. He might have been more interested in her accounts of pilgrimages to the heretical colonies in the United States. She knew Laurence Oliphant, the English disciple and dupe of the notorious Thomas Lake Harris; she had interviewed Madame Blavatsky. She had made a pilgrimage to the Oneida colony, discovering everywhere the mysterious intervening of the antinomian heresy (which had led to the downfall and disgrace of her husband Robert) and the masked eroticism of suppressed sexuality. But on such matters one did not discourse with one's son-in-law.

As for Robert Smith, Santayana seems the only one of the literary guests at Friday's Hill who noticed him enough at this period to record his impressions. With his Spanish courtesy still undimmed by his American experience, Santayana made a comforting and receptive listener for the old man who was now the extinct meteor of his former fiery self, completely overshadowed by his wife and daughters and their radical circle of friends.

"Don't tell Mrs. Smith," Robert said while showing Santayana his garden, "but I am not a Christian at all! I am a Buddhist!" He pointed to what he called his Bo tree, a great oak in the midst of which he had constructed a windowed cabin. He led the Spaniard up a ladder into it, a single small room with a black horsehair couch and a small bookcase filled with old-fashioned American books, among which George spied *Prue and I,* a novel by his own Aunt Sarah's son-in-law, George William Curtis. And he had expected the

Dhammapada or the Upanishads! "Vain flight of the American puritan to softer climates! He carries his horizon with him and remains rooted at home."

In his mid-seventies, Robert Pearsall Smith's mind seemed to have burnt itself out, and he became a faint and ghostly figure at the intellectual banquet set before him in the hospitable country house in the quiet Surrey countryside. He slipped out of life on April 17, 1899, his turbulent and spectacular career forgotten on both sides of the Atlantic.

With characteristic unpredictability, Hannah resigned herself to this loss. Experience in life, she stated, had taught her to look upon the male portion of the human race as one must upon avalanches or earthquakes—as phenomena that could not be stopped nor altered, but must simply be avoided with as little inconvenience to oneself as possible. And of all the male portion of the race, she was most disillusioned about husbands.

Bertrand Russell in his twenties was seeking some sort of political group with which he could affiliate; and the Webbs persuaded him to join the Fabian Society. But neither then nor later did he find himself in intellectual agreement with these two prophets of the Welfare State; beneath the surface of young Russell's consummate courtesy lurked an obdurate enemy of all conventional idealism. Fastidious in his choice of friends and acquaintances, Bertie detested idealistic platitudes and hated any kind of self-seeking egotism. He gazed at humanity from a pinnacle of aristocratic detachment; maliciously he diagnosed people and tried to demolish all world-saving causes.

In addition to his political relationships with the Webbs, for Alys's sake Russell endured friendship with them. He was bored by their famous dinners, but he went with Alys to 41 Grosvenor Road, the house which the Webbs shared with Frank Costelloe. Beatrice and Sidney continued to live in the house after Frank's death—altogether they occupied it for nearly forty years, and it became famous in the annals of Labour politics.

Beatrice had arranged the little house carefully. The work-room was on the ground floor, and also served as a dining room. This long, narrow room, running east and west, was lined with books and factory reports. Whatever space was left over was covered with steel engravings and with large photographs of three generations of the Potter family. There were portraits of Beatrice's earlier friends and associates: Herbert Spencer, Haldane, Marie Souvestre. On the half-landing, between the ground and first floors, Beatrice placed her secretary's office with its oilcloth floor, its large deal writing table and shelves filled from floor to ceiling with boxes of pamphlets. On the first floor a conventional sitting room was furnished with long seats fitted into alcoves, a table heaped with books, three easy chairs—no sofa, but an *escritoire*. Mrs. Webb, who managed with two maids, carefully planned her policy of entertainment; the rooms were designed to accommodate the largest possible number of guests, standing or sitting.

At 41 Grosvenor Road, the Webbs were at the hub of the political universe in London. Like two industrious spiders, they sat at the center of a vast web of politics, in which they caught and frequently devoured, for the highest social purpose, every kind of person from prime ministers and millionaires to indigent writers and shorthand typists. They knew everyone who counted for anything in politics, society and letters, and knew everything that was going on both before and behind the curtain. They were highly trained, expert social scientists with encyclopedic omniscience of the history and anatomy of Labour politics.

Russell's eventual revolt against the Webbs and the Fa-

bians never became an open one like that of young Herbert
Wells, who took his revenge in print after he had been practically expelled from the Fabians. But Russell could appreciate Wells's *The New Machiavelli,* in which the Webbs were
satirized as Altiora and Oscar Bailey, and the house on Grosvenor Road was cruelly lampooned. Bertrand appreciated
Wells's reaction to the Barmecide feasts presided over by
Beatrice Webb. Afterwards, out on the Embankment, Bertie
felt an immense relief just at the sight of the lamplit Embankment; at all the wasteful, colorful stir and confusion of
London. Later he would chuckle as he read Wells on a
typical dinner with the Webbs:

". . . then with all this administrative fizzle, this pseudo-
scientific administrative chatter, dying away in your head,
out you went into the limitless grimy chaos of London streets
and squares, roads and avenues lined with teeming houses.
. . . You saw the chaotic clamour of hoardings, the jum-
ble of traffic, the coming and going of mysterious myriads,
you heard the rumble of traffic like the noise of a torrent; a
vague incessant murmur of cries and voices, wanton crimes
and accidents bawled at you from the placards; imperative
unaccountable fashions swaggered triumphant in the dazzling windows of the shops; and you found yourself swaying
back to the opposite conviction that the huge formless spirit
of the world it was that held the strings and danced the put-
pets on the Bailey stage. . . ."

Every year Beatrice and Sidney were invited for a six- to
nine-week sojourn at Friday's Hill. They arrived with their
heavy burden of bulging notebooks and statistics. Derided as
"two typewriters that clicked as one," and pigeonholed as
"useful but inhuman freaks," the Webbs were denounced by
their enemies as soulless survivors of the Utilitarians. But to

Alys, Beatrice's bond with Sidney was an example of perfect and undeviating love, knitted out of comradeship and tenderness, delicacy and mutual understanding. And to Beatrice, Alys and Bertie seemed the most attractive couple she had ever known. They combined youth and beauty, personal charm, unique intelligence—Alys embodying beauty and Bertie intellect. Beatrice was certain of the permanence of this marriage. In the realm of social reform, Alys became her loyal disciple, while Bertrand concentrated upon higher mathematics.

Following the example of the Webbs, the Russells organized their lives at Friday's Hill upon a strict schedule: breakfast was served in their study at nine o'clock; Bertrand then worked at mathematics until twelve-thirty. Then the two read together and strolled for a quarter of an hour in the garden before luncheon at one-thirty. Cigarettes and coffee with the Webbs followed, croquet with Logan, and then tea at four-thirty. More mathematics for Bertie until six o'clock, followed by reading aloud with Alys until seven-thirty. Dinner with the Webbs and other guests was served at eight. At nine-thirty Alys and Bertie retired to their room and read to each other until ten-thirty.

But after a few years, Mrs. Webb was brought to a reluctant realization that all was not going well with this marriage she herself had encouraged. The knowledge came to her during a holiday in Normandy in 1902, where for a week she and Sidney joined the Russells in a little Norman village. The young couple could not enjoy their holiday in the cramped and uncomfortable lodgings in which Beatrice found them. They were still reading together, but Beatrice found "a tragic austerity and effort in their relations." "They are both so good in the best and most complete sense," Beatrice noted in her diary. "Alys has so much charm and Ber-

trand so much intellect, that it is strange that they cannot enjoy lighthearted happiness in each other's love and companionship—but there is something that interferes, and friends
can only look on with respect and admiration and silent
concern. Perhaps, they will grow into a more joyful union;
certainly they have the big essential condition—a common
faith so far as personal conduct is concerned. . . . Fortunately his splendid morality outweighs his tragic propensities
and I doubt whether Alys realizes that he thinks his married life an heroically lived tragedy."

Finally Alys and Bertrand Russell came to the decision
that their marriage was a mistake. Both were sensitive
enough to appreciate the irony of their situation, for after
having surmounted so many obstacles, and having defied the
opposition of his family and kinsfolk, they found themselves
compelled to admit that there might have been wisdom in
such opposition. The failure of this first marriage exerted a
profound influence upon Bertrand Russell's subsequent
thought and conduct. His insistence upon the desirability,
even the necessity, of premarital initiation may have been
derived from his own unhappy first marriage. The young
Russells were perhaps too idealistic and high-minded in their
love, if we may accept the testimony of Beatrice Webb, who
observed them both during their earliest years together. Had
children come, their personalities might have merged more
closely.

Mathematics offered young Russell an escape from his unhappy marriage. In 1900, he had gone with Alfred North
Whitehead to a philosophical congress in Paris, where they
listened to the eminent Italian logician Giuseppe Peano, who
had invented a new system of symbols for use in symbolic
logic. Whitehead and Russell decided to collaborate on a
book that would bring order out of the chaotic study of the

foundations of mathematics. That task took up ten years of their lives—from 1900 to 1910—and the achievement was published as *Principia Mathematica,* which has been acclaimed as perhaps the most important philosophical work of this century. Most of the work was done at Cambridge, where Russell had returned as a don in 1900. It required long absences from home—absences which intensified Alys's misery. Consciously she realized that these prolonged separations were legitimate, but unconsciously she knew them to be voluntary. In her desperation she invited Beatrice to join her in a trip to Switzerland, a holiday during which Alys sought to adjust her spirit to the final separation which now seemed inevitable. Bertie was rebelling not only against his own marriage, but against all the conventions of the caste and status in which he had been brought up. He became an energetic champion of women's suffrage, of social reform and antimilitarism.

Alys could not stand in his way. But she could take a secret pride in his intransigent courage; it was due to her influence, she felt, that he had earned his spurs in public controversy as a champion of women's suffrage. However, it was not until 1914 that Russell became famous as a rebel. Then past forty, and too old to be considered a "conscientious objector," he made his protest as a public speaker and pamphleteer. He was physically assaulted when he mounted to public platforms to protest the war; he was dismissed from his lectureship at Cambridge; he was jailed, and he throve on persecution.

A Frenchman has said: "Every man is a radical at twenty, a conservative at forty." But this truism was reversed in the case of Bertrand Russell. At forty, he became at last free of all the Victorian conventions, those of Friday's Hill as well as those of Pembroke Lodge. He was later to confess that he felt no disgrace in serving a prison term for his unpopular convictions. Prison, he discovered, was not altogether disagreeable. "I had no engagements, no difficult decisions to make, no fear of callers, no interruptions to my work. I wrote a book, 'Introduction to Mathematical Philosophy,' and began the work for 'Analysis of Mind.' I was rather interested in my fellow-prisoners, who seemed to me in no way morally inferior to the rest of the population."

But this prison experience came to him long after his separation from Alys. As a Quaker born and bred, Alys might have sympathized with Bertie's defiant pacifism. Their break had come not from any discord in the realm of intellect, but rather from their innocence and lack of experience in the physical basis of love. Their marriage might have lasted if they had known that it must derive its strength, like Antaeus, in periodically touching earth. But their paths had diverged now, and Bertie and Alys were not to come together again until a second war had devastated their Europe and their London.

When the First World War ended, and there was such an intense and very natural reaction against the war and all the Victorian values that had made it possible, Russell found himself a spokesman of the intellectual *avant-garde,* indeed of a whole new generation, bitter about the past, but also filled with zeal for new ideas, the Russell ideas of peace and social justice, of sexual freedom and progressive education and, above all, of happiness.

Alys tried to persuade herself that her husband would return to her one day. They had not been living together since 1911, but after the excitement of the war years she felt he might have a change of heart. Meanwhile she was schooling herself to accept, in the civilized and sophisticated postwar

code, the rumors that came to her ears of Bertie's friendship
with Lady Ottoline Morrell, the wife of one of Logan's closest friends. Philip Morrell was the son of a wealthy brewer,
and Logan, a self-appointed social arbiter, had vehemently
objected to his friend's alliance with the daughter of the
great house of Cavendish-Bentinck, descendant of a long
line of the Dukes of Portland, and half-sister of the Sixth
Duke. Logan had refused to attend their wedding in 1902.
But later, flattered by the attention paid to him by Lady
Ottoline, Logan forgave his Balliol friend for marrying so far
above his station. "I think I *can* go on seeing you after all,"
Logan remarked to Morrell. "I find Ottoline very interesting,
so I shall be able to keep on coming to see you, not as your
friend, but as Ottoline's." How could Alys hope to compete
with the brilliant, eccentric and generous patroness of the
arts, who collected celebrities as others collected masterpieces?

Inevitably, Alys's brilliant husband was added to
the great collection at Garsington, Lady "Ott's" great country house near Oxford. Bertie became a frequent guest there,
discreetly housed in a farmhouse on the Garsington estate.
His hostess introduced him to Joseph Conrad, for whom
Russell developed a lifelong admiration. But the meeting
with D. H. Lawrence was not so successful. That misplaced
messiah resented Bertie's cool, aristocratic anarchism, and he
broke off their friendship with a characteristic outburst. Lady
Ott liked to mix her celebrated guests and enjoyed the clash
of temperaments. She persuaded Bertrand to bring George
Santayana to her house, little realizing that the shy Spaniard
could be as incurable a gossip as he was a distinguished philosopher. Behind the façade of friendship, Santayana detected a love affair between Bertie and his hostess. Later, in
My Host the World, Santayana was to leave a vivid portrait

of Lady Ott—with her aristocratic beak, her straggling locks, her pale blue eyes, her tall thin figure, her blue flounces and yellow cross-gartered stockings, all combining to give her the aspect of a bird of the tropics. Love affair or not, this friendship exerted a profound influence on Russell. It destroyed the final vestiges of his Victorian virtues and freed him from the inhibitions implanted so long ago at Pembroke Lodge.

There could, as Alys realized, be no question of a marriage with Lady Ottoline. Divorce was not a custom of her high caste; and moreover, she remained true in her fashion to her darling Philip. Morrell was not infrequently snubbed by the celebrities his wife gathered together, but Ottoline loved him with a tender, maternal love, and took to the hustings when Morrell stood for Parliament. "Some have said that I do not care for the common people!" Lady Ottoline is said to have cried at a crowded meeting. "But I do! Oh, I do! Didn't I marry one of them?"

After the Armistice, Russell joined a group of liberals and leftists going to Russia to inspect the fruits of the Bolshevik revolution. He returned disillusioned with his discoveries there; and then promptly set out for China, where he was invited to lecture to university students. He was accompanied by his secretary, Dora Winifred Black, the daughter of Sir Frederick Black. She shared all his advanced views on love and marriage. Upon their return, Bertie finally asked Alys for a divorce, which was granted. His marriage to Miss Black followed promptly, and on November 16, 1921, Bertrand Russell's first son was born. He was named John Conrad, and when his father succeeded to the title of Earl Russell, the boy became Viscount Amberley.

Chapter 9 · Logan's Career

To trace the metamorphosis of Logan Pearsall Smith from his beginnings as a birthright New Jersey Quaker to a well-nigh perfect English country gentleman and an arbiter of literary taste, we must go back once more to the mid-nineties, when young Mr. Smith stepped out of Balliol with a clipped Oxford accent and a vast appetite for culture. As described by one of his contemporaries, he had grown up into a refined and gentlemanly bachelor, with a pretty talent for turning out sentences and a taste for collecting bric-a-brac. Tall, delicately featured, and always courteous, Logan was still the prey of deep-seated melancholy, aggravated, perhaps, by a long record of self-conscious failure to become an artist in words. Britain was proving too complex for him to grasp—he was perpetually breaking off before he had mastered even the smallest portion of it. He was trying to find a career, or even a wife, to suit him.

After leaving Balliol, Logan at once decided upon a year's stay in Paris. There, in Montparnasse, he rented an apartment for twenty pounds a year. His three rooms opened on a little garden and a great cherry tree. It was all quite shabby and provincial and Henry-Jamesian, but the great boulevards were not too far away.

Hannah went over to inspect his new quarters and reported herself delighted with their simplicity and cheapness. But

135

Hannah's perpetual distrust of art in all forms remained. To her, aesthetic pursuits seemed a fearful waste of enthusiasm and effort, particularly the art of painting. ". . . for of course most of this Art studying comes to absolutely nothing. I shudder to think of the thousands of wretched daubs that are being turned out year after year in these Paris *ateliers,* each one representing a whole world of enthusiasm and earnest work, and often an infinity of sacrifice on the part of the parents and friends, and all to end in hopeless failure."

With his friends Roger Fry, Lowes Dickinson, Charles Conder and the lovely flower-like Kinsella ladies (adored from a proper distance), Logan made expeditions to Giverny and Les Andelys (where the great Poussin was born). But his first interest remained in what he was always to call "the lovely art of writing." Even posing for the celebrated Jimmy Whistler became tiresome. That master showman of the brush was beginning a portrait of the famous—or infamous—Count Robert de Montesquiou-Fezensac. The Count was posed standing in full evening dress with a magnificent fur coat draped over his arm. But the aristocrat could not be expected to pose for this accessory, and Logan was delighted when his compatriot asked him to serve as a substitute, a "stand-in." On and on Jimmy painted, until Logan, ready to drop, would beg for a rest. "In a moment! Just a moment!" Whistler would reply, and this moment would stretch into half an hour. The portrait of the Count may now be studied in its fading glory in the lecture hall of the Frick collection in New York. This Parisian eccentric was the prototype for Huysmans's arch-aesthete Des Esseintes, and was later to serve as the model of Marcel Proust's repellent homosexual Baron Charlus.

Paris soon proved too distracting, too seductive for a serious student of the "lovely art of writing." For that, loneliness

and solitude were the prerequisites Henry James had counseled in 1895. Logan had sent the Master his first little volume of short stories, published at his own expense, entitled
The Youth of Parnassus. Henry James mislaid Logan's book
riding in the Underground, and sent the author a letter
dripping apologies. But later he found another copy and
graciously invited Logan (thirty years of age at that time) to
come for a talk about his stories. James's praise was kindly
but tepid—he possessed a fine gift for discouraging all fellow
countrymen who aspired to enter the field of fiction. Logan
left, not depressed, but positively exhilarated by James's part-
ing remarks, which nearly fifty years later Logan remembered well enough to quote: "My young friend," James in-
toned, "and I call you young—you are disgustingly and, if
I may be allowed to say so, nauseatingly young—there is one
thing that, if you really intend to follow the course you indicate, I cannot too emphatically insist on. There is one word
—let me impress upon you—which you must inscribe upon
your banner, and that," he added after an impressive pause,
"that word is Loneliness."

After his Paris year, remembering this advice of the Master, Logan decided to retire to the English countryside. Not
far from Friday's Hill, near the Sussex border, he found an
old farmhouse which he could rent for the lordly sum of
thirty pounds a year. For recreation he would develop the
enclosed garden—Logan prided himself on his green thumb.
There, at High Buildings, he could toil like an industrious
apprentice in polishing his precious prose—composing jewel-
like paragraphs of Aesopian brevity. These he named *Trivia*,
and in 1903 he published three hundred copies at his own
expense.

But his interests remained academic and he returned to
Oxford for a master's degree, which was awarded him in

1906, when he had passed the age of forty, three years after the publication of his first volume of *Trivia*. In 1907 he published *The Life and Letters of Sir Henry Wotton,* an academic compilation of interest only to specialists in the literature of the early seventeenth century. However, this effort won the praise of that captious critic Lytton Strachey.

During all these years, Logan's friendship with James, which might have been terminated by the hurt feelings of a budding author, actually flowered into mutual affection. James used to refer to his younger friend as "poor dear *good* Logan!" and he mischievously encouraged Logan in his mimicry of literary celebrities. Henry, Logan later remembered, used often to say, "Do so and so for me!" and Logan would oblige with an impromptu impersonation. On occasion Henry James himself would "do" a character for Logan. "Do Gosse!" said Logan one day; but for that Henry James must be in exactly the right mood; Logan must wait. Health, place, time, in fact all external circumstances must be entirely propitious.

Often James became a willing, if unresponsive, listener to Logan's strictures against his native land—that "sandy Sahara of culture." Once the two of them were walking together in the wide-horizoned expanse of Romney Marsh, near Rye. As is habitual with certain expatriates, Logan was attacking his native land. How could he speak so bitterly of his own country and countrymen, Henry James protested. It was altogether shocking. He stopped and, turning full circle, surveyed the empty landscape. Then, reassured that they were quite alone, "My dear boy," James said, putting his hand upon Logan's shoulder, "I can't tell you how passionately I agree with you!"

Logan accepted every invitation to visit the great novelist

at Lamb House, Rye, and wrote Alys ecstatic letters of his
pilgrimages there.

In the autumn of 1904, Hannah Smith's public appearances, her speeches and sermons were brought to an end.
Rheumatism or arthritis put her in a wheel chair, from which
she was not to escape. She gave up Friday's Hill, as well as the
house in Grosvenor Road, and with her granddaughters,
Ray and Karin Costelloe, moved to a London flat; it was in
Morpeth Mansions, very near Westminster Cathedral. Mrs.
Smith was glad to be free of the dark little Grosvenor Road
house, and enjoyed the new, light, airy all-on-one-floor flat.

Two years later, when Logan had received his master's degree from Balliol, he leased a house named Court Place, at
Iffley, on the river near Oxford. Since now neither the beloved Mariechen nor Alys was free to be with their mother,
and as Logan greatly preferred Oxford to London, Hannah
and he decided that this old house on the banks of the
Thames, near a beautiful church, was exactly the place for
both of them. Court Place sat in the midst of eight charming
wooded acres. In her wheel chair on the green lawns, Hannah
looked down on the river, or turned occasionally to receive
pilgrims from overseas who had read her books, heard her
speak, or simply heard of her good works. They came to pay
homage to one they revered almost as a secular saint.

Hannah still considered herself "Broad, Broader, Broadest," and her outspoken advice to young girls was often not
what they expected. "Girls," the majestic old lady might
admonish, "there is one thing in life you ought to know.
Don't be too unselfish!"

Logan acquired a launch with which he could expedite
guests from Oxford for lunch or dinner. One of these guests

was William James. When he was lecturing on pragmatism at Oxford in 1908, "he said that I was only the second person," Hannah reported to Mariechen, "who had said a word to him about his work since he came to Oxford four weeks ago. He longs to talk his philosophy over with the thinkers here, but they are all too shy to introduce the subject, and he does not like to do it himself."

Death came for Hannah at Court Place in 1911. She was glad to die, would have preferred "flying off astride the tail of a comet." Her last months were full of pain, and she did not end her days on a bed of illness, but, stiffened by disease, was compelled to sit bolt upright in a chair. But she would not give up her *idea* of the happy life even as she was dying.

It was inevitable that now, with Hannah's passing and Alys's separation from her husband, Logan and Alys should decide to live together.

Near Arundel in Sussex, Logan found an attractive Georgian house. Soon Alys and he were established in Ford Place, which both decided would become their country home. Alys shared Logan's enthusiasm for its early Georgian façade and the forecourt, the potentialities of its formal garden. Logan planted stock and delphiniums, and set out a long rose bed in the center of the walled enclosure. Across a meadow or two, on its way to the Channel, lazily flowed the river Arun. While Logan exerted his energies to revive the garden, Alys organized the household within. Both worked hard to prepare the new house for their series of distinguished weekend guests. During the summer months they entertained many friends from Oxford, Cambridge and literary London. Alys had acquired poise and a new kind of beauty. Her coloring was still vivid, although her hair had turned to an iron gray; her voice (at least to visiting cousins from Philadelphia) had become very, very English. She still took a lively interest in all reform movements, including votes for women, and still remained loyal to the Fabian ideals of her friends the Webbs, who became frequent guests at Ford Place.

Even as he approached fifty, Logan retained the naïve enthusiasm of a juvenile. Expectant eyes peered at guests through gold-rimmed spectacles; his long nose was becoming more prominent. Although he spoke with a fashionably clipped Oxford accent, a slight lisp remained in his speech. Yet in his quiet way Logan could dominate a room full of distinguished guests. A master of deft questioning, his exclamations were also perfectly timed. He could make silence eloquent, and knew how to change the subject swiftly and effectively. Did Logan's gentlemanly diction ever recall to Alys the dictum of her old friend Graham Wallas? Just as it is impossible to sing, or to speak a foreign language well, with one's mouth and throat in a "gentlemanly" position, Wallas had observed, so it may prove to be the case that one cannot think effectively if one's main purpose in life is to be a gentleman.

Together, Logan and Alys became the perfect host and hostess at Ford Place. There they celebrated the established rituals of their weekend hospitality. Logan felt that his standing in the London literary aristocracy was quite definitely, if intangibly, elevated by the marriages of his nieces Ray and Karin Costelloe. Both had married into the emerging Bloomsbury set (Desmond MacCarthy's wife had coined the name "Bloomsberries" around 1910 or 1911), becoming members of its "first families." Ray married Oliver Strachey, Lytton Strachey's elder brother, and Karin became the wife of the irrepressible, fun-loving Adrian Stephen.

Adrian was the son of Sir Leslie Stephen and the brother

of Virginia, who at about the same time married Leonard Woolf, and whose first novel, *The Voyage Out,* was soon to be acclaimed by the critics, in 1915. Adrian was the last of four children born to Julia and Leslie Stephen in the first few years of their marriage. Close in age, the four were as closely linked in feeling. First came Vanessa, so dearly loved by Virginia that no words could ever express her feelings. She was the rock, the refuge, as well as the playmate, the friend, the co-conspirator, the secret sharer. Then came Thoby, whom Virginia adored, whose approval she sought, whose memory remained always bright, the golden, glorious brother. Adrian, the youngest, was merry, mischief-loving, incomparably comic, the brother to whose defense she was ready to rush if ever he should be in need. Come the four corners of the world in arms, the four young Stephen children were ready.

In 1907, Adrian and Virginia had moved from Gordon Square to Fitzroy Square, when Vanessa married Clive Bell, one of Thoby's oldest friends. Adrian and Virginia, in Fitzroy Square, had both been principals in a prank that provoked scandal and laughter when it was perpetrated. This was the so-called Dreadnought Scandal. Swathed in colorful robes as the Emperor of Abyssinia and attended by such disguised courtiers as her brother Adrian, Duncan Grant and a few others, Virginia paid a "state" visit to a British battleship, and emerged from this burlesque ceremony undetected. Adrian acted as interpreter; he needed only a little sunburn powder and some false hair as a disguise, it was considered, though his height (he was six feet five inches tall) made him eminently recognizable. Adrian later published a pamphlet recording this hoax, a prank typical of the gay malice and irreverence of the children of Sir Leslie Stephen.

A few doors away from Adrian and Virginia in Fitzroy Square, Duncan Grant, a cousin of Oliver Strachey, shared rooms with John Maynard Keynes. Later these four shared a house for a short time.

Mary might have hoped for a son-in-law closer to Ray's age group than the distinguished Oliver Strachey, who was in his late thirties, but she accepted her daughter's engagement with philosophical resignation. Like his Scottish ancestors since the sixteenth century, Oliver had served as a civil servant in the East. He had returned to London in 1910, and had been introduced to the Bloomsbury group by his younger brother Giles Lytton. He was the son of that formidable Lady Jane Maria Strachey who between 1860 and 1887 introduced no less than ten Stracheys into this world, of whom Oliver was the sixth, having been born in 1874.

Between 1910 and 1920 the Bloomsbury group, which began with a group of old Cambridge friends, grew into the spirit known as "Bloomsbury" and included, besides the Stracheys and the Stephens, such men as Arthur Waley, Francis Birrell and David Garnett.

Adrian Stephen was about ten years younger than Oliver Strachey, and thus only a few years older than Karin Costelloe. Karin had made her literary debut with an essay on Bergson in a philosophical journal. She went on to take a doctor's degree, and became a practicing psychoanalyst.

With Ray and Karin established among the elite of Bloomsbury intellectuals, I Tatti became even more identified as the Italian outpost of Bloomsbury. It seemed that every artist and writer from Gordon Square and the streets that clustered about the British Museum eventually found their way to Settignano and the doors of I Tatti. The clan of Stracheys there could not be counted, there were so many family ramifications.

In 1913, Logan came to a decision he had long put off: he became a naturalized British subject. An avowed Anglophile since his Balliol days, he had delayed taking this momentous step during the lifetime of his mother, from whose domination he had never liberated himself. For Logan the experience was more than a mere change of country: it was a sort of equivalent to the "second experience" once preached so powerfully by his parents, a mystical rebirth. It would banish from the depths of his spirit the inner conflict that never ceased to torture it. But it was not merely his love of England that motivated his decision: it was his dislike of his native land as well. Logan was one of those exiles from the United States of whom it was said: "Those who become expatriates out of hatred for their homeland are as bound to the past as those who hate their parents."

Having taken this momentous step, Logan tried to persuade Henry James to do likewise, but he was more directly influential in getting the Master to meet his friend Santayana. Among his cherished memories of James, Logan treasured most the role he played in bringing about that encounter. "Will you come to lunch to meet him?" Logan asked. "Come!" Henry James cried, according to Logan, uplifting his arms in a sacerdotal pose. "I would walk across London with bare feet on the snow to meet George Santayana!"

That memorable occasion, in Logan's little London *pied-à-terre,* was limited to five—James, Santayana, their host, Alys, and Mary Berenson, who happened to be visiting in London. For Logan, the long luncheon became almost a sacred ceremony, so closely did the five of them seem united in a community of spirit. There was an unconscious suggestion of a Last Supper. He was more than gratified that Santayana found the Master so congenial—far more to his liking, as he was later to confess, than James's elder brother William. Later, Santayana recorded his impression: "By that time Logan Pearsall Smith had developed his amiable interest in my writings and the Berensons had showed me the greatest kindness. Now the brother and sister asked me one day to lunch with Henry James. Those were his last years and I never saw him again. Nevertheless in that one interview he made me feel more at home and better understood than his brother William had ever done in the long years of our acquaintance. Henry was calm, he liked to see things as they are, and to be free afterwards to imagine how they might have been . . ."

Events moved too swiftly for Henry James ever to visit Logan at Ford Place. When war was declared in August 1914, James suddenly found himself engulfed in a tidal wave of patriotism—not, indeed, any new-found love for his native land, but for the country of his adoption. His patriotism swept away every other interest and overwhelmed the neat order of his life at Rye. His anger against the Kaiser became almost hysterical. He hurried up to London, to his lodgings in Chelsea, and enrolled with the American Ambulance Corps; he worked for the refugees from Belgium. When Logan met him at lunch at Edith Wharton's, James was a ruddy volcano of righteous wrath. A blaze lighted up his eyes. "This is a war for men only," James sputtered; "it is a war for me and poor Logan." Logan years later detailed his version of this memorable scene:

"But surely we must discriminate," Logan mischievously but mildly suggested to this master of discrimination; "surely we must look to the right and left, and proceed, all eyes, with care and strategical caution. This is certainly my war, as I am a naturalized British subject; but you, I believe, are a neutral, as neutral as Switzerland or Sweden. Why don't you come into it?" he asked. Panting, Logan paused to wipe the imagined gore from his face. "Why don't you enroll yourself as a British subject?"

During the winter that followed, Logan would end his telephone colloquies with James on this trumpet note: "When are you coming into the war? . . . How long are you going to sit with the Roumanians on a back seat in the Balkans?"

One day the Master's elaborations of phrase, the parentheses, the polysyllabic evasions, which made any talk with Henry James so amazing an adventure, were replaced by a terse query:

"Logan, how—you know what I mean—how do you do it?"

"You go," Logan tersely replied, "to a solicitor."

"Of course. I know just the right person," and the great novelist rang off with a bang that almost smashed the receiver.

Simon Nowell-Smith, in his anthology, *The Legend of the Master*, doubts the strict accuracy of Logan's "decorative pen," admitting that "I cannot conscientiously say that I believe it to contain any appreciable element of literal truth"; but he admits it to his canon as "spiritually true." In later years, the legend remained that it was Logan who first persuaded James to apply for naturalization, but such evidence as is available does not support Logan's claim. In his *Recollections of Logan Pearsall Smith*, Robert Gathorne-Hardy states that Logan was one of James's sponsors in these proceedings, but he is in error; the records show that as sponsors Henry James secured Prime Minister Asquith, George Prothero, Edmund Gosse, and his own literary agent, J. B. Pinker. The great decision was taken in June 1915. Papers of naturalization were granted on July 26, when Henry James took the oath of allegiance. But his days as a British patriot were numbered. For a man past threescore and ten he worked too hard, drove himself too relentlessly in his war work. On December 2 he suffered a stroke, in his quarters in Carlyle Mansions, Chelsea, and, a few days later, a second one. On New Year's Day, 1916, Logan, Alys and the rest of literary London read in the *Times:*

"The King has been graciously pleased to make the following appointment to the Order of Merit:

HENRY JAMES, ESQ.

"Mr. Henry James recently became naturalized in this country to mark his sympathy with the cause of the Allies. The high honour now conferred on him will give the keenest satisfaction to lovers of literature all over the world . . . He joins Mr. Hardy in the Order, membership of which is the highest distinction attainable by a writer, and in which they are the only two representatives of pure literature."

The insignia of the Order was carried to James's bedside by Lord Bryce. Sir Edmund Gosse asked permission to tell Henry of the great honor awarded him, but found his old friend lying inert with closed eyes in the light of a flickering candle. Leaning over, Gosse whispered: "Henry, they've given you the O.M." No expression lighted up the immobile features, but when Gosse closed the door James opened his eyes and whispered to his nurse: "Nurse, take away the candle and spare my blushes!"

James died two months later, on February 28, 1916; his funeral was held March 3, in Chelsea Old Church.

Mrs. W. K. Clifford wrote to William Lyon Phelps: "His own country must not think for a moment that he forgot it, for he didn't, and he left directions that his ashes, after cremation, were to be taken back to it. There was much talk of a service in Westminster Abbey; the Prime Minister approved of it and the Dean was quite willing there should be one . . . But Mrs. William James refused all idea of it. The simpler service in the little church not a stone's throw from his flat, was more in accord with his life, she said . . . better befitted the New Englander. So thus it was . . . most beautiful and dignified . . . in the little church that is now centuries old and will now forever be identified with him."

Logan, who could scoff and ridicule the primitive faith of his father and mother, could nevertheless express something closely akin to adoration in his attitude to James—an expression articulated in a letter he wrote to his friend Ethel Sands: "I feel as if a great cathedral had disappeared from the skyline, a great country with all its civilization been wiped from the map, a planet lost to the solar system. Things will happen and he won't be there to tell them to, and the world will be a poorer and more meagre place. We shall all miss the charm and danger of our relation with the dear elusive man, the affectionate and wonderful talks, the charming letters, the icy and sad intervals, and the way he kept us all allured and aloof, and shone on us, and hid his light, like a great variable but constant moon."

Today this seems overwritten rather than sincere; but for the remaining thirty years of his life, Logan reverently kept alive his memory of Henry James. He became, indeed, what we may name the last of the synoptic disciples. He became a priest of that enigmatic cult that has increased and multiplied around the works and the legends of the Master—a cult, or a sect, the growth of which can perhaps best be explained in religious rather than literary terms.

One of Logan's later distinctions in literary London was voiced in the three words often whispered behind his back: "He knew James!" He liked to think that he found himself in situations that could have furnished the plot of a Jamesian fiction. When he took the sun in Burton's Court, he always spoke of the seat he habitually took there as "my bench of desolation."

Hardly had Logan brought Ford Place in Sussex to near-perfection in spite of war, than he discovered an Elizabethan manor house on the Solent, the channel that separates the Isle of Wight from the mainland. The house captivated his imagination; he liked its rose-colored brick walls, its steep tiled roof, and the fact that it overlooked Southampton Water. Even its name amused him—for this house in southern England was known as Big Chilling. The garden was simpler than that of Ford Place, and presented a new challenge to this impassioned gardener. Alys, as usual, acquiesced in her brother's swift decision; and soon, as though by magic, peaches were growing along the sun-warmed walls, and cantaloupes ripening in the greenhouse. Logan acquired a sailing dinghy and moored it at the mouth of a nearby river. He took weekend guests skimming over the reaches of Southampton Water, incidentally demonstrating his prowess as a yachtsman. The land immediately surrounding Big Chilling was flat, but it was elevated at least fifty feet above sea level, high enough for Alys and Logan to watch the ships in the distance, and on clear days to catch a glimpse of the Isle of Wight—at least from the upper floors. They watched, in fine weather, the horizontal bands of colors—the brown, green or golden yellow of the surrounding fields, the blue of the Solent, glistening or glittering, or at night the great ships departing from Southampton, darkened and silenced by wartime regulations.

Logan still retained an air of youth, even of juvenility. American cousins who came to visit him were impressed by his invincible boyishness. To visiting Whitalls, Logan's spirit remained what it had been in far-off Germantown days. And Logan revealed himself still the skilled conductor of the conversational symphonies that took place on week-ends at Big Chilling, when the visiting stars were the Webbs, or Bernard Shaw, or the omnipresent Desmond MacCarthys. With her gray hair and vivid coloring, her charming deference, Alys was still a gracious hostess for her brother. After the death of Henry James, Logan's most carefully protected friend was Bernard Shaw. Logan kept the visits of the Shaws inviolate from the vulgar curiosity of less distinguished intimates. Shaw came with the Webbs to Big Chilling as a weekend guest the first week in June 1917. This triumvirate of the Fabians put their stamp of approval on the house set in the midst of cornfields and only five minutes away from the Solent. In April 1919, the Webbs came to spend almost two weeks with their old friends of Friday's Hill days. Beatrice delighted in her long strolls by the seaside in the brilliant sunshine of midspring, but Sidney, as in the old days, preferred to sound off in his pontifical fashion. Alys, as usual, provided him with a perfect, passive listener. In the evenings Logan read selections he was making from the philosophy of Santayana, who in his opinion combined perfect style with the truest wisdom. Tactfully he avoided any mention of Henry James, since Beatrice had met James in her pre-Webb London days and disliked him heartily— an aversion which was as thoroughly reciprocated.

In her diary for April 29, 1919, Beatrice Webb presents a vivid picture both of Logan's house and of his literary success. "A delightful twelve days with Logan Pearsall Smith and Alys Russell at Big Chilling . . . The walks by the sea in mid springtide in brilliant sunshine—waves, birds and buds—were healthful and happy. We enjoyed the companionship of our hosts: Logan spent his time in cross-examining us about our experience, thought and feelings. He is an observant and thoughtful psychologist. The publication of his *Trivia* has brought him literary fame through

his invention of a new literary form. His particular specialty
is to represent, with scientific accuracy and literary charm,
the actual content of his own mind as an example of the
mind of most intellectuals. He exercises this new craft with
consummate skill and with ruthless and cynical frankness,
revealing how much of the stream of thoughts and feelings,
even of the enlightened and moral man, are pathologically
trivial in their vanity and egotism."

Ever since the first private printing of his *Trivia* in 1903,
Logan had worked over these miniature prose cameos with
the infinite patience of the craftsman. He wanted to become
a disciplined chaser of phrases—using this word both in its
sense of pursuit and in terms of artisanship.

Constable accepted these *Trivia* and published the revised
volume in 1918, fifteen years after the private printing. It
was an auspicious moment. Here was a gay little volume well
fitted to provide an antidote to the long strain and anxiety
that would come to an end only with the signing of the Armistice. Here was a new form in English letters, as Logan's admirers pointed out; they could find no counterpart for these
polished brevities. They were not essays, nor could they be
described as aphorisms, anecdotes or short stories. Rather,
they captured in words brief moments of apprehension or
illumination—sometimes visual, but oftener emotional or
intellectual insight. They seemed to take the reader to the
edge of life's profundities, but glanced only fleetingly into its
depths. Some reviewers saw in the author a Montaigne in
miniature, and others mentioned the wit of another Smith—
the unparalleled Sydney.

"Here is a handful of chosen flowers," archly wrote an
anonymous critic of the *Times Literary Supplement*, "a dinner of exquisite little courses, a bunch of various coloured
air balloons . . . Nevertheless he is conscious of belonging

to that sub-order of the animal kingdom which includes the orang-outang, the gorilla, the baboon and the chimpanzee. His usual mood toward himself and the rest of us is one of ironic but affectionate detachment, befitting an elderly Pierrot conscious of grey hairs."

Reviewers were pleased with the sight of a book in which the virgin whiteness of the pages so charmingly surrounded shimmering pools of precious prose. This seemed to promise gaiety, ease, unconcern, facetious levity—a promise that was fulfilled. Logan's greatest satisfaction came with the reviews of the American edition. One reviewer characterized *Trivia* as one of the few perfect books of our time. Don Marquis later praised Logan's levity: "When the weight, the gravity, the terrible heavy solidity, of the social order seem to bear down upon him and crush him out of existence, with a twitch and flicker of his pinions he darts from the impending crash, and a moment later you see him perched shimmering above the avalanche, like a dragon-fly which has just escaped an earthquake."

Logan hoped that his Quaker cousins in Philadelphia would read these reviews. He might send them to Cousin Carey Thomas at Bryn Mawr—Cousin Carey who had these many years ago urged him to give up business, to sever his apprenticeship with Whitall-Tatum. Or to his cousin John Whitall, who was now head of the works in Millville and all its satellites. (Mary Berenson had persuaded Cousin John to allow his own son to come across the Atlantic for the completion of his aesthetic and cultural education.) Now it seemed to Logan that *Trivia* became in its deprecatory fashion the apologia *pro vita sua*. On both sides of the Atlantic his publishers were asking for more. He would be fifty-three years old on his next birthday. Fame had reached him at last.

Chapter 10 · Duveen

At I Tatti the Berensons housed favored and privileged guests in their *villino,* hidden by the olives and cypresses. For a few weeks in 1906 the special guests were their friends Hutchins Hapgood and his wife, who wrote under her maiden name of Neith Boyce. With his boisterous, convivial laughter, "Hutch" was the polar opposite of the meticulous B.B. Yet somehow they had always been congenial companions.

To Hapgood, obsessed with what he considered radical philosophy and the spirit of labor, B.B. appeared as a true cerebral, his mind occupied with a *participation mystique* with works of art. Berenson, he said, seemed "lean, intense, and winged" like a Donatello statue, uprooted from all the basic interests of humanity. Everyday aspects of life he left to Mary. The Berensons conducted Neith and Hutch on long tours of the Uffizi and Pitti galleries, to Florence's innumerable churches, so rich in frescoes. Berenson preached the integral relationship between the intensity of art and the enchantment of life—"life-enchancing" was one of his favorite verbal coins. His scholarship, the Hapgoods agreed, was truly passionate. "Berenson could not understand any person not wanting to learn all he could; and often grew impatient with his wife and mine on this ground; they would not apply themselves intensely to acquiring knowledge."

153

But there was another Florence at which B.B. only vaguely hinted—the Florence of the forgers and the counterfeiters. Far removed from the villas lived and worked these craftsmen, the restorers, the copyists, black-market dealers who operated with their spies and accomplices among the dealers of Paris, London, and New York. The traffic in fake Old Masters had prospered for decades. In 1852, Herman Melville denounced the effrontery of foreign picture dealers in America who christened their spurious "masterpieces" with the loftiest names known to art. A few years later James Jackson Jarves, obsessed pioneer in the acquisition of Italian primitives, discovered that old copies, as well as originals, secmed as inexhaustible as the coal pits of Britain. For centuries Italy had been supplying the world market with Old Masters, yet somehow the supply was never exhausted. Lumber rooms were stored with them, he said; streets were lined with them; every tailor had his gallery. Jarves presented a glimpse of the Florentine art market that had not radically changed when Berenson first introduced the Hapgoods to his adopted city. In Jarves's day, there seemed to be a wholesale, as well as a retail, buying and selling of painting: "A speculator arrives, and gives out that he is a purchaser of pictures by the wholesale. A flock of crows cannot light sooner upon an open corn-bag than do the sellers upon him. He is not after good pictures, but the trash that can be bought for the value of the wood in their frames. They are brought to him by wagon-loads. He looks at the pile, and makes an offer according to its size. In this way he buys several thousand daubs at an average of a few dimes each, spends as much more in varnishing, regilding, and a little retouching, sends them to America, where they are duly offered for sale as so many Titians, Vandycks, Murillos or other lights of the European schools. One lucky sale pays for the whole lot."

In 1868, Alexander Foresi had published *Tour de Babel,* an exposé of the international traffic. And in 1891, in an essay in *The Nineteenth Century,* J. C. Robinson had denounced the growing trade in spurious works of art. Later, Paul Eudel exposed current methods of trickery, and in 1888, in an article in *Lippincott's Magazine,* William Sheppard detailed some notorious hoaxes. Waldemar Kaempffert described the race of art counterfeiters as the world's most "cultured" criminals, and their secret skills as the best-paying crime. In 1901 an exhibition of fakes was organized in London, as a warning to private collectors, and from the turn of the century, a literature on the subject gradually accumulated. The chief market for the forgeries was without doubt the United States and the unwary and credulous collectors who aimed to follow in the footsteps of John Pierpont Morgan. In 1906 the *Nation* published a denunciation of the "artistic underground railroad" and the methods by which unscrupulous dealers unloaded their false wares. The *North American Review* warned American collectors against the traffic in spurious pictures. William le Queux in the *New York Times* exposed the methods by which American art collectors were swindled by Italian tricksters in antiques.

A variation of Gresham's law was operating in this field: a flood of debased and meretricious counterfeits drove the precious and authentic off the open market. Hence the necessity for the professional art experts, each specializing in the art of certain periods. Most of them were museum curators, men such as the redoubtable Herr Dr. Wilhelm von Bode, who had been elevated to the august post of director general of the royal museums of Prussia, whose knowledge of Dutch and Flemish art was reputedly unsurpassed and whose advice was sought by American museums and collectors to authenticate works they considered buying. Such independent experts sometimes expected and exacted *douceurs,* gifts and fees for opinions "gratuitously" given. During some interminable litigation involving an art forgery, an English judge uttered the dictum that there were three kinds of liars: liars, damned liars, and expert witnesses. B.B. disdained Von Bode's book *Florentiner Bildhauer der Renaissance,* and considered all scientific Germanic expertise, from the work of Lipps to that of Meier-Graefe, pedantic and pretentious.

Because of this acute need for authoritative opinion, Joseph Duveen came to Florence in 1906 to meet Berenson. Mary was fascinated by the strange little dealer who was destined to play so great a role in her native land, and who had come to Italy on a still hunt for an expert—an authority who could certify the authenticity of the masterpieces he might offer to the great American or British collectors. His offer of at least a temporary collaboration was a tempting one to Berenson. To get the house and gardens of I Tatti into satisfactory shape was becoming an endless task, one into which all of Mary's income was pouring, as well as his own less reliable resources. Berenson felt the need of stabilizing his finances and his knowledge of art would help him to do so. And so he accepted the offer to act, as the occasion might arise, as expert for this international dealer in Old Masters. Years later Berenson was to admit that he took the wrong turn when he swerved from purely intellectual pursuits for a troublesome reputation as an expert. But like Saint Paul and Spinoza, he needed a means of livelihood. At the end of it all, he would still regard himself as a failure, and in his diaries and memoirs would refrain from mentioning his spectacular collaborator.

B.B.'s acceptance of Duveen's offer is easy to defend and rationalize: it might help to defeat the traffic in the fake and counterfeit art which was being unloaded upon the American market. Had this not been his true mission in life for years—this avowed campaign?

Duveen was not the first pioneer art dealer to invade the American market, nor was J. P. Morgan the first important collector. But Morgan set the pace in the acquisition of all that was unique and beyond the reach of lesser financial rivals. In this endless quest, his interest—or that of his experts —turned from painting to unique manuscripts, to incunabula, to the reliquiae of past cultures and ages. The Morgan Library is the monument to this quest. The great industrialists, the entrepreneurs, the financiers and merchants discovered that collecting brought them cultural status, gentility and the respect of press and public. And leaving these collections to museums brought posthumous reputations for philanthropy and generosity. Out of these private collections grew the public museums, so that now the United States can boast of being the possessor of no less than one-fourth of all the museums in the world.

With his innate genius for showmanship and salesmanship, Joe Duveen became a past master in the art of stimulating the inner drive toward acquisition and possession, and of diverting it to his own profit. But he could not have established and maintained his prestige in this cutthroat battle without the collaboration of Bernard Berenson. Without his *imprimatur,* Duveen's reputation could not have been sustained. And it is with accuracy that someone has noted that Berenson is the "secret hero" of S. N. Behrman's lively book on Duveen.

Duveen modestly looked upon *his* role as that of a teacher, his true vocation to teach Yankee Midases how to become Maecenases, to reveal to them the necessity of paying the highest prices for unique treasures of art. Only so could forgeries and counterfeits be driven out of the market. Every master must be certified, verified, authenticated. This was how Berenson could help.

Who could withstand Duveen's sanguine enthusiasm, the war he had declared against the fake Corots, fake Titians and Murillos, against the genuine Dagnan-Bouverets and the Alma-Tademas treasured in American mansions?

From the effervescent Duveen, Mary and B.B. learned some of the basic beliefs of the art dealer. It was far easier, Duveen assured them, to find good buyers than good pictures. Duveen bought pictures and other *objets d'art* wherever he could find them—from private collectors in need of money, in the great auction rooms or from individuals who called on him "off the street." It was a profession that required endless scouting, endless travel, the employment of secret agents.

After Berenson accepted Duveen's offer, in September 1908, he and Mary began a journey to America. They stopped off in England to gather up Ray and Karin and take them for their first prolonged visit. The young Costelloe girls met their Quaker cousins in Philadelphia and Baltimore, and were the guests of Carey Thomas at Bryn Mawr, but Ray remained tactfully loyal to English Newnham. The year before, Ray's first novel, *The World at Eighteen,* had been published, and the twenty-one-year-old novelist could hardly be impressed by American young men.

The Berensons were exhibited by Joseph Duveen to his most affluent clients: Mary and B.B. were taken to inspect the great private collections of Henry Frick, J. G. Johnson of Philadelphia and P.A.B. Widener; B.B. was eventually to authenticate and catalogue the Italian masters in the latter two collections. With his neatly trimmed Vandyke beard, his well-coifed hair, and his expertly tailored suits, Mr. Berenson was, in appearance as in fact, the worldly scientific expert. His was the voice of authority on Italian art. His three volumes on the subject were already in two editions, and Joe Duveen could now exhibit him as the private Duveen expert in authentication. With the Berenson *imprimatur,* who could question the authenticity of the Old Masters which Joseph Duveen placed on the market?

During this 1908 sojourn in America, Berenson made the unexpected gesture of defending Henri Matisse from the charge of charlatanry that had been made against him by a Paris correspondent of the *Nation.* This communication, published in the weekly for which B.B. had been a correspondent since his earliest days in Italy, remains of interest not so much for its defense of the ultramodernist Matisse, who had been brought to meet the Berensons by the Steins, as for its respectful allusions to such nineteenth-century painters as Rousseau (not, however, *le douanier*) and "the stupendous Millet."

Examining museums and private collections in the United States, the Berensons uncovered all styles in the dubious, the unauthentic, the outrageously counterfeit. Chaos prevailed. Every copy, every counterfeit was boldly tagged with the name of some famous master, new or old. The meretricious overshadowed, all but obscured, the few examples of authentic painting. New York still remained a profitable market for the overflow and the backwash of academic Paris. In most private collections, Mary and B.B. were shown the inevitable Corot—usually an obvious counterfeit. "Corot is the painter of some three thousand pictures," commented a French wit of the period, "of which ten thousand have been sold in the United States."

Berenson and Mary were the guests of Miss Belle da Costa Greene, J. P. Morgan's erudite and expert librarian. Many considered Miss Greene the brains behind the vast Morgan collections. They met John Jay Chapman, like B.B. a Harvard graduate of the late eighties, who had abandoned the practice of law to pen his iconoclastic essays. They dined at the tables of the rich, in *châteaux* imitating those on the Loire, or Florentine *palazzi* of dubious ancestry. It required all of Mary's tact and finesse to comment on the "collections" exhibited to them—galleries awash with fakes and with all too authentic works by Bouguereau, Dagnan-Bouveret, Millet, Ziem, Bonnat and other now long discarded "masters" of the late nineteenth century.

When B.B. and Mary returned to Tuscany in 1909, B.B. was enraged by the spectacle of everything gone wrong at I Tatti during their prolonged absence. Mary could not blame him—it was more than human nature could be expected to bear. But soon they were both immersed once more in their study of art.

Mary found herself drawn into a group of bluestockings and *femmes savantes* who wrote or planned to write definitive studies upon the Old Masters of their choice. Maud Cruttwell had already published her great, beautiful book on Pollaiuolo, illustrated by many reproductions. Miss Cruttwell was supposed to have pronounced the last word on Pollaiuolo, although others were always looking for new facts, searching through the painter's laundry lists, scratching around in every conceivable corner for something new to add to his history. But Maud had found out everything there was to be known and put it all in her big volume.

These women were all learned and sophisticated, and inclined, at the same time, to be emotional. They had no men in their lives except the men they wrote about. Vernon Lee and Mrs. Robinson and Maud Cruttwell were all writers, and those who were not had semiartistic, almost historical associations with men; none of them had love affairs with them. Flora Priestley lived with her mother and was a friend of John Sargent. He painted her many times, for she was very beautiful. Everyone who knew her knew that she had sat for his "Carmencita," so Carmencita became Floracita to their friends. Marguerite Michel, Gabrielle Borthwick and the Baroness de Nolde belonged to this group. The fact that she was married seemed to set Mary somewhat apart from these ladies, however. Besides, B.B. derided them, making fun of them all with his vitriolic tongue. He said especially mean things about Maud Cruttwell. He did not sympathize with other people who wrote about the Italian painters.

In her memoirs Mabel Dodge ridicules all the aesthetes of the Tuscan hills: "Everybody in Florence was like that. The life was built up around the productions of the dead. At the Berensons' they played a guessing game that consisted of spreading a lot of photographs of paintings on a table and then, taking one, somebody would cover it with a piece of paper out of which a little hole was cut, so that only a fold of a cloak, or a part of a hand or face would be seen, and everybody would guess, by the treatment, who had painted it. That was considered the way to pass really gay evenings up at I Tatti!"

Mary wrote about Italian art because she had for so many years been an apt pupil of her husband's theories and methods of detection, indeed his collaborator. If she had been encouraged to strike out on her own, she might not have been eclipsed by her husband's reputation. After a pilgrimage to Poland, she published in an Italian magazine an essay on the *Dipinti Italiani a Cracovia,* another on Botticelli's portrait of Giuliano de' Medici. These and similar efforts are now buried in the archives of connoisseurship. Mary's humor and humanity found no outlet in these essays.

During the years preceding the First World War, Berenson was busy in America, preparing his catalogue of the Italian Masters in the J. G. Johnson collection in Philadelphia, and later cataloguing the great P. A. B. Widener collection at Wynnewood Hall. The alliance with Duveen, which had begun almost casually, light-heartedly, as a temporary arrangement, was gradually becoming more exacting. Duveen's enemies, who increased as his spectacular success grew, hinted that B.B. was the art dealer's "paid expert" and that his fee was five percent of the selling price of every canvas that bore his signed attribution. But the financial agreement between the two men has never been made public and probably varied with circumstances. "I never baptize outside my parish," Berenson is quoted; but this "parish" remained the vast field of the Italian Renaissance.

Close as the relationship between Duveen and Berenson became with the passing of the years, it was not without its embarrassments. One of these was the suit for damages brought against Duveen by Mrs. Andrée Hahn, owner of a so-called Leonardo *Belle Ferronnière* which had somehow turned up in Kansas City. Upon the announcement of this discovery in 1921, Duveen expressed loud doubts as to the authenticity of the picture. Mrs. Hahn promptly filed a suit for "libel of goods" against the art dealer. To facilitate taking the testimony of European art experts, the case was finally transferred to the consul general in Paris. This procedure also facilitated comparison with the *Belle Ferronnière* which was treasured in the Louvre. The first expert called was B.B. Berenson asserted that its technique and style were unlike Leonardo's and placed it as a French copy of about 1775. The following day he was cross-examined by Mrs. Hahn's attorney, an impudent lawyer with the picturesque name of Hyacinthe Ringrose, whose intent was to destroy

Duveen's reputation for honesty, and to expose B.B. as his paid hireling. Berenson's testimony was supported by nine distinguished European art experts, including Sir Martin Conway, Captain Douglas, Dr. Schmidt-Degener, Roger Fry and Professor L. Nicolle. After comparison with the Louvre picture, and the testimony of the experts, the Hahn picture was declared a copy, but there were unpleasant repercussions anyway. Duveen's enemies asserted that B.B. was "the chief authenticator in Sir Joseph's stable." With his staff of salesmen, his scouts, and his own supreme court of certification, Duveen, they said, was "tops" in the business of fancy packaging. How, demanded these enemies, could connoisseurship be entrusted to those who stood to profit by its exploitation? They attacked the methods employed by Duveen's unnamed restorer, boldly declaring that "a publication of the disclosures made by this restorer concerning so-called Old Masters now in American collections and public museums would throw the art world into a panic. The traffic in dubious paintings and outright fakes, which have been certified as genuine by various experts . . . has been enormous." Years passed in the Hahn litigation; Duveen finally made a settlement.

Discouraged and humiliated by this enforced descent into the muddy arena of litigation, B.B. and Mary returned from Paris to I Tatti. To be forced to submit to the poisonous insinuations of Hyacinthe Ringrose, who claimed that Berenson's decisions were determined solely by expected profit, that he was nothing more than an employee of the most famous dealer in the world—these accusations were acutely painful. Though never substantiated, they were bruited about in the press and gossiped about by Joe Duveen's enemies. Why had Joe dragged Berenson into this sorry international scandal?

If Duveen were to sound off every time a false Leonardo da Vinci turned up, he could find time for little else, for sixty or more copies of the celebrated *Mona Lisa* alone were known to every informed expert. The resentment of the Berensons against their friend was only half-conscious, but the suggestion of deliberate charlatanry stung to the quick —the idea that B.B. could be bribed by Duveen to attribute to a great master anything Duveen placed on the market. B.B. confessed himself tired of his role of infallible expert. In having turned from purely intellectual and aesthetic pursuits to collaborate with Joe Duveen, he felt a sense of failure, of guilt.

Years were to pass before the final break with Lord Duveen of Millbank (Duveen was elevated to the peerage in 1930 for his benefactions to the Tate Gallery and other national museums). In the early thirties, Duveen learned that one of his best clients, Andrew Mellon, was in the market for a Giorgione—a real, truly authenticated example of the work of the much disputed young Venetian who had died of the plague in 1510, at the age of thirty-two. Duveen put his grapevine to work to find a Giorgione that might be sold; in the collection of the Viscount Allendale was an *Adoration des Mages* which the owner might be persuaded to part with for a price. Duveen hopped a transatlantic liner and offered the Viscount a sum that was too large to refuse. In a few weeks he was back in America exhibiting this treasure to Andrew Mellon in a velvet-lined salon.

"What does Berenson say?" demanded the taciturn Mellon.

"This is a true Giorgione, certified as such!" protested Duveen. "But I'll send him a cable."

The cablegram finally reached B.B. as he was traveling

on the island of Cyprus. He was familiar with the Allendale Giorgione; long ago he had decided that it was an early Titian. But Duveen could not accept this reply and he sent the disputed masterpiece by special messenger to Berenson, when B.B. returned to I Tatti. As he studied the disputed painting, Berenson kept the Duveen messenger waiting for days. He was thoroughly familiar with the Giorgione problem. He could remember the days when "every cigar-boxy prettiness" was attributed to Giorgione, until the revaluations by honest experts, from Morelli to Venturi and to the Frenchman Hourticq, had reduced the Giorgione "canon" to four or five indisputable paintings. There was, he well knew, a softly gliding transition from Giorgione to the youthful Titian. His opinion still remained that this Allendale *Adoration* was an early Titian. He would not risk his reputation for integrity and he gave his verdict against Duveen. Lacking Berenson's certification, Andrew Mellon refused to buy the Allendale picture. Undaunted, Duveen sold the disputed painting to S. H. Kress, a rival of Woolworth, and a newcomer in the field of connoisseurship. Eventually it was given, with other Kress treasures, to the National Gallery, where it is still attributed to Giorgione.

While Duveen was almost continuously tangled in litigation with rival dealers in New York, he went on gathering honors and prestige in his native England. And while involved with the American government over income-tax deficiency or settling a damage suit, he was indulging in shrewd benefactions; for example, to divert public attention from the sensational Hahn litigation, Duveen made a slyly timed gift of a Carpeaux *Venus* to the W. R. Nelson Gallery of Art in Kansas City. To his friends, Duveen claimed to be the originator of the idea for a national gallery to house the Mellon collection in Washington.

The Berensons noted the triumphal progress of their former associate with detached amusement and not without a tincture of regret. Without the co-operation of Berenson, Duveen could never have attained his eminence as the Napoleon of dealers. But he was not to survive for long after his break with Berenson over the disputed Giorgione. He died in 1939, at the age of seventy.

Chapter 11 · The Observer Unobserved

Logan and his sister Alys spent the final years of their lives at 11 St. Leonard's Terrace, in Chelsea. As age crept in, Logan lost interest in the beauties and attractions of Big Chilling, in yachting and gardening and the expenditure of bodily energies. The great success of *Trivia* in 1918 on both sides of the Atlantic and the demand for *More Trivia* (1921) contributed to this decision. From his ivory tower in the seclusion of Chelsea, Logan could observe with Olympian detachment the dismal world outside. Through the windows of his book-lined study, he gazed out upon the open spaces of Burton's Court. Through the plane trees which lined the road opposite, he could glimpse the Chelsea veterans' hospital and the broad façade of Wren's noted building. Before his fireplace Logan placed a needlework fire screen that Alys had embroidered, and in front of the hearth there was a rug designed by Duncan Grant. Above the bookshelves which lined this room were plaster busts of his favorite French authors, casts bought in Paris and painted to soften the glaring whiteness. A dedicated collector of old books, particularly of the authors he fancied he had discovered, Logan was often praised by literary visitors for the catholicity of his taste, as a "beautiful reader."

As all his friends well knew, Logan had a malicious tongue, and witty, too, and was not unready to use it against anyone. His very love of words led him on and on to astonish and amuse an audience. And it is this habit of embellishment and exaggeration that makes him a rather unreliable source of information. His tales were always founded on truth, but often wandered far from their beginnings.

Before the war, Logan was a regular annual visitor at the great villa of the Berensons, even when his hosts were away on their own explorations. At home in the library of forty thousand rare volumes, he nevertheless sometimes felt paralyzed in front of the shelves and did not know where to begin. He felt happier when some of his own contemporaries were there, and the luxury and splendor of I Tatti could be enjoyed at its best—such guests as Edith Wharton, or Santayana. They made up "a little group of not unsuccessful people," as he wrote; "a group old and ill and gay and disenchanted, with tongues wagging as freely as any on the Continent, with their ironic observations and reflections, their improper anecdotes."

Logan loved to travel; his journeyings were in the nature of pilgrimages, for he liked to visit shrines that were tinctured with the presence of some saint or holy man of literature. More sinister locales of history or crime might also be visited, but these were the exceptions. What he searched for was "the Platonic essence of the past." And as he grew older he began to feel the need of a companion, guide and courier for these jaunts.

The interests of his sister Alys found satisfaction elsewhere. After her separation from Russell, she had become an addicted joiner. She had gone through many phases of good works—from her beloved Beatrice's Fabianism to the "simple life," and from temperance and birth control to child welfare. Her models in democratic reform remained

Graham Wallas and Beatrice Webb. She found time to be active in the League of Nations Union and the Labour Party. To these causes, Alys added nearly a dozen others, so that her life became passionately busy, though undoubtedly less important than she believed, whether she called her interests "social service" or "intelligent philanthropy." Even after exposure to Bertrand Russell's mind, Alys had never been introspective, had never worried about the origin and meaning of life. She simply felt committed to it, with the obvious duty of making it a better life for other human beings.

But now, living with her brother Logan, she asked only to make herself contented and happy. How had life molded her, and what experience and resources could she draw on for a peaceful old age? First, she told herself, she could hope to call on her Quaker training in patience, serenity and optimism. This gave her, first of all, acceptance of the inevitable, aging, and of being tired and useless; it was real acceptance, with serenity and a happy, hopeful outlook.

With the mellowing of age came liberation from the old Quaker inhibitions, more tolerance for other people's characters and views, a tolerance learned partly in committee work. Having worked in Women's Institutes and with local Labour Party groups, having lectured in academic circles and in aristocratic drawing rooms where she was acceptable because she was the only speaker who could deal with the subject of expectant and nursing mothers with enough delicacy for the ears of duchesses—in all this work Alys had learned to know and like many kinds of people, especially the young and ardent reformers with views and methods which differed from her own. She came to learn the detachment and tolerance so necessary in dealing with the young, and now she found that it was important not to give too much advice, nor to insist on her own experience and views, if she wanted to keep their friendship and love.

In October 1921, Logan made his first and only return to his native land since leaving Whitall-Tatum to enter Oxford in 1890. This return was for the purpose of undergoing a delicate—or indelicate, as he felt—prostate operation at Johns Hopkins Hospital in Baltimore. On the westward voyage his companions were the writers J. C. Squire (later Sir John) and A. P. Herbert (later Sir Alan). He spent most of his time in the United States in "the immense red building . . . devoted to one of the least glorious of our human organs."

Logan renewed his acquaintance with his Thomas cousins of Baltimore, and paid a short visit to Carey Thomas. However, he showed a minimum of interest in the phenomenal expansion of the Whitall-Tatum company, though it remained the source of his assured income. He still condemned the United States as a cultural desert: ". . . no interest in the life of the mind." A cultural colony, but without a head, according to Logan's prejudiced complaints to his friends in Europe. He wrote a letter on the subject "to the wisest man I know." In reply George Santayana, even though he considered himself an alien in the United States, came to the defense of Logan's native land. Logan had published his *Little Essays Drawn from the Works of George Santayana* (with the collaboration of Santayana) and the reception had been gratifying to both.

This most articulate defender of America against Logan's strictures was himself one of its acutest critics; but Logan's derisive criticisms seemed to embody the "genteel" and "cultured" attitude that most annoyed Santayana. Santayana condemned America's sophomoric patter about art, its "lady-like" religion—but, he pointed out to Logan, all learning and all mind in America was not of the ineffectual sophomoric sort. Why had Logan crossed the Atlantic except to find a great surgeon at Johns Hopkins? And in a letter from Rome, Santayana reminded him: "It does not seem to me that we can impose on America the task of imitating Europe. The more different it can come to be, the better; and we must let it take its own course, going a long way round, before it can shake off the last trammels of alien tradition, and learn to express itself simply, not apologetically, after its own heart."

On his return to England, Logan again became active in the Society for Pure English, a group of philologists and grammarians pledged to combat the defilement of the English language. Logan had been one of the leading spirits in the founding of this organization in 1913, under the chairmanship of the poet Robert Bridges, and with the collaboration of such linguistic authorities as Henry Watson Fowler, Sir William Craigie, A. Clutton Brock, Henry Bradley and others. This little *praesidium* of purity sought to preserve English from defilement and corruption, especially from overseas. Its aim was asserted to be, not "foolish interference with living developments," but to inform popular taste along sound principles, to guide educational authorities and to introduce into practice certain "slight modifications and advantageous changes." Logan's interest in the English tongue led to his book *Words and Idioms*, which was published in 1925. *Words and Idioms* is a group of related essays, including "English Sea Terms," "The English Element in Foreign Languages," "Four Romantic Words," "Popular Speech and Standard English," and "English Idioms." One of the most interesting of these was "Four Romantic Words" (though why four?—there were more!), which discusses the journeying of English words into other languages and their return to English usage, showing the enriching effects of their travels. The discussed words included "genius" and "talent," which called forth this comment from Logan:

"There can be no doubt that the spontaneous, inspired daemonic genius—or at least, since it is more a matter of degree than of absolute distinction—that the genius who possesses more conspicuously than others this character, has existed in all the arts: El Greco in painting, Michelangelo in sculpture, Wagner in music, are analogues of original poets like Shelley, Blake, or Walt Whitman; but the emphasis laid upon the type of genius possessed by these great originators, and the depreciatory contrast with mere talent, has tended, I think, to make us forget that the daemonic genius is not the only kind of genius, and indeed not by any means always the greatest kind."

Words, the infinite shadings of meaning, the delicate precision of choice—these were a fanaticism with Logan. "It is natural to the literary mind to be unduly observant of the choice of words," wrote Evelyn Waugh on Logan's mania. "Logan Pearsall Smith was the classical case. I met him only once. He did not speak to me until we stood on the doorstep leaving. He then said: 'Tell me, how would you describe the garment you are wearing? A greatcoat? An overcoat? A top-coat?' I replied 'Overcoat.' 'Ah, would you? Yes. Most interesting. And, tell me, would that also be the usage of an armigerous admiral?' "

When Logan's confessed ambition to "live on after his funeral in a perfect phrase" was questioned, this was his answer: "The ever-baffled chase of these filmy nothings often seems, for one of sober years in a sad world, a trifling occupation. But have I not read of the great Kings of Persia

who used to ride out to hawk for butterflies, nor deemed
this pastime beneath their royal dignity?"

In the late twenties Logan felt the need of a literary apprentice—some ambitious youth who could "devil" for him
in the British Museum and the London Library, who might
act as pupil, disciple and traveling companion as well. Logan
set down two prerequisites: his disciple must promise not
to be involved in romantic affairs with girls, and never, however tempted, get married; nor should he harbor any secret
ambition to write a best-selling novel. Young writers who
marry, it was Logan's firm conviction, were bound to ruin
their gifts by writing for money.

Eventually Logan struck up an agreement with a bright
young man who turned up at St. Leonard's Terrace, a restless, inquisitive aesthete in his twenties. Born September 10,
1903, educated at Eton, and, like Logan, at Balliol, Oxford,
he was the son of Major Matthew Connolly. His father had
served many years in the regular army. His grandfather,
Admiral Connolly, had been the son of a General Connolly
and nephew of various veterans of the wars with France, and
had belonged to a naval family long resident in Bath. His
full name was Cyril Vivian Connolly.

Logan was duly impressed by this substantial background
—it was quite evident that Cyril came of a "good family."
Frugal, blue-eyed, long-lived, quiet, tidy, the older Connollys
appeared to be an obstinate race of soldiers and sailors; the
Admiral's uncle, Captain Matthew Connolly, had been an
arbiter of Bath elegance in the reign of George IV.

Logan and Cyril soon came to a working agreement—
without any vulgar mention of a definite salary. Logan appreciated Cyril's originality of mind. Already a gourmet in
Parisian pleasures—vintages, gossip, memorable meals, exotic pet animals, coigns of euphoria and melancholy—this

young Francophile in crumpled dinner jacket shocked the Chelsea mandarins by smoking cigars with their bands still on. Connolly was too restless and too impatient to fit into the precious milieu of literary Chelsea, into this caste in which, in his own words, "aged mandarins or superannuated monks worshipped at the shrine of the literature of past centuries, who lived beside one another in neat little Georgian houses, secure with their assured incomes—this 'leafy, well-to-do fig-ripening Chelsea . . .' from Carlyle Mansions to Ebury Street," where a good luncheon party could last until lamplighting. George Moore, Henry James and Augustine Birrell had been the high priests of that secular cult. Now, in the mid-twenties, their traditional rites were fulfilled by Logan. Logan reminded Connolly of a Chinese sage—"aging, sedentary, angry and ironical"—deploying all his vast store of scholarship, erudition and banter to his adopted spiritual heir and perpetual apprentice.

But as Logan soon had to confess, Cyril "proved something of a disappointment." He announced that he was leaving—and to be *married!* However, they parted amicably and their friendship grew warmer with absence and the passing of the years. Logan took a vicarious delight in Connolly's subsequent adventures and misadventures among masterpieces, in his growing influence upon writers even younger than himself. Connolly became a catalyst for youth —expressing its ambitious, its exotic yearnings, its ingrained laziness. "Yours is a life of dizzy heights and deep abysses," Logan wrote to him. "I envy it in a way, for it is a life of that poignant reality which is the stuff of art; but my serene and pleased indifference, the constant mood of my calm thoughts, suits best my temperament and my years."

A decade or so later, Connolly launched and edited his intellectual monthly named *Horizon*. As its senior patron,

Logan read each number meticulously, sent in contributions, and persuaded B.B. to do so as well.

Logan discovered his second disciple in an antiquarian bookshop. Puttering about, hunting for first editions of Jeremy Taylor—for he was making a volume of selections from the sermons of that seventeenth-century master of English prose—Logan came upon Robert Gathorne-Hardy, a copartner of the shop. This book dealer revealed to his caller that he himself was a Taylorian, and happened to be working on a bibliography of the noted bishop. He was naturally immediately invited to luncheon in St. Leonard's Terrace, and was soon persuaded to relinquish his partnership in the bookshop, to become Logan's perpetual apprentice.

About a year older than his predecessor, Gathorne-Hardy was the son of the Third Earl of Cranbrook and Lady Dorothy Boyle. In Logan's mocking words, he was "one of the finest flowers of English civilization, Eton and Christchurch." Twenty-seven years old at the time of their meeting, he was to remain for the next seventeen years Logan's secretary-companion, the courier of his travels, and, at times, the victim of his rages. The two men came together as *milvers*— a word which Logan invented to fill a longfelt need and which he defined in *Afterthoughts*. "But what festivals of unanimity we celebrate when we meet what I call a *milver* —a fellow-fanatic whose thoughts chime in a sweet ecstasy of execration with our own!" A proud claim of Logan's was that a stranger had once asked him the etymological origin of milver.

Robert Gathorne-Hardy began working regularly as Logan's apprentice and researcher in 1931. One of his first tasks was to help assemble the materials for Logan's essay on Shakespeare. The master kept asking the advice of the ap-

prentice, but so completely did he assimilate his proposals
that when the essay first appeared in the September 1932
number of *Life and Letters,* Gathorne-Hardy could not discover any trace of his own suggestions. Later the essay was
expanded into a slim little volume published by Constable
in 1933. Into its 136 pages, Logan managed to cram all the
recondite knowledge of Shakespeare he had assembled for
years. The book was frequently reprinted and remains,
with its liveliness of style and impudent suggestions, one of
the better introductions to Shakespeare—not profound, perhaps, but provocative and stimulating. The success of this
little effort led to the making of a Shakespeare anthology,
The Golden Shakespeare, which was published after Logan's death.

Gathorne-Hardy was also called upon to help his master
in the preparation of tracts for the Society for Pure English.
As the young man discovered, Logan was an industrious and
generous contributor to these publications. It was as though
this effort might eradicate from his speech and pen the last
vestiges of the Yankee vernacular. Often his unconscious
aversion for his homeland would infiltrate his scholarly
prose. " 'Why, good Heavens!' I cried to my companion, as
I pointed to the broad face of that great, unanimous, uni-
vocal Republic, 'why, from the point of view of Style, the
whole Continent could sink beneath the sea, and never leave
a ripple!' " he wrote in Tract Number XLVI.

In his sixties, Logan lost all the appearance of boyishness that had been so remarkable even in his fifties. His increasing bulk became too much for his legs, and locomotion
grew difficult. His spectacles rested at the end of his long,
pointed nose. His expensively tailored clothes could not be
made to fit the stiffened stoop of his back, legs and shoulders.

Whenever we indulge in any of the seven deadly sins, some unobserved observer is said to register this failure and, possibly, to record it. Between his tasks of deviling in the British Museum, correcting proofs, and acting as courier on Logan's pilgrimages to literary shrines, Robert Gathorne-Hardy became the unobserved observer of Logan, of his benefactor's self-indulgence, and, eventually, of Logan's undulating moods of elation and depression.

He did not realize until long after his first meeting with Logan that his patron was projecting a manic-depressive pattern. Gathorne blamed himself when the friendly light of welcome that glowed in Logan's eyes was replaced by one of hostility, when high spirits were killed by a period of gloom. But gradually the psychic alternations became more apparent to the younger man. Logan's periods of exuberant gaiety, with their incessant, irresponsible chatter and their outrageous practical jokes, were succeeded by weeks of sullen gloom. At such times Logan plunged into solitary reading —usually of a single author.

With the passing of the years, those periods during which Logan preferred to remain in solitude became more frequent and of longer duration. Then suddenly he would be swept up to the crest of euphoria. During the depressed periods, Gathorne-Hardy's life was his own—Logan used to dismiss him at the end of twenty minutes of gloom.

In the dualism in his employer's secret nature there was, on the one hand, the Logan who was a wise older friend, the enchanting host, the erudite lover of letters who could deteriorate into a boring teller of stories, a monopolist of table talk. And there was the almost impossible, gloomy Logan. Gathorne-Hardy somehow learned to live with the two Logans and remained with him for almost the rest of Logan's life.

Gathorne-Hardy soon became aware, also, of how completely the three women who managed the little household in St. Leonard's Terrace pampered its eccentric master. It was mainly Alys's self-effacing efficiency that made every detail of comfort as the master wished it. Mary, the cook, and Hammond, the nurse-housekeeper, sacrificed their lives to Logan's.

First engaged as a sort of half-nurse, half-housekeeper, Hammond was a picturesque character of a type only to be found in London, or in Shakespeare. Someone described her as a sort of female Sancho Panza. She shared Logan's practical jokes. Her devotion to him was complete, yet she could give as good as he gave. Although Hammond could scold and answer back, she served her peevish master twenty-four hours a day, jumping to answer his peremptory bell and looking after his enormous bulk as though he were a baby.

Logan and Gathorne-Hardy traveled together to the shrines of Logan's favorite authors in the British Isles, to Holland, to France, to Spain, to Madeira. Gathorne-Hardy made the unsettling discovery that Logan's recurring recession into one of his periodic glooms might come in the middle of some interesting pilgrimage; but when in 1938 Logan suggested a trip to Iceland, the apprentice found this invitation hard to resist. Logan was excited about the cruise, but after their arrival at Reykjavik he began to complain about the hotel, about Stefan Stefansson, the guide and courier, and many other things. His descent into the pit of depression was beginning. They drove to Thingvellir, historic site of the earliest European parliament. One day Gathorne-Hardy went on to further exploration of that fantastic territory, and when he returned, he was met with the announcement that Logan was ill, and had been taken to a hospital. This illness developed into double pneumonia, and from delirium Logan crossed the border line to madness. Eventually, his traveling companion records, "the pneumonia was over, his temperature was down, but he had gone mad."

Gathorne-Hardy has published a detailed record of his ordeal. "In his madness the devil entered right into him, through a breach which the sickness had made, and which, it seemed, was never to be repaired. At any time during the rest of his life the devil might take charge of him; he would always be liable to various degrees of a very dreadful possession."

When at last they left Iceland, two nurses were in attendance upon Logan for the return voyage. The unhappy travelers were met at Copenhagen by Logan's niece, Dr. Karin Stephen, and his nurse Hammond. In London, Gathorne-Hardy was questioned about Logan's illness by Alys. The Icelandic doctor's moral verdict had been: "A spoilt old man." "I have spoilt him," commented Alys. "But then he has given me a home to share . . . for thirty years. I couldn't help it!"

At the very moment of Logan's madness in Iceland his gay, spicy *Unforgotten Years* was being published—his reminiscences of his childhood and youth. The book became an immediate success on both sides of the Atlantic. Logan's polished prose, his irreverent and merciless thrusts at the religious pretensions of his mother and father, were bound to arrest attention, and his spinsterish wit evoked chuckles. The most notable portrait in the book was that of Walt Whitman. To Robert Gathorne-Hardy, this volume of memories, suddenly broken off, seemed a history of escapes—Logan's attempted escape from the religion of his parents, from the glass business of Whitall-Tatum, and from the United States of America.

But for another friend, Santayana, who always addressed his

letters to "Dear Smith" instead of "Dear Logan," the mandarin of St. Leonard's Terrace had never succeeded in making good his escape from Yankeedom, even though he took so great a pride in his British citizenship. With his uncomfortable perspicacity, Santayana found in Logan's *Unforgotten Years* fresh evidence of its author's rooted and persistent Americanism. For Santayana, an experienced observer of American exiles in Europe, Logan remained "terribly conscious" of not being at home in England, although it had so long been his home. These recollections offered Logan "an escape to his childhood and youth, to his beloved sisters and the oddities of his parents, to his intimacy with that arch-Yankee, old Walt."

The book revealed to Santayana an ineradicably American Logan. "He is intensely so," Santayana wrote to his friend Mrs. C. H. Toy, "only of the expatriate tribe. If he were young now he would return and live in Greenwich Village. England itself is no longer comfortable or congenial to the would-be aesthete of 1890." To Logan himself, Santayana praised the portrait of Walt Whitman, which "alone would suffice to justify the book," but he begged for a more detailed autobiography, to record the relations existing between "cultured England and America. . . . You may say that Henry James has done it once for all: but he, you, all Americans in print, are too gentle, too affectionate, too fulsome. The reality requires a satirist, merciless but just, as you might be if you chose."

Chapter 12 · Retreat in Tuscany

After the First World War, the sybaritic life of the aesthetes in the villas surrounding Florence was resumed, with some cast changes but with the same rituals. This resurgence of social life among the Tuscan exiles and expatriates, the thronging visitors and pilgrims to I Tatti, became a trial to Mary. Even before the war she had secretly complained to her mother of the strain. Now it was worse. She was fed up with being *la locandiera,* the mistress of the inn.

There were at least forty rooms in the villa at Settignano, and when B.B. was in residence they were filled with students and pilgrims to this vatican of the fine arts, as well as friends. Typewriters clicked, photographs were microscopically studied. I Tatti took on the atmosphere at once of a library, a museum and a shrine. The villa also had the reputation of serving the best food in Tuscany, a fact which did not exactly deter pilgrims. Life seemed to be one continuous stream of visitors, not only students and experts and curators from American museums, connoisseurs and collectors, but friends and relatives from London and Philadelphia. Among B.B.'s serious students were the promising Kenneth Clark, and the extraordinary American Arthur Kingsley Porter, who dared to differ in many controversies with the master.

To Mary Berenson, devoted to the ordered routine of her

days and the luxurious habits of her comfort, many of these pilgrims were boresome in the extreme. Their platitudes reminded her of M. de La Palice, that semimythical French character who is credited with such remarks as: "A few minutes before he died, he was still alive."

One distinguished exception—and decidedly a friend rather than a pilgrim—was Edith Wharton. The Berensons' friendship with her had not matured, however, until years after their first encounter. They met before the First World War at the villa of their neighbor, Henry Y. Cannon, but it was seemingly impossible for B.B. to establish contact with the imperious and contemptuous Edith—perhaps a case of rival prima-donnaism. To Berenson that first meeting seemed composed entirely of sniffs, of sneers, of jeers—all on the part of Mrs. Wharton. She was, he remembered, addicted to the wounding epithet and the venomous phrase, and she expected the deference paid only to royalty. The Berensons left exasperated by this meeting with a great literary lady, resolved never to see her again. Later, in 1909, they did meet again, by chance, as guests of Henry Adams at the Voisin restaurant in Paris. Then B.B. discovered that he and Mrs. Wharton had the same loves and hatreds in the realm of art, and the friendship was sealed on the sure basis of shared aversions. During the years following the war, Edith Wharton became a frequent and welcome visitor at I Tatti. As a friend and disciple of Henry James, she was, of course, an intimate of Percy Lubbock; and she was a friend of Mary's brother Logan from the old Jamesian days. As they grew to know each other, Mary discovered the real Edith, no longer formidable, smooth and dry as porcelain. As Edith talked with the Berensons, felt their interest, her face softened, even the steely spine relaxed. She was not the trim, hard European hostess, but a nice old American lady.

"Writers who write for money, don't write for me," used to be one of Logan's catch phrases. The other guests at I Tatti might tacitly scorn Edith Wharton's popularity as a novelist—taking their cue from James, the Master, they might disapprove of her instinctive awareness of the reader at the end of her pen, her intuitive power of direct communication—but they were compelled to acknowledge that she was an erudite and cultivated person.

Although she shared with the other guests the interminable colloquies in the great library at I Tatti—discussions usually directed and paced by B.B.—she was more at ease with her own little court of admirers. These included the Frenchman Charles du Bos, the American expatriate historian Gaillard Thomas Lapsley and Percy Lubbock, who became her equivocal memorialist.

The friendship between Mrs. Wharton, the Berensons and Logan lasted throughout their lives, and at least one incident of their association bore literary fruit. In 1926 Mrs. Wharton invited Logan to join her and other guests for a cruise of the Greek islands, on the chartered steam yacht *Osprey*. During the voyage three of the company were writing books of memoirs which would include accounts of the cruise—Edith Wharton's *A Backward Glance*, Logan's *Unforgotten Years*, and Margaret Terry Chanler's *Roman Spring*.

To seek respite from the endless procession of visitors, the Berensons finally acquired a modest hideaway in Vallombrosa, named Casa al Dono. But mostly they escaped by embarking on artistic explorations of the entire Mediterranean Basin, in Berenson's opinion the birthplace of civilization and the humanistic arts. And for these journeys they now had the help of a young companion.

In 1918, Baron Egbert von Anrep and his family had been driven out of Estonia by the Bolshevik invasion. Their country house on the Baltic was burned to the ground and all its contents destroyed. Later, their entire estate was confiscated by the Soviet authorities. The Anreps escaped with their lives and a few trinkets—jewels, miniatures and such valuables as they could conceal on their persons. Their flight was typical of that of many of their compatriots, differing in that they soon were able to establish themselves in a charming old house overlooking Florence's old bridges, with its entrance on the Borgo San Jacopo. There the Baroness Alda soon became a hostess to other exiles from her native land, and to many men of letters, musicians and artists as well as distinguished Florentines. There they brought up their son Cecil. There they were joined by the Baroness's younger sister, Elizavetta Mariano—renamed "Nicky" by their friends.

It was inevitable that the Anreps should be received at I Tatti. B.B. was especially attracted to Elizavetta: a buxom, sturdily built young woman from the German-speaking Baltic who recalled his native province. Inevitable, too, that she should eventually join the staff at the villa. Nicky came first as a secretary and reader; a polyglot, as were so many of the White Russian exiles, Nicky read Goethe and Racine aloud in English, translating as she went. Mary, too, welcomed the presence of Nicky. In Mary there was no trace of jealousy, but a sort of all-embracing generosity to her fellow women. As the years passed, Nicky Mariano became indispensable to the aging couple, especially on their travels. Every year they journeyed from I Tatti to London and Paris, to Rome, to Sicily; they knew Italy and Greece, and ventured across to Egypt and the Near East. Yet B.B. was a difficult traveler, a victim of what he termed *xenodochophobia*—foreign hotels which threw him into a rage. He complained of accommodations; he could not stomach the standardized hotel food. Noises and odors kept him awake. And it became Nicky's function to solve or at least to minimize these annoyances. So she became not merely secretary, but nurse, dietitian and cook, as well as companion, on these frequent expeditions.

When the Berensons traveled, they traveled in royal fashion. With her advancing years, Mary came to depend upon her personal maid, and sometimes her husband was attended by a valet. Nicky always packed different pills for different kinds of illnesses; sets of eyeglasses—for far, near, and the glare of desert and cruel sunlight; umbrellas, parasols, sticks, fly whisks, luncheon and tea baskets, peppermints, brandy, camomile, dry biscuits, discreet jams, indiscreet honeys; but most of all books, books, books—books for information and books for leisure hours. These ventures in travel were in pursuit of Berenson's ambition to see and know at first hand the whole art of the Mediterranean Basin. Year by year, they covered not only the countries of western Europe but Egypt, Palestine, Syria, Sicily, Tunisia and Algeria.

One spring in the late twenties, the Berensons set out on a pilgrimage of the Near East. Nicky Mariano as usual acted as companion and dietitian; Mary took along her maid. There was a guide or dragoman. Mary felt guilty at the expenditure of energy and money and work involved in the comfort of a "lazy old lady" of sixty-five. But somehow the appreciation of the beauty of the world, and the deeper understanding of the achievement of men which these explorations brought, quieted her misgivings; and besides, it meant so much to B.B. In no matter what entrancing environment a heap of ruins was set, the surroundings might be improved —the heap of ruins, never. In and out between the fallen stones B.B. would dart like a lizard, shouting to Nicky and Mary to join him in his minute inspection of some tumbled and fractured classical sculpture, or to call for some of the books to help him reconstruct the plan of the ruins. Sometimes, as B.B. and Nicky undertook some of the more arduous expeditions, Mary was left behind. When their dragoman Iskander saw her walking with a stick he decreed: "This lady cannot go to Petra!" It was a great disappointment, but when she heard from other people who had been there about the long and difficult scramble, on indifferent mounts, over rocks and down steep declines where the horses literally had to slide, a scramble which reduced even youthful and hardened travelers to a sorry state of stiffness and fatigue, Mary realized that the dragoman's order, disappointing as it was, was also sensible.

Eventually the time came when B.B. and Nicky Mariano went together on a journey and Mary remained at home to write a book about it, which she called *A Vicarious Trip to the Barbary Coast*. She much preferred this arrangement —it was one of the great advantages of physical infirmity that she now had the opportunity, undistracted by social engagements and responsibilities, to survey the whole development of Greek and Roman civilization in Libya, the colonization by Greece and Rome of the north coast of Africa.

During the autumn of 1936, the Berensons took Lady Horner's house in London for a prolonged visit. Alys lay gravely ill in the little house in St. Leonard's Terrace, and Logan was persuaded to relinquish his quarters there to nurses and attendants. He moved in temporarily with the Berensons, into a house adorned with drawings and canvases by the

Pre-Raphaelite Edward Burne-Jones. It was evidence of the catholicity of their appreciation that B.B. and Mary could find merit in a fire screen painted by that English painter, whose reputation is now eclipsed.

For Mary, this London visit was a fresh opportunity to renew her intimacy with her daughters. Ray Strachey was living in the country. As she approached her fiftieth birthday, this flaming feminist of earlier days had grown into a heavy woman with a thatch of gray hair surmounting a quizzical and intellectual visage. She was completely absorbed in the process of building walls with blocks of compressed mud, and the Stracheys' country place was appropriately called the "Mud House." It was a British form of the adobe habitations of the American Southwest, but for Hannah Smith's granddaughter it became a new form of unconscious fanaticism. Inside the "Mud House," Logan found the halls cold and the bathroom untidy "beyond imagination." But such details of housekeeping were outside the zone of Ray Strachey's interests.

Despite her absorption in building walls, Ray found time to carry on her work for basic feminism. Only the year before, her book *Careers and Openings for Women* had been published by Faber, following another book, *The Cause,* a short history of the women's movement in Great Britain. She also edited and wrote an introduction to her grandmother's papers on *Religious Fanaticism.* Although Ray's faith in Catholicism had apparently vanished, Mary found in her daughter qualities of the old religious energy of Hannah Smith and something of the Irish fervor of Frank Costelloe. Ray also wrote several more novels after her early *The World at Eighteen;* her final one was *Shaken by the Wind,* subtitled *A Story of Fanaticism.*

During the thirties, Ray's daughter, Barbara, had been permitted to join a cruise into northern waters. On shipboard she fell madly in love with a Finnish mariner, and became his bride at one of the ports of call. This breakneck marriage did not last, but one of its results was to make Ray a grand-mother (before she was fifty) and Mary Berenson a great-grandmother. Barbara was invited to come to I Tatti for a prolonged stay with her little son, who was only three or four years old when, in 1938, he was first presented to Mary. He broke into her old age like the rise of the sun. Enthroned in her great bed, she fell in love with the little boy. Even B.B., who had always equated babies with confusion, noise and domestic disorder, was converted, and expertly decreed this step-great-grandson of his to be a masterpiece of beauty—so merry, so playful, so graceful—more merry, more ecstat-ically happy to B.B. than the babies of Luca della Robbia, or even Donatello's in Florence. "I suddenly realized what heaven-sent playthings such babies might be," wrote the childless B.B., "and how not only mothers but even fathers craved to have one on hand, with new ones coming on as the first were growing too old. And how grandparents and even great-grandparents revelled in them more and more as their own age increased."

With her own delightful treasury of nursery rhymes, sto-ries, games and verses, Mary established a close bond with her great-grandson. She too realized freshly how the circle of life was balanced and steadied by the newcomers into the world. Her own world was coming to an end, and here before her eyes, not merely a new generation but, indeed, a new universe came gamboling, whirling, dancing into exist-ence.

It was one of Mary's last deep joys, to brighten her in the dark that was descending. The little boy broke the lonely

hours when B.B. and Nicky were away on some expedition
—to Dalmatia, to Spalato, or Venice. In Venice for the great
exhibition of Paolo Veronese, B.B. had run across George
Santayana. They had had one good talk, but their second
colloquy had dwindled away into an awkward silence. Berenson was spending day after rapt day at the Veronese exhibition, always discovering new beauties there. To Santayana, as
he confessed to his confidante Mrs. Toy, there was something
juvenile, something of arrested development in this undying
enthusiasm about "art." He too had been an aesthete, at least
an aesthetician, but now he wondered how B.B. could still
keep the flame alive; he suspected by forced draft, by social
and intellectual ambition, and by professional pedantry. If
he were a real poet, would he turn away from the evening
sky to see, by electric light, how Veronese painted it?

It was the absent Mary, Santayana realized, whom he had
found *simpática;* not B.B., but Mary with whom he had
laughed at the tribe of exiles; Mary who had nursed him at
I Tatti, and who had brought him, during his convalescence,
those naughty volumes of the *Arabian Nights.* Santayana
grieved to hear of her illness and infirmities, but he was
never to see her again.

It was 1939 and wartime; communication with England
became difficult, then impossible, and in common with the
world's millions, the Berensons were cut off from family and
friends in other countries.

Indirectly, news came to Mary of the death of Ray—her
daughter Ray who was more "Gram's" child than Mary's
own; Ray a grandmother, dying at the age of fifty-three, so
ambitious and yet defeated, her energies finding their outlet
in building walls with bricks of pressed mud. Virginia Woolf
wrote in *A Writer's Diary,* on Wednesday, July 24, 1940,
"No, I can't go on to Ray's death, about which I know noth-

ing, save that that very large woman, with the shock of grey hair . . . that monster . . . I remember typical of young womanhood, has suddenly gone. She had a kind of representative quality, in her white coat and trousers; wall building; disappointed, courageous, without—what?—imagination?"

After Pearl Harbor, the American authorities in Florence advised the Berensons' immediate return to the United States—indeed, practically ordered them to go. But Mary's frailties were stronger than the command, and at length Mary and B.B. decided to stay in the house they had lived in and loved for more than forty years. Some of the close-knit group of friends urged their going mainly because Berenson's enemies were accusing him of spreading propaganda. A hostile atmosphere began to envelop I Tatti. But Mary and B.B. realized that besides the difficulties of returning to America, they could not take up life there again at their ages—Mary nearly seventy-eight and Berenson only a year younger. Moreover, I Tatti was their creation. Forty years of life had gone into it, and they identified themselves with the little community which depended upon them. They could not desert it now.

So at the beginning of 1942, B.B. and Mary found themselves in the status of aliens and civilian prisoners in the country that had for more than four decades been their home. Largely because of Berenson's great international celebrity, they expected to be treated humanely, but he had been warned that he was a target of the Fascist propaganda against Jews, and of the false accusations that he was an agent of a "Judeo-demo-plutocratic" plot to strip Italy of her art treasures. The Berensons were tolerated and allowed to remain at I Tatti, but now as ostracized "untouchables." On January 11, 1942, Berenson noted in his journal: "Just a month ago war was declared between the country and people I love most on earth and the people to whom I owe whole-souled allegiance."

The dangers which constantly threatened to engulf the elderly Berensons and their community of dependents at I Tatti were all too real. Although the Italian armistice with the Allies was signed on September 8, 1943, most of Italy was still smothered under the Nazi occupation. The Allies were operating in the foot of Italy, but the Nazis, moving northward in retreat, were leaving their signatures in unspeakable destruction and devastation. Before Florence heard the first guns of the Allies, Tuscany had been cut off from the south for fifteen months. The citizens of Florence, of all Tuscany, were famished, thirsty, angry, and had no hope for themselves except mere survival. Hitler's earlier declaration that Florence would be treated as an open city had lulled its inhabitants into the belief that it would at least escape physical destruction. Nevertheless its great treasures of art had been long removed to hiding places: pictures from the Uffizi, the Pitti, and the Accademia were concealed in four outlying castles: Montegufoni, the property of Sir George Sitwell; the Villa Bossi-Pucci, at Montagnana; the Villa Guicciardi; and the Castello Guido at Poppia—all of which stood in sight of each other.

By nationality, origin and unconcealed political conviction, B.B. was a shining target for Fascist hostility. During the years before the war his international importance was such that the Italian Fascists were able to do little to harm him or to hinder the life at I Tatti. But a new and more virulent form of fascism was blazing out again under the German occupation. This intensified the danger to Berenson, at the hands of the SS or of Fascist terror gangs.

From her own refuge on the second floor at I Tatti, Mary could hear the sounds of the hurried removal of pictures, books and the glorious art library which were to be sent into hiding before the arrival of the Nazis. Some of these treasures were to be hidden at Le Fontanelle, the villa of His Excellency the Marchese Filippo Serlupi-Crescenzi, Minister Plenipotentiary to the Holy See. Thirty-two smaller pictures were hidden in the home of the Anreps in the Borgo San Jacopo, in the center of Florence. Books and the great collection of art photographs were taken to Quarto, a Noah's Ark owned by the Baroness Ritter de Zahony, née de Fénelon-Salignac.

On September 10, 1943, B.B. and Nicky Mariano were whisked away from I Tatti by the Marchese Filippo Serlupi, who enjoyed the prerogatives of an active diplomat. They drove to his villa near Careggi, built on the site of the house where the Platonist Marsilio Ficino had lived five hundred years before. Le Fontanelle stood high over the palace of Careggi, which had been built by Cosimo de' Medici on the brow of the Montevecchio.

When they had offered Berenson shelter, at serious risk to their peace of mind, and even their personal safety, the Marchese and Marchesa Serlupi-Crescenzi knew him only as an acquaintance. They treated him not as an aged refugee, but as if it were an honor to protect the illustrious man. "It was *caritas* in the most human and Christian sense of the word."

Mary, bedridden at I Tatti, was beyond the zone of indignation or fear. She realized that it was necessary for B.B. to hide in the *macchia de luxe,* for at seventy-eight he was still an enemy alien and a Jew. But Mary was lovingly cared for. On the day of Nicky and B.B.'s secret flight, the Anreps came to stay with her; Alda and her husband, Baron Berti, and their son Cecil, those German-speaking exiles, were eminently capable of handling Nazis who might come to occupy I Tatti.

Under the care of her nurse, in her large room on the second floor, Mary was left in peace. But this peace was disturbed by the steady rumble of cannon fire and the whine of hand grenades in the distant hills. Despite Mary's seclusion, rumors reached her that the Nazis were threatening to destroy Florence. Just before the coming of the Germans, in December 1943, the Florentine art authorities furnished placards warning that I Tatti was under their special protection and was not to be occupied.

Nevertheless, Nazi officers appeared and inspected the house to see if it would suit them. Berti Anrep received them, and they let themselves be persuaded that they had better look elsewhere. Later, other Germans showed up, medical officers prepared to take up quarters at I Tatti. At first it was five or six with their orderlies; then it was one entire medical staff, comprising at least fifty persons. Had they chosen to stay it would have been disaster; for Mary, in her helpless invalid condition, to be moved from her own special bed, her familiar surroundings, could well have been a life-and-death matter. Through the closed door of her bedroom Mary could hear the Anreps pleading in German with the officers of the Wehrmacht. *"Koennen Sie nicht etwas menschlicher sein?"* (Can't you be a little more human?) The old lady, the Germans insisted, must be removed from the villa for her own safety. They would even provide transportation and a safe-conduct to any hotel or nursing home she might choose.

It was impossible, Berti and Alda insisted in their fluent Baltic German, that the mistress of the villa be moved. If she were not safe in her own home, where else could she be? The Nazis were "correct" but insistent. They needed the two lower floors. They could not promise safety, for I Tatti might be under heavy fire, might even be destroyed, or, at best, brutally damaged. But while the Anreps were packing up their belongings, the Germans suddenly decided that Poggio Gherardo, a neighboring estate, suited them much better, and ordered the tenants there to clear out. And Mary chose to remain at I Tatti, even though she might yet be confined to a little room under the tiles, on the top floor. Every night the windowpanes rattled and the walls shook with terror, as the gun flashes lit up the distant skies. Every morning massive formations of four-engine bombers thundered overhead and were outlined against the cone of Mount Cetona. As they moved north in full retreat, Nazi troops were unable to carry their booty with them; their sadistic, destructive impulses were intensified by defeat, and they smashed everything they could lay their hands on with determined frenzy. Wherever they stopped, nothing was left untouched—water pipes and electric wires were torn out; clothes, underwear were torn to shreds by bayonets; books and music scores were torn to bits page by page; wardrobes were split open and their contents ruined; walls were meticulously defaced, curtains torn down, china smashed, cooking utensils crushed, knives, forks and spoons twisted. Those who saw the results describe them as what might have happened if some tribe of anthropoid apes had indulged in an orgy.

Mary passed the endless hours in her own nest, hardly aware of the ever tightening network of isolation that closed in on I Tatti. Cut off from news of the outside world, except as rumors filtered through the Fascist and Nazi press, only vaguely conscious of the disaster soon to sweep northward over Tuscany, she was warmed by the loyal friendship of Igor and Kyra Markevitch, who lived in the *villino* that the Hapgoods had occupied forty years ago. A brilliant composer and conductor, Igor Markevitch was born in Kiev and was brought up in Switzerland by his *émigré* parents. Later he became a pupil of Nadia Boulanger in Paris. The first per-

formance of Igor's *Concerto Grosso* had been given in Paris
when he was only seventeen. Later he married Kyra Nijin-
skaia, daughter of the great Nijinsky. The Markevitch son,
five-year-old Funtyki, became a regular visitor to Mary's bedside.

By March 1944, the Germans had given up the pretense
that Florence would be treated as an open city, and were reported to be installing air defenses at every suitable eminence around the city. It was not until the first of June that
news came of the Nazis' evacuation of Rome, and their retreat homeward became accelerated. Now the dull thud of
distant guns again shook the walls of the villa, and the roads
past I Tatti were crowded with military traffic.

At the end of July the parched, famished, terror-stricken
residents of Florence were ordered to shut themselves up in
their own houses, forbidden to appear on the streets under
penalty of execution, cut off from all public service as the
water mains, the gas and electric conduits were blown up.
On August 3, a great explosion burst from the heart of Florence. It threw up a serpentine jet of smoke that reached the
sky, and then bent to the right as if to meet the flames of
the conflagration. Flashes and many-colored rockets kept
lighting up the horizon. After nine days, the Florentine pop-
ulace was "liberated," and emerged into the sunlight as
from some dreadful epidemic—pale, emaciated and almost
stunned into catalepsy. Then they discovered that the bridges
across the Arno—with the exception of the Ponte Vecchio
—had been blown up and the nearest building destroyed.

The destruction of the Ponte Santa Trinità symbolized for
art lovers all over the world the climax of the Nazi fury. (It
would require thirteen years to replace this jewel of the Arno
with a facsimile.) "We shall never see the like of it again.
Its moldings were too subtly delicate to be copied; and be-

sides, the whole fabric has been caressed by centuries of sun and shadow and given a patina, a color, between ivory and honey that restoration cannot supply," wrote B.B.

In their hiding place at Le Fontanelle, Berenson and Nicky were no safer than they could have been at home. Nicky wrote in her diary, ". . . We live most of the time behind barred windows and doors, with small oil lamps or candles, in a small room or in one of the hallways. From Friday to Saturday the grenades whined all night above our heads. In the early afternoon some quietness, and B.B. proposed we should enter the library and read there together. While we crossed the front drawing room, again an ear-bursting close hit. It seemed to me as if I would see fire snakes along the window shades, and one heard glass splinters fall, and we returned quickly into our dark protective section. Hardly had we arrived, when we heard one close hit after another, aimed at our house. Most of them exploded on the terrace, close to our door; one hit the door to the drawing room in which we were a few minutes ago. Fortunately B.B. endures all this quite well, is without any fear and uses every quiet moment to occupy himself in his usual manner, reading and writing. His nerves are far better than mine."

After the retreat of the Nazis, Frederick Hartt and Sheldon Pennoyer of the American Forces, and Eric Linklater, of the British, rushed to Le Fontanelle to find the villa perforated by shells. They were informed by Serlupi-Crescenzi that Berenson was alive and well, and in a few minutes Hartt was taken to him. He was lying on a chaise longue in an upper room, terribly pale and suffering somewhat from shock, but otherwise unharmed. Hartt recalls:

"It had been a difficult experience for a man of seventy-nine. The villa had been hit by more than thirty small-caliber shells during a bombardment that lasted seven days and nights. Berenson and the Serlupi family had taken refuge in two small rooms at the back of the villa, safer than any of the others because hollowed out of the side of the rock. Shells had passed through the villa quite near this shelter, and at one time Berenson had narrowly escaped being struck by a shell when he left the room for a few minutes. Shells had burst in the living room, which contained the precious paintings, but only one or two small fragments were embedded in the masses of protective cushions, blankets and upholstery, and the surfaces of the pictures themselves were unscratched. The fighting in the area had ceased only the morning before, and shortly afterward Major Sampson, the AMG Displaced Persons officer, had arrived, depriving me of the honor of being the first Allied officer to reach Berenson."

On September 1, Igor Markevitch appeared at Le Fontanelle bringing news from I Tatti: Mary was bearing up well under the hell of German occupation; the reservoirs had run dry due to the Germans' wastage of water; the house was in not too impossible a state of repair. But the gardens were ruined because they had not been taken care of. Markevitch reported that the entire population of Ponte a Mensola had crowded into the villa for safety from air attacks and other alarms. On September 2, a car was sent by Major Sampson of the British Army to carry Berenson and Nicky home for a visit. That gesture was taken as a sure sign that the danger was past. "I found my wife no better for the year, less one week, that has separated us," Berenson noted in his diary. "She was suffering spasms of acute pain, and her speech was clogged. I carried away a sad and painful impression."

All of the gardeners and half the domestics had gone. The cook returned, but there was nothing to cook. Berenson gazed in dismay at the surroundings which he had spent so many years cultivating; now all was reduced to a combination of refuse heap, motor junk yard and Gypsy camp. That summer had been dry and drought-ridden, and military vehicles pursuing the Nazis left clouds of stifling dust. American units were placing heavy guns in the fields of the estate, warning that all windows and doors must be left open, as blasts might smash them. The fields were trodden to powder. Berenson returned to Le Fontanelle in speechless discouragement.

On September 23, Berenson was at last permitted to return to his home permanently. At twilight, as he came within sight of the broken-down walls and scorched fields, he sank into a pool of despair. But his spirits were lifted by the sight of Berti and Alda Anrep at the door, and the household staff gathered to welcome the master home. "Everything was in place," he noted in his journal. "Upstairs my study, my bedroom, the adjacent passages, in a most unexpected magical fashion, looked exactly as I left them, September 10th, 1943—looked in fact more peopled with dear and half-forgotten *objets d'art,* chiefly Chinese, that had been stored out of view for several years." Mary, too, was in a less painful state of health than he feared.

By the middle of October, Berenson discovered that they would have to spend the winter in three rooms small enough to be heated—for stoves were to be installed, hideous terracotta monstrosities, quite ruinous to space relations and color harmony. Firewood was practically nonexistent in Tuscany, and had to be transported from a distance of thirty miles. It was an ironic fact that the Anreps' house in the Borgo San Jacopo, where some of B.B.'s art treasures were secreted, was destroyed by the dynamiting of the bridges, while no object left at I Tatti suffered any damage.

But at last I Tatti was liberated, and restoration of the property began. The pictures were gradually returned to their places, the books to the great library, from the refuge in which they had been concealed in Florence. Berenson began anew his life of communication with innumerable Italian friends and Allied visitors. Eventually even the shattered pictures from Borgo San Jacopo began to return. Through the skill of Giannino Marchig, B.B.'s restorer, most of them were saved; only nine of the thirty small paintings had been damaged beyond redemption. But I Tatti, with its illustrious occupant and its priceless treasury of books and paintings, was once more safe. An Off Limits sign was to remain on the gate below the cypresses for many years.

In the seclusion of her darkened bedroom, Mary became only intermittently conscious of the renewed activity in the enormous villa—the return of the treasures, the reinstallation of the valued books to their proper shelves, the restoration of the gardens and fields outside. Igor Markevitch, who loved and appreciated her character, has written:

"The Nazis lived a very short time at I Tatti. Mrs. Berenson was allowed to lead a fairly quiet life, and at the time, she had a nurse looking after her, as always. Of course, she suffered from not seeing either her friends or any of her relatives, whom she was unable to see in the last years of her life.

"Fortunately, she managed to see B.B. again before dying. They had a very curious relationship. Both were very attached to one another. But she probably was the only person who dared to laugh at him and judge him with her strong critical sense, which used to irritate B.B. very much. In the last period of her life, Mrs. Berenson could hardly move. Her body was almost completely paralysed and she always had to remain in bed. I knew her only as an invalid and already when I first met her in 1935, she moved with great difficulty only with the use of crutches and she needed to be helped when going down for meals.

"She had a regal appearance. Her features were extremely regular until her very last breath. She was passionate, very unjust in her likes and dislikes, finding everything natural with the people she loved and having no forgiveness for the others. She was very fond of children and had a real passion for my little boy. When he was learning English, she knew every nursery rhyme he was reciting. In fact, she gave the impression to have known all English poetry completely by heart, which was a phenomenal feat. She used to allow my little boy to do anything. He played the doctor with her and she would have swallowed any sort of concoction he presented her with."

Mary died early in 1945, resigned to this final release, as Leo Stein, who had come again to I Tatti, noted in his journal. One curious omission in Berenson's two books of memories, *Rumor and Reflection* and *Sketch for a Self-Portrait*, is that no mention is made of Mary's final days. But he dedicates his *Sketch* "In Memory of My Wife and Fifty Years of Companionship."

Chapter 13 · The War Within

After the declaration of war in September 1939, Alys and Logan decided to remain in St. Leonard's Terrace—even to be bombed out, if that were to be their fate. Logan could think of nowhere else he might prefer to be, and his life was Alys's life. Better to live from day to day and to put the unseeable future out of mind. Logan was flattered to receive a request from the Library of Congress in Washington asking him to send papers and letters for permanent safekeeping. This was gratifying evidence of his fame in America, and Logan decided to send the papers as soon as possible, before the Terrace could be bombed out of existence.

Some two hundred of Logan's letters to members of his family, covering a period of more than fifty years, were sent in a diplomatic pouch to the Library of Congress; with them went fourteen precious letters from Henry James, most of them dated just before the outbreak of the First World War. There were also thirty-three letters from George Santayana; letters from Robert Bridges; the complete correspondence between Logan and Virginia Woolf. Along with these precious documents Logan also included his notes for unpublished *Trivia* and his preliminary sketches for *Unforgotten Years*.

It was at this time that he decided to spring to the defense of John Milton, who was then under attack from T. S. Eliot. One phase of Logan's "complex" was that he forgot, or pretended to forget, his American ancestry. He no longer considered himself an expatriate, and had long sought to expunge from his vocabulary any trace of American vernacular. He detested American writers—particularly Ezra Pound and T. S. Eliot, because of their being fellow expatriates—and this aversion led to his determination to undertake one of his last books, *Milton and His Modern Critics*, an essay which gave him excuse for attacking these two. This led Logan into a study of other cultivated compatriots who had crossed the Atlantic to seek literary fame and fulfillment in London, and this in turn inspired a tentative scheme for a satirical *Who's Who* of expatriate Yankees. His essay on Milton began half as a joke, but he soon became absorbed in the more serious aspects of his subject.

Ezra Pound became the special *bête noire*—the egregious Ezra who, though born in Idaho, had passed through Philadelphia before becoming the *enfant terrible* of poetry in London. In January 1940, Logan sent a postcard to his literary apprentice: "I want your help. I am trying to get at the history of the fall of Milton—I believe it happened on the banks of the Mississippi where T. S. Eliot spent his youth. I dare say Ezra Pound helped to bring him down. I am coming more and more to believe that the great Ezra is the originator of this anti-Milton stunt. In the book . . . *Make It New* [1934], he writes of his 'year long diatribes' against Milton. He is older than T. S. Eliot, who only echoes with feeble squeaks Ezra's full-mouthed denunciations. I should like [to] make certain of this if possible—it would be a fine stunt if the most slipshod and illiterate of published writers should have toppled from his august throne the most finished and scholarly of our poets . . ." In the final version of his essay, he toned down his attack on Pound and Eliot, although he could not resist the temptation to twit Eliot with his birth on "the banks of the Mississippi." Although Logan's defense of John Milton was motivated less by his love of the noble poet than by his temperamental hostility to two fellow expatriates who were attracting attention in London, *Milton and His Modern Critics* is a scholarly and worthwhile essay.

In the first months of the Second World War, the "phony" phase, Logan was relatively undisturbed, because he was entering his period of euphoria. Cheerfully he sent extra furniture for the refugees—the Dutch, Belgians and Luxembourgeois who were now pouring into Chelsea—hoping however that none would be quartered at 11 St. Leonard's Terrace. He spent days going over the old Smith papers, photographs and letters. He sat every afternoon on his "bench of desolation" in the public gardens near his house. He enjoyed what he called the afflictions of old age—that "softening of the brain" which made everything he wrote or said seem delicious. Logan did not like even to mention the wretched war. "We must suffer what we must, and there is nothing to be said about it." In spite of all, Logan managed during this euphoric phase to lead quite a pleasant existence, lying abed each morning polishing phrases, and during the afternoon watching cricket and tennis matches.

Then the "phony" war came to an abrupt end, and the war over England began in earnest. Bombs fell continuously on the vast, sprawling expanses of greater London, and day raids over inner London came with increasing frequency. Although Logan had announced that he would rather be bombed in his own house than spend the rest of the war in any other, by September 15, 1940, Alys and he moved to a nearby hotel in Sloane Street. Twice they had been ordered to vacate their house upon five minutes' notice, and this became too great a strain on Logan. But the hotel was no safer than St. Leonard's Terrace, and Alys and Logan decided to move to Bishop's Stortford, in Hertfordshire, some twenty-seven miles northeast of London. From that chilly and miserable refuge, Logan sent out a long wail of anguish. To Gathorne-Hardy he wrote: "Altogether everything is too wretched for words, and the charming civilized world I have lived in so long seems to be crashing to pieces." He sent Alys back to Chelsea to see whether the house was still standing. If so, they would return; he preferred bombs to the life forced upon him—such a life for one so harried and ill, in his seventy-fifth year, was no life at all. So the two returned to their Chelsea "refuge."

With the coming of the real war and with disaster hovering over London, Logan for the first time took comfort in his American blood. "I've suddenly discovered an American eagle in me," he proclaimed. American patriots cannot claim that he was returning, piously, to any love of his homeland— he found no fresh feeling for the United States. It was only that he loosed his animus against his adopted country. "I think we're beaten, and we deserve to be beaten," he snapped with fury. He foresaw defeat and ruin, all due to the failure of British statesmen, British strategists, British character. He poured venomous contempt upon the faintest optimism.

But by the spring of 1941, Logan found himself swept out of his depression once more, although his moments of gaiety and good humor and generosity were interrupted by the renewal of the bomb warfare. A parachute mine fell on a block of flats on the west side of Burton Court, barely two hundred yards from St. Leonard's Terrace. Luckily, Logan was in his euphoric phase when the windows of his house were blown in. Plaster fell down from ceiling and walls; the front door was cracked and askew. The door of Alys's room fell over her bed, but she was rescued uninjured. Shattered panes were replaced with oiled silk, wallboard, or black-out material. Logan joked about having "gone with the bombs"; he described this as a grandiose experience, though it left his home still habitable. On April 21, 1941, he could announce: "Here we shall stay until we are blitzed to heaven." And later: ". . . having lived for seventy-five years on the world, but unspotted from it, I have now after being nearly bombed from its surface, emerged from under a shower of broken glass and plaster as world-loving, as mundane as the most pushful social climber. All I want is titles and social glory . . ." They might eventually be bombed out of Chelsea, but in the meantime they planned a bomb-proof refuge, to which they might repair and find safety even if the house were demolished.

Under such conditions, Logan gave up any attempt at long-sustained literary efforts. Yet he did produce essays, sketches and book reviews. He sent them to *Horizon* and his sketch of Henry James to the friendly *New Statesman and Nation*.

Commenting on a number of *Horizon* to which he himself had contributed, he wrote: "I liked in the current number Philip Toynbee's letter he prints from that American manufacturer of barbed wire for the great concentration camp— vast beyond imagination—in which America will imprison the 'Spirit of Man.' That is the ultimate fate of this planet —to become an immense sanitary concentration camp, wisely regulated and run by hygienic Americans—a great Sahara of dreary dust like the Moon—that awful unheeded warning and forecast of our ultimate fate."

But by the end of 1941, an obsession of impending ruin took possession of the old man, an obsession from which he would not be free for the remaining years of his life. He was seized by a fear of poverty—that his royalties from *Unforgotten Years* might be swallowed up by the excess profits tax; that his income from America could not reach him. The penury and stinginess of his depressed periods returned with repellent intensity. Was not Bob slyly trying to trick him? Was not Alys planning to desert him? Logan turned in fury on Alys, on the faithful Hammond, on Mary the cook. He could make a generous gift and then angrily demand its return. In 1943, he managed to attend the celebration of Sir Max Beerbohm's seventy-first birthday, but could describe it as a dismal occasion—"a most horrible performance in his dishonour." He repaired this dishonor by a tribute to Max in the *Observer*. He sold another American mortgage, to find money to keep going for a few months, noting that "we are all in the same boat, which now seems to be leaking badly," adding that "it's a great thing to be old and to have no children, and to be fated to leave this disastrous planet soon."

Logan's complaints of poverty became so chronic that Gathorne-Hardy offered to lend him a hundred pounds. But the wolf, Logan admitted, was not actually at his door. Never in his long life had Logan been even within speaking distance of poverty; he had always enjoyed a comfortable home attended by faithful females. If by this offer of a loan Bob was now turning the other cheek, he was following "the dirtiest trick ever invented by Our Saviour." Now Alys, Hammond and Mary the cook sacrificed their own needs to give the master the few eggs that came into the house, all the delicacies from the food packages that came from overseas admirers. Logan demanded all these as his right; he felt himself the chosen victim of a conspiracy, a plot against his security.

The demon in his unconscious took possession of the bedridden old man, and he began to blame all of his miseries upon the presence of the three attentive women. So insistent became his mania that Robert Gathorne-Hardy reluctantly advised Alys to become selfish for once, and to seek a flat of her own. Alys's encounters with her brother became so cruelly painful that she could no longer sleep, and her doctor finally forbade any meeting between the two. Logan himself at last demanded that Alys leave his house and go and live elsewhere. But Alys, the handmaiden of his life, could not bear to leave Logan, in his final days, in the care of others, and stayed on.

Logan now communicated with his sister in brief, incoherent messages scribbled on the backs of used envelopes, or on bank slips; he was obsessed with the compulsion to drive her out of his house. Whenever Gathorne came, he managed to snatch a few words with Alys, but to talk to Logan was like communicating with a soul at some incalculable distance. Where was the real Logan? To this disciple suddenly came the monstrous reply: "Where else but in hell?"

"Don't you know what she's planning to do?" Logan asked Hardy one day. "She's going to fetch a van and take all the bed linen away so that I shall have none left! I don't know what else she may take . . . she may take all the furniture away and leave nothing for me!"

"Your sister has made her arrangements to leave you," Hardy explained. "Don't interfere! She's going to go. Let there be a truce. . . . Be friends now!"

But Logan was beyond any reasonable appeal. Early on the morning of Saturday, March 2, 1946, Alys telephoned to Gathorne-Hardy. "It's over," she said. "Logan died early this morning." The young man hurried into London. "I wept for Logan when I thought he was dying in Iceland," he said to Alys, "but I can't weep now."

There were only five people present at the funeral of Logan Pearsall Smith. Later his friend the Dean of Westminster conducted a memorial service in St. Margaret's Westminster. But this worshiper of words was more fittingly commemorated by those who worshiped in the same chapel. Cyril Connolly paid an eloquent tribute to his old master in the pages of the *New Statesman*.

"His own unique resonance was a perpetual warm ironical appreciation of life heightened by a never-failing passion for the best in literature and the human heart. . . . He would write some long essay in which the gleanings of his dark winter hibernations were set down in those long shining sentences, where intelligence and feeling and scholarship and strange bleak flashes fetched from his spiritual underworld were integrated into that peculiarly radiant prose, so limpid and seeming-artless, so penetrating in insight, so warm in texture, which constituted his own secret weapon against chaos and time. Two weeks before his death, a friend asked him half-jokingly if he had discovered any meaning in life. 'Yes,' he replied, 'there is a meaning, at least, for me, there is one thing that matters—to set a chime of words tinkling in the minds of a few fastidious people.' 'And the State, Logan,' the friend went on, 'the Family, the International Situation, Russia, India?' Propped up on his pillows he waved all this away with his hand, 'A chime of words,' he repeated, 'a few discriminating people.'

". . . Just as it seemed that Logan could never have lived anywhere except in St. Leonard's Terrace . . . so it is impossible not to imagine him still living there, in his high study which looked over the Wren gates, 'with cloudy trophies hung,' to the Hospital that symbolized that seventeenth century which he had loved so well and helped so much to elucidate, the England of Shakespeare, Milton, Donne, Taylor, and Wotton, for whose sake he had become a British subject. To us who knew him in those war years Logan Pearsall Smith personified an indispensable quality in civilization. Civilization will not lose by his death for it has his books, but his friends will all feel less civilized. Who will care now how we turn out, or warn us when we decline, or advise us how to surpass ourselves? This is the real burden of mortality; a human spirit shines out for so long that it becomes encrusted with memories, the oracle of wisdom for a whole tribe, a fountain of humorous affection. 'And yet, as with Tolstoy and with Proust, all is slowly changing beneath the unimaginable lapse of time, until suddenly the unimaginable happens; the shears of destiny snap together, the sun goes out, the curtain of darkness falls.' And round us, not him, the shades gather."

The relation between the master of St. Leonard's Terrace and the younger disciple Gathorne-Hardy reminds us of the literary fables of Henry James. The companionship of seventeen years was a long endurance test for Gathorne-Hardy, and it left him with a grievance, which he sought to exorcise by writing and publishing a detailed volume of recollections. Gathorne-Hardy's *Recollections* present an embarrassing, though well-documented record of Logan's last years. But the Jamesian "turn of the screw" revealed that the apprentice, in painting the unflattering portrait of his master, had also consciously or unconsciously revealed himself. It is impossible to agree with those British critics who feel that Gathorne-Hardy's book was written *con amore,* or with Alys's reference to it as a "glowing picture" of Logan's work and personality. But it must be admitted that it is a painfully convincing and detailed diagnosis of the disintegration of a frustrated person. We are indebted to Robert Gathorne-

Hardy for most of the details of the final period in the life of this self-proclaimed expatriate.

Robert Gathorne-Hardy believed that Logan never freed himself from the silver cord of maternal domination. As he saw it, Hannah Smith unconsciously attempted to break Logan's spirit in his earliest infancy, and psychologists would probably discover that she almost succeeded in doing so. He shared his house at Court Place with her until she died, but even her death did not bring the freedom he thought he wanted. He was continually searching for what some psychologists have termed a surrogate mother.

Following publication of Gathorne-Hardy's personalized case history, young John Russell was persuaded to edit Logan's diaries and letters. His book, *A Portrait of Logan Pearsall Smith, drawn from his letters and diaries,* was published in an expensive edition by the Dropmore Press, at two guineas the copy. This tribute may have been intended to counterbalance the unpleasant impression created by Gathorne-Hardy's *Recollections.* "First comes Mr. Robert Gathorne-Hardy to perform an autopsy," wrote Stephen Spender; "now comes Mr. John Russell to line the coffin with satin." Spender represented the revolt of a younger generation from the preciosity of the ivory tower mandarin as revealed in Smith's letters. For Spender, literature could not be divorced from life. Logan did not care for sex, Spender wrote, nor music, nor painting; he did not care for any kind of intensive living, except vicariously through his friends—and he made irreconcilable demands on them. He had a passion for correctitude in the writing of English; an excellent thing, said Spender, except that his disciples often confused it with artificiality. To Spender, moreover, the spectacle of Logan polishing and repolishing his little jewels of self-denigration was painful. No writer was ever so serious about not taking his own personality seriously. "I don't want respect. Treat me with affectionate derision," Logan is quoted as saying. But finally this lack of self-respect became "a kind of sniggering derision at life."

After Logan died, Alys went on living in the little house in St. Leonard's Terrace. Even as she approached her seventy-ninth birthday, in spite of the defeats of life that she had suffered, she manifested a marvelous resilience. She had refused to be crushed by Logan's mad spite. Alys had had every reason to feel battered and embittered and downcast, in anguish over the state of the world and the psychopathic behavior of her brother; but she remained an incurable optimist and humanitarian. Mariechen had gone the year before, and Alys was the last survivor of their faraway childhood days in New Jersey. Her memories kept returning to Mill-ville, to old Walt and his cottage in Camden.

Alys had practically adopted Julia Strachey, Oliver's daughter and Ray's stepdaughter. When Gathorne-Hardy came to write his *Recollections of Logan Pearsall Smith*, he asked Alys's permission to dedicate to her this story of a friendship. She gave her permission willingly, and in her foreword she wrote: "My brother would be the first to wish the whole truth to be told, as a partial portrait can never be a faithful nor a lasting one. From time to time younger friends would ask for his opinion when they were at work on memoirs or recollections. His advice was always firmly given, 'Tell the truth.' But I cannot do better in this respect than to quote the words of our old friend who, as my brother has written, had so profound an influence on him, 'Do not prettify me,' said Walt Whitman to Horace Traubel. 'Be sure to write about me honest: whatever you do, do not prettify me: include all the hells and damns.' "

Through the efforts of Barbara Strachey, Mary's grand-daughter, Alys was persuaded to broadcast twice for the Home Service of the British Broadcasting Corporation. In one of these broadcasts she recounted vividly her memories of the early Fabians—of Beatrice and Sidney Webb, of Bernard Shaw, of Graham Wallas and all the guests on the Sunday terrace at Friday's Hill. In her second broadcast, she told her listeners how to enjoy life at eighty. In this she described herself as the product of the early feminist movement in an American Quaker family with a rebellious mother. In this broadcast, Alys reverted once more to Walt Whitman, because he seemed to her "a perfect example of an old age of calm serenity, whose placid sun and skies diffused about him an atmosphere of peace and leisure, which made his companionship so genial, and induced endless discussions with him which were the greatest pleasure. Old and poor and half-paralyzed, he never spoke of his poverty, nor of his physical disabilities. He looked forward to the future as 'old age flowering free, with the delicious assurance of death,' and he was content and even happy in the thought. I can never approach his beautiful 'Am I exacting, am I querulous? Am I a nuisance, or am I a comfort?' For just as old people can be a nuisance by their demands and their complaints, so they can be a help by their cheerfulness and their sympathy. They need never grunch nor grouse, never be more of a nuisance and a bother than they can help, but can aim at being a blessing and a treasure. Grumbles, like measles, spread like wildfire, and people get tired of wiping our tears from our eyes. I should like also to be self-regulating or self-organizing, and to settle my petty crises and troubles without bothering."

Alys had one gratifying reward in her last years. Bertrand

Russell had returned from the United States, where he had been marooned during the war years. Chance brought Alys and Bertie together, and he came often to see her. Nearly forty years had passed since their estrangement, yet with a certain vicarious pride Alys had always followed his career. He had spent many of those intervening years in the United States, and the newspapers were all too generous in reporting the adventures and misadventures of the radical aristocrat—the more so because Bertrand had become the Third Earl Russell, a title to which he succeeded in 1931, upon the death of his elder brother, the incorrigible Frank.

In America, his luck had not always been so conspicuously good. Alys could recall his marriage to Dora Black in 1921. Her own divorce, Bertie's marriage to his secretary, and the birth of his first son had all been telescoped together in a few months in that eventful year. Dora, who was a fiery radical, defied in word and practice the conventions of middle-class Britain, wrote a shrill treatise on *The Right to Be Happy* and persuaded Bertrand to become cofounder of a school where the freedom of children could be encouraged. Their son, John Conrad, was born in November 1921, and a daughter followed a year or two later. That second marriage lasted until 1934. Its final years placed the master of symbolic logic and rationalism in a rather absurd and humiliating position. Alys could not shut her ears to the gossip of those years that echoed and re-echoed between Bloomsbury and Chelsea.

In 1936, Bertie married his third wife, Patricia H. Spence, nicknamed "Peter," and many years his junior. A son, named Conrad in honor of Bertie's old friend the novelist, was born in 1937. But in 1946 that marriage was on the rocks, though the decree of divorce had not been signed.

Alys could appreciate the reversal in their positions, for Bertie had become almost an expatriate from his native land, so frequent and so prolonged were his visits to the United States; frequent, despite the controversies his presence stirred up in the academic world and in the press. His enemies were the Roman Catholics; he was a sort of whipping boy for the unco guid. His appointment at the College of the City of New York became a *cause célèbre,* uniting the liberals in his defense. To appoint this distinguished mathematician and logician would be to establish a "Chair of Indecency," said one of his opponents. He was smeared by his enemies, as his father had been smeared because of his association with the Drysdales and the early Neo-Malthusians.

Through his old friend John Dewey, Russell was introduced, in the early forties, to Dr. Albert Coombs Barnes, the collector of modern art and the autocrat of the Barnes Foundation at Merion, near Philadelphia. Russell signed a contract to deliver a yearly series of lectures at the Foundation for a period of five years. He began with some success in 1941. During 1942 the youthful Lady Russell ("Peter") attended her husband's course, bringing her knitting with her into the lecture hall. Her presence and her knitting are said to have aroused the ire of the terrible-tempered Dr. Barnes (he was, like Bertie, seventy years of age), who ordered Peter's banishment, and, confronted by the protest of Earl Russell, dismissed him as well. Russell filed a suit claiming his salary for the unfinished term of his contract. The court ruled that Barnes had broken his contract, and after prolonged litigation, Russell won his suit.

Another adventure plunged Bertrand into icy water, instead of the customary hot water of transatlantic controversy. He was en route to a lecture engagement in Norway when the flying boat on which he was a passenger capsized abruptly in the harbor of Trondheim, and the seventy-eight-year-old philosopher was shoved by one of the crew into Trondheim's chilly water, to sink or swim. There was no choice, and so, although he was wearing a heavy overcoat, the indomitable Bertie swam until he was rescued. He was one of the twenty-three who survived this disaster, and he suffered no serious injuries.

On his visits to his aged ex-wife in London, Bertie discussed many of his early intellectual adventures in her native land, and she recalled the scandal she herself had precipitated at Bryn Mawr fifty-odd years before, when she advocated a maternity wage.

They recalled the old days at Friday's Hill and laughed together at memories of Beatrice Webb's peculiarities when the four of them were in Normandy. Mrs. Webb preferred to remain upstairs in the morning because she could not bear the spectacle of her companions enjoying their good French *petit déjeuner*. The first morning Mrs. Webb had sent down a message: "We do not have butter with Sidney's breakfast." Another message was her order to a waiter that "We do not take sugar in my husband's tea."

Knowing of these renewed visits, friends in Bloomsbury and Chelsea suggested, in jocular fashion, that Alys and Bertie might be remarried. Could it be possible that a reconciliation with Alys might take place? Alas, Alys was past eighty—a remarriage between an old lady of eighty-three and a man of seventy-eight was an absurdity not to be considered. And Bertie had already chosen his fourth wife, but this marriage did not take place until after the death of Alys. Earl Russell spent long hours at her bedside, and her going must have come to him as a sharper blow than he had anticipated, for she was the last survivor of the old and happy days of Fernhurst and Friday's Hill.

And she was also the last survivor of her branch of the Smith family. Mary had died at I Tatti in 1945; Logan had died in 1946; Alys, happy in her forgiving, new-found companionship with her still-beloved Bertie, lived on until 1951.

On December 15, 1952, Lord Russell married for the fourth time. His bride was Edith Finch, a graduate of Bryn Mawr as Alys had been. The third Earl Russell was eighty years of age, his fourth bride was fifty. Not only was she a graduate of Bryn Mawr, but she was also the first and only biographer of M. Carey Thomas, Alys's older cousin, the stiff-necked autocrat of the female college she had created. The bride had received a master's degree from Oxford and had studied at the Sorbonne. She had made her debut as a biographer with a book on Wilfrid Scawen Blunt; and with her biography of "Cousin Carey," Miss Finch had made herself almost a member of the Thomas-Whitall clan. The new Countess possessed something of Alys's energy and vitality. There were whispers among the irreverent that she was a "stand-in" for the departed Alys when, by the eight-minute civil ceremony at the Chelsea Registry Office, the former Bryn Mawr instructor became the Countess Russell.

Certainly Lord Russell needed a wife to husband his resources, for he found himself now the Grand Old Man of English philosophy. It was not so much that he had changed since the old days at Friday's Hill, as that Britain had grown up to him. He felt, and the press felt, that he had lost none of his unquenchable vitality. First had come the Order of Merit and then the Nobel Prize for literature. There were increasing demands for his appearance on television, on the Sunday "Brains Trust," and for radio broadcasts. His agent in America cabled for "think pieces" on every available topic, and his publishers were quite excited about his roguish ventures into the realm of fiction. It is not surprising that an Australian interview described the philosophical peer as looking like "a sophisticated koala bear which had just thought of a funny story." Had not his whole career been a funny story? Had those who awarded him the O.M. and the Nobel Prize forgotten that he had served four and a half months in Brixton prison, forgotten his efforts to undermine the moral conventions of those days long past? He was uttering the same subversive thoughts he had uttered in his twenties and forties, but because he was eighty and the world was older, they were now accepted as the wisdom of a sage. No wonder he looked like a naughty koala bear.

One of his published books was entitled *Portraits from Memory*, really a printed version of a series he had tape-recorded for the BBC. Lord Russell gave amusing anecdotes of Sidney and Beatrice, of Bernard Shaw and H. G. Wells, and limned in acid a little etching of his old friend George Santayana. There was a tribute to his grandfather Lord John Russell and his almost-godfather John Stuart Mill. The little volume was padded out, with six autobiographical essays to make a book. But there was not a word about his first wife Alys, not a word about his first mother-in-law, nor his first father-in-law, nor his brilliant sister-in-law Mary. Here is evidence of a technique of forgetting as well as of remembering. He did mention his brother-in-law Logan, who had given him advice on how to write. We cannot believe that Lord Russell is other than facetious when he says that Logan advised him: "Put a comma after every four words," and "Never use *and* except at the beginning of a sentence." This

is merely Russell's way of telling us that he could not abide
Logan.

Eventually the day arrived when Countess Russell came
to the realization that there were too many demands upon
the time and energies of the Grand Old Man of British
thought. They had been living in Richmond, not far from
Pembroke Lodge (now converted into flats) and there were
too many causes to support, too many manifestoes to sign,
too many protests against nuclear bombs. After all, no human being can remain in a state of perpetual indignation.
So she persuaded the gentle gerontocrat to retire to Wales,
to a place with the difficult name of Penrhyndeudraeth, in
Merionethshire.

On May 18, 1957, Lord Russell celebrated his eighty-fifth
birthday. And there in Wales he received the tribute of a
full-length biography written by a reverent Australian-born
disciple, Alan Wood, called *Bertrand Russell: The Passionate Skeptic*. In it, the Grand Old Man states his ultimate beliefs: "The secret of happiness is to face the fact that
the world is horrible, horrible, *horrible*—you must feel it
deeply and not brush it aside. You must feel it right in here
—[*hitting his breast*]—and then you can start being happy
again."

Mankind collectively, he said, under the guidance of fools
(i.e., statesmen) and by the ingenuity of slaves (i.e., techni-
cians) , is busily engaged in the great task of preparing its
own extermination. But despite these dicta, which recall the
pessimism of his early essay on "A Freeman's Worship," Lord
Russell, so Philip Toynbee assures us, still has faith in
Hope: "I find men in our dangerous age who seem to be in
love with misery and death, and who grow angry when hopes

are suggested to them. They think that hope is irrational
and that, in sitting down to lazy despair, they are merely
facing facts. I cannot agree with these men. To preserve
hope in our world makes calls upon our intelligence and
our energy. In those who despair it is very frequently the
energy that is lacking."

Chapter 14 · Retrospect

Alys Russell died in 1951, one hundred years after the marriage of her parents. Looking back over that century in the lives of our five transatlantic Smiths, we cannot fail to be impressed by how vividly they demonstrate the part played by unconscious motivation. Mary Berenson must have had her own family in mind when she exclaimed: "God knows by what unconscious impulses we are moved!" How otherwise may we interpret Robert Pearsall Smith's mad pilgrimage to Britain to promulgate his good news of immediate and complete salvation? That Quixotic quest brought about the uprooting of his family from the austere, close-knit community of the Society of Friends, of which they were all birthright members. His "call," his vocation, which welled up to suffuse the bright little circle of consciousness, was respected by all, and given priority over his duties with the Whitall-Tatum company. Robert was released to pursue his career as a teacher and preacher. Such was the beginning of the momentous changes that came to the Smiths, and eventually made them all exiles from their native New Jersey.

Nothing had indicated that Robert and Hannah might not live out their quiet lives in Millville, Haddonfield and the more aristocratic Germantown as upright members of the Philadelphia Meeting. But then Robert received his call to

summon Christians to the second experience of immediate
and complete salvation. Today, from our point of vantage,
we can detect in this sudden call, this "mystical" experience,
the symptoms of the manic-depressive configuration; but in
those days there was less acknowledgment of the unconscious.
One phase of Robert's madness, as we have seen, was an
overpowering need to communicate this message to the
world of believers, and this need led to an insatiable search
for more and more audiences. Madman or mystic, he took his
leap into the unknown, and eventually he led his family
with him. Such was the break, irreparable and irreversible,
from the closed and stable society in which they had been
born and reared.

Robert Pearsall Smith moved as a triumphant spiritual
prophet from London to Oxford, from Oxford to crowded
Brighton, and to a succession of country homes, bringing the
promise of release from the crushing hardships of external
law, the promise of immediate and everlasting personal salvation, and the ushering in of a new age of love, forgiveness
and spiritual liberty. The overwhelming response to these
promises stimulated the overseas prophet to further audac-
ities. Unconsciously, in his benign madness, he became a
new spokesman of the antinomian heresy, that doctrine
of the covenant of grace that had brought Mistress Anne
Hutchinson into conflict with the established authorities
and the organized church back in Boston more than two and
a half centuries before. Suppressed and driven underground
time after time by orthodox theologians, the antinomian
tradition, nevertheless, emerged in the bold challenge of
a William Blake, in the transvaluation of all values proclaimed by Friedrich Nietzsche, in the strange sects and mes-
sianism of the frontiers, a challenge to all man-made codes—
particularly those relating to sexual taboos.

In Germany, it was as though Robert Pearsall Smith were indeed "speaking in tongues," as he knew not one word of German. This was truly the expression of the charismatic gift, a direct communication with the masses. His madness was in tune with their madness.

But in the end, Robert Smith's flame was extinguished by a small group of sponsors, the close-knit committee of respectability. And it was, as we have seen, the undular pattern of his manic-depressive personality that precipitated his apostasy. This *Weltmissionar* found sanctuary again in the offices of Whitall-Tatum, his story killed by a conspiracy of silence of which he himself was the chief instigator. He who had been acclaimed almost as a messiah was now hidden behind the *persona* of the solid and sound businessman. And yet his influence was felt for decades after, as the fellowship movement spread in Great Britain and Germany.

Beneath Hannah Smith's Quaker decorum vibrated a violent, though disciplined, nature. Her chastisement of little Logan when he was scarcely six months old is but one example of her innate violence. She had the fierce protective affection of the tigress for her own children. Hannah possessed none of the mental unbalance of her husband, but a native common sense. One of the ironies of her history is that this "great" lady, who banished secular poetry and fiction from her universe, who ridiculed the aesthetic pronouncements of Oscar Wilde, who could not come to terms with the family guest Walt Whitman, who failed to appreciate the Old Masters, who had her suspicions of a philosophy that banished the Deity—that she should become the mother-in-law of Bertrand Russell and Bernard Berenson. Her Quakerism concealed a woman of the world, shrewd and skillful in establishing enduring friendships with the titled

ladies of England. In writing home, as we have seen, Hannah
became something of a name-dropper, and innocently admitted that were she English she would prefer to be a member of the aristocracy. Her humor was a mixture of flat-
footed common sense of the native Yankee brand and unconscious snobbery.

Hannah was one of the first of our "inspirational" writers, the ancestress of a long line of popularizers of spiritual
platitudes. She made use of an artless casuistry in promising
her thousands of readers happiness no less than sanctity. She
became a best seller long before that term was invented.

Mary Berenson would have vehemently denied that she
had ever made a synthetic religion of art. It is true that
Pater's *Marius* had been the testament of her London years,
but as she matured she demanded a clearer exposition of appreciation than the shimmering but misty veil in which
Walter Pater wrapped his aesthetic hero. But she dared to
live out her convictions, and left her husband and two baby
daughters to follow in the footsteps of Berenson in the
study of the art of the Italian Renaissance.

We can imagine the supercilious and even contemptuous
little smile flashing across B.B.'s lips as he overheard his
Mariechen referred to as a "Philadelphia Quakeress." Quakeress? This was the last word to describe her. All her life she
had been in determined rebellion against the puritanism of
her ancestors. Returning from Cambridge, Massachusetts,
she had shocked all her Quaker relatives with her proclama-
tion of the duty of self-development for every woman. Walt
Whitman's "bright particular star" a Quaker? Never! But
her conversion to art may have been a variety of religious experience. Only in some such way can Mary's desertion of
home, husband and children be understood.

Did she become disillusioned in the final years of her life? She confessed that she could utter the unpardonable heresy at I Tatti—that she had come to prefer nature to art. Much to his annoyance, she learned to laugh at Berenson. The unending stream of pilgrims who found their way to I Tatti must have bored her. The unchanging ritual of its luncheon table, its captive conversation, and the inevitable tour of inspection of the treasures of the villa may have driven Mary to the seclusion of her own quarters; may have awakened her to the truth of Aldous Huxley's perception (published in 1927) that the "cultivation of art for its own sake has become a substitute religion" and that the lives of aesthetes are a far from edifying comment on the religion of beauty.

After Mary's death in 1945, her memory seemed eclipsed at I Tatti and few questions were ever put to B. B. about his debt to her. But without Mary's help and encouragement the villa at Settignano would never have been purchased and developed. Without Mary, B.B. could never have established his unique authority among the high caste of collectors and connoisseurs. Without Mary, the complex pattern of entertaining the right persons at the right time could never have been successfully accomplished over a period of decades. Without Mary, Berenson's books could not have presented those qualities of simplicity and lucidity of style.

It was not until his ninetieth birthday in 1955, just ten years after Mary's death, that Berenson finally confessed his debt to his wife. "They say that when I was young I was quite handsome. But—I was insufferable. It took my beloved wife and my good friends to make a human being out of me."

The inner conflict between the conscious and the unconscious that raged deep within Logan Smith's soul was never terminated. Robert Gathorne-Hardy, that close observer of

Logan's latter years, believes that his life was a history of attempted escapes, all of them unsuccessful. His "spirit" had been tamed if not broken in infancy by his domineering though well-meaning mother. Later, he recoiled from all that was associated with that domination—the blazing faith of his parents, his own homeland, the family business; from all mundane and commercial ambitions. We prefer to emphasize the conflict, rather than the attempted escape. For it was the inner conflict that prevented Logan from growing to maturity. He remained "little" Logan until the day of his death. It was his perpetual adolescence or preadolescence that was responsible for his delight in hoaxes and "practical" jokes, for the facile levity that marred even his best writing. As Santayana warned him, even in fooling there must be an underlying philosophy. And Berenson declared that his brother-in-law's besetting sin was an all-enveloping facetiousness. Juvenile too was Logan's habit of self-limitation, of never attempting anything that was beyond his tested powers. So eventually he sought a sanctuary from the rough-and-tumble world of Grub Street, and became a monk or perhaps the Father Superior in his own Abbey of Thélème. But as we have seen, even in the seclusion of his refuge in Chelsea, the inner conflict not only raged on, but brought tragedy with it.

In vain Logan had sought his salvation, his religious experience, in the worship of words, *le saint langage,* in the words of Paul Valéry. Once again we cannot avoid the analogy of the substitute religion: Logan's habitual pilgrimage to the holy places of English literature; his compilation of a roster of the saints of letters; even his tracts written for the Society of Pure English may be compared to the missionary tracts little Logan distributed as a small boy in the streets and trams of faraway Philadelphia.

All this is not intended to deny that he was a master of

words, a keen student of English style and usage. In this he resembles another master of the word, John Ruskin, who like Logan was a victim of a psychic conflict that prevented the full fruition of his genius and at the end of his life plunged him into madness. Logan was no Ruskin, yet despite his inner tragedy he succeeded in winning a place for himself in English letters. He was a still small voice above the clangor and sirens of the society that was collapsing around his head.

Of all our transatlantic Smiths, Alys, the youngest of them all, was the most equably balanced. She did not possess the brilliance of her sister Mary; she was not defiant of conventions and decorum; she was free from the dominating though masked egotism of her mother; she revealed no trace of the wild, mad mysticism of her father. Alys was predestined to play a secondary role in life—secondary first to her mother and sister Mary; then as a close friend of Beatrice Potter Webb; after that to her brilliant young husband Bertrand Russell; and still later to her brother Logan. Her marriage ended in heartbreaking disappointment, but Alys lifted herself out of defeat courageously and gallantly. She was the truest Quaker of them all, working selflessly in all good causes that came her way, becoming an inveterate "joiner" in the cause of feminism, working alongside her beloved Beatrice in furthering the Fabian ideal, speaking out for the Liberals and later the Labour Party. For thirty-five years she served as a substitute mama for her erratic brother. And when, in the end, he turned against her, Alys possessed the resiliency of character and the inner resources to meet this crisis with dignity and nobility.

Alys possessed that enigmatic and perhaps feminine power of coming back. Evidence of her charm and courage are to be found in her broadcasts for the British Broadcasting Corporation. Alys retained her serenity and her Quaker kindness to the end. We discover no obvious inner conflict in her nature, perhaps because she was content with the secondary and sustaining role she was assigned to play in the Smith drama.

"But is not all this written in the book of Henry James?" Logan asked in his memoirs. And in the opinion of Edith Finch, the present Countess Russell, Logan's own family carried out "with singular accuracy the international theme of Henry James." She commends their impulsive kindness, their immense awareness of the mellow, elusive and desirable English scene. She stresses their appetite for new experiences, the freshness of their observance, the sharpness of their discriminations, the warmth with which they embraced new loyalties. Their good looks and their generosities combined to endear them to groups upon whose doors many transatlantic visitors knocked in vain. But, examined more closely, their success was not characteristic of the tragic heroines of Henry James. We need only glance at these transatlantic Smiths to realize how little they conformed to the figures in the Jamesian carpet. How did Henry James portray his American pilgrims to the Old World? In the novels of his major phase, James depicts two types: the newcomers, deluded by what he terms a "superstitious valuation of Europe"—innocent, idealistic, naïve to the point of gullibility, and all mysteriously affluent; and the permanent exiles, hardened, ruthless, often penniless, living on their wits and therefore parasitical, often working in collaboration with unscrupulous and cynical native Europeans. Even though James invariably awarded the "moral" victory to his innocents abroad, the discriminating reader carries away the impression that they are no match for their ruthless, unscrupulous and relentless adversaries, who somehow are the representatives of Old World "art" and culture.

But for the Smiths this Jamesian conflict did not exist. From Millville and Germantown to the stately halls of Broadlands and the aristocratic circles of English Evangelicals they moved as honored guests, received with a warmth and hospitality we find difficult to explain even today. For the transatlantic Smiths, there was no prolonged "siege of London" in the Jamesian sense.

There was one Jamesian similarity, however. Not unlike the outstanding characters in the Master's later works, the Smiths were the forerunners of a new generation of American expatriates, the elite of what Santayana has described as "an international intelligentsia adrift amid unsuspected currents and wrecked, one by one, on the reefs of El Dorado." Their culture was in a sense sterilized, cleansed of the final vestiges of regional provincialism, uprooted from the industrial soil which made it possible.

If in these last pages the interweaving of conscious motives and unconscious drives in the lives of one small family has been oversimplified and overemphasized, it is not with the aim of being merely a gossip and, like Autolycus, a snapper-up of unconsider'd trifles, but to reveal in one small group of humans a microcosm of the larger human community. Ideas and ideals are embodied in individuals, who must live out their convictions and translate into their conduct the hidden values—some of them illusory—of their faith.

Bibliography

AGA KHAN: *The Memoirs of Aga Khan: World Enough and Time.* New York, 1954.

RICHARD ALDINGTON: *Life for Life's Sake: A Book of Reminiscences.* New York, 1941.

——: *The Religion of Beauty: Selections from the Aesthetes.* London, 1950.

NOEL GILROY ANNAN: *Leslie Stephen: His Thought and Character in Relation to his Time.* London, 1951.

S. N. BEHRMAN: *Duveen.* New York, 1952.

BERNARD BERENSON: "Painting and National Income." London, *The New Statesman,* January 25, 1947.

——: *Rumor and Reflection.* New York, 1952.

——: *Sketch for a Self-Portrait.* New York, 1949.

MARY (SMITH) BERENSON: *Across the Mediterranean.* London, 1937.

——: *A Modern Pilgrimage.* London, 1932.

——: *A Vicarious Trip to the Barbary Coast.* London, 1938.

——: "Walt Whitman in Camden." (Reminiscences by Mary Costelloe.) London, *Pall Mall Gazette,* December 23, 1886.

HENRY BRYAN BINNS: *A Life of Walt Whitman.* London, 1905.

CYRIL CONNOLLY: "Logan Pearsall Smith." London, *The New Statesman,* March 9, 1946.

ANANDA K. COOMARASWAMY: *Why Exhibit Works of Art?* London, 1943.

BENJAMIN FRANCIS CONN COSTELLOE: *The Abuse of Indulgences.* Catholic Truth Society, London, 1913.

BENJAMIN FRANCIS CONN COSTELLOE: *Aristotle and the Earlier Peripatetics.* Being a Translation from Zeller's "Philosophy of the Greeks" by B. F. C. Costelloe and J. H. Muirhead. London, 1897.

———: *The Church Catholic. An Address Delivered on February 19, 1888, at the South Place Institute, to a Non-Catholic Audience.* London, 1890 (?).

———: *Ethics or Anarchy. An Essay Concerning the Relation of Modern Philosophy to Morals and Religion.* London, 1895.

———: *Frederick Ozanam.* Catholic Truth Society, London, 1892.

———: *The Housing Problem.* A paper read on January 11, 1899, and published by the Manchester Statistical Society. Manchester, 1899.

———: *The Incidence of Taxation. With the Text of the Owner's Rate Bill, and an Appendix on the Equalization of Rates.* London, 1893.

———: *The Mass. A Second Address at the South Place Institute.* Catholic Truth Society. London, 1889.

———: *Notes and Statistics Concerning the Irish Franchise Committee on Irish Affairs.* London, 1884.

———: *The Reading of the Scriptures in Alphonsus O.S.F.C. "The Popular Use of the Scriptures."* London, 1900.

———: *The Reform of the Poor Law.* London, 1891.

———: *The Teaching of the Twelve.* Catholic Truth Society, London, 1895.

J. H. DUVEEN: *The Rise of the House of Duveen.* London, 1957.

RAOUL ERHMANN: "The Chances of a Dialogue: Berenson and Malraux." New York, *Diogenes,* Number 7, 1957.

"MICHAEL FIELD": *Works and Days.* London, 1933.

EDITH FINCH: *Carey Thomas of Bryn Mawr.* New York, 1947.

HELEN WHITALL (THOMAS) FLEXNER: *A Quaker Childhood.* New Haven, Conn., 1940.

ROBERT GATHORNE-HARDY: *Recollections of Logan Pearsall Smith: The Story of a Friendship.* New York, 1950.

HUTCHINS HAPGOOD: *A Victorian in the Modern World.* New York, 1939.

R. F. HARROD: *The Life of John Maynard Keynes: A Personal Biography.* New York, 1951.

FREDERICK HARTT: *Florentine Art Under Fire.* Princeton, New Jersey, 1949.

ALDOUS HUXLEY: *Proper Studies.* London, 1927.

"In Honour of Bernard Berenson." London, *The Burlington Magazine,* July, 1955.

RUFUS M. JONES: *The Later Periods of Quakerism.* 2 vols. New York, 1921.

ALFRED KAZIN: "From an Italian Journal." *The New Partisan Reader (1945–1953).* New York, 1953.

PERCY LUBBOCK: *A Portrait of Edith Wharton.* New York, 1947.

MABEL DODGE LUHAN: *Intimate Memories.* Vol. 2: *European Experiences.* New York, 1935.

IGOR MARKEVITCH: *Made in Italy.* London, 1949.

WILLIAM MOSTYN-OWEN: *Bibliografia di Bernard Berenson. A cura di William Mostyn-Owen.* Milan, 1956.

LADY MOUNT TEMPLE: *Memorial of William Francis Cowper, Baron Mount Temple.* London, 1890.

SIMON NOWELL-SMITH: *The Legend of the Master.* Compiled by Simon Nowell-Smith. New York, 1948.

EDWARD REYNOLDS PEASE: *A History of the Fabian Society.* London, 1925.

ROBERT GEORGE REISNER: *Fakes and Forgeries in the Fine Arts. A Bibliography.* New York, 1950.

WILLIAM ROTHENSTEIN: *Men and Memories: Recollections of William Rothenstein.* 3 vols. Cambridge, 1931–1939.

ALYS (SMITH) RUSSELL: "How to Enjoy Life at Eighty." London, *The Listener,* Nov. 11, 1948.

———: "When The Fabians Were Young." London, *The Listener,* Jan. 27, 1949.

BERTRAND RUSSELL: *Portraits from Memory.* London, 1956.

——— and PATRICIA S. RUSSELL: *The Amberley Papers. The Letters and Diaries of Bertrand Russell's Parents.* 2 vols. New York, 1937.

JOHN RUSSELL: *A Portrait of Logan Pearsall Smith, Drawn from His Letters and Diaries.* London, 1951.

GEORGE SANTAYANA: *The Letters of George Santayana,* Edited, with an Introduction and Commentary, by Daniel Cory. New York, 1955.

GEORGE SANTAYANA: *Little Essays Drawn from the Works of George Santayana by Logan Pearsall Smith,* with the Collaboration of the Author. New York, 1921.

——: *Persons and Places.* Vol. 1: *The Background of My Life.* Vol. 2: *The Middle Span.* Vol. 3: *My Host the World.* New York, 1944–1953.

ROLLO G. SILVER: "The Bright Particular Star." (Letters of Walt Whitman to Mary Smith Costelloe.) New York, *The Colophon:* New Series, No. 2, 1937.

HANNAH WHITALL SMITH: *Philadelphia Quaker: The Letters of Hannah Whitall Smith.* Edited by her son Logan Pearsall Smith. With a Biographical Preface by Robert Gathorne-Hardy. New York, 1949.

——: *Religious Fanaticism.* Edited, with an Introduction, by Ray Strachey. London, 1928.

LOGAN PEARSALL SMITH: *All Trivia (Trivia, More Trivia, Afterthoughts, Last Words).* New York, 1945.

——: *English Idioms.* S.P.E. 1923.

——: *The English Language.* London, 1942.

——: *Fine Writing.* (S.P.E. Tract No. XLVI.) Oxford, 1936.

——: *Milton and His Modern Critics.* London, 1941.

——: *On Reading Shakespeare.* London, 1933.

——: *The Papers of Logan Pearsall Smith,* writer and scholar, including 209 letters of Smith to various members of his family, dated 1883–1938, concerning travel, literature, gossip and society; 14 letters of Henry James to Smith, dated 1892, 1912–1914; 33 letters of George Santayana to Smith, dated 1917–1933, 1938; letters of Robert Bridges; the correspondence of Virginia Woolf and Smith; and various literary manuscripts of Smith, including his notes for "Unpublished Trivia" and *Unforgotten Years.* Washington, D. C., The Library of Congress: Manuscript Division.

——: *Reperusals and Recollections.* London, 1936.

——: *Robert Bridges, Recollections.* (S.P.E. Tract No. XXXV.) Oxford, 1931.

——: "Saved from the Salvage." London, *Horizon.* March 1943.

——: "Slices of Cake." London, *The New Statesman.* June 5, 1943.

LOGAN PEARSALL SMITH: *A Treasury of English Aphorisms.* London, 1928.

———: *A Treasury of English Prose.* London, 1947.

———: *Unforgotten Years.* Boston, 1939.

ELIZABETH SPRIGG: *Gertrude Stein.* London, 1957.

KARIN (COSTELLOE) STEPHEN: *The Misuse of Mind: A Study of Bergson's Attack on Intellectualism.* London, 1922.

———: *Psychoanalysis and Medicine: A Study of the Wish to Fall Ill.* Cambridge, 1933.

LEO STEIN: *Journey into the Self: Being the Letters, Papers and Journals of Leo Stein.* New York, 1950.

RACHEL (RAY) (COSTELLOE) STRACHEY: *The Cause: A Short History of the Woman's Movement in Great Britain.* London, 1928.

———: *Frances Willard, Her Life and Work.* London, 1912.

———: *A Quaker Grandmother.* New York, 1914.

———: *Shaken by the Wind: A Story of Fanaticism.* London, 1927.

———: *The World at Eighteen.* London, 1907.

HORACE TRAUBEL: *With Walt Whitman in Camden.* 4 vols. Boston, New York, Philadelphia, 1906–1953.

GIULIANA ARTOM TREVES: *The Golden Ring: The Anglo-Florentines, 1847–1862.* Translated by Sylvia Sprigge. London, 1956.

BENJAMIN BRECKINRIDGE WARFIELD: *Studies in Perfectionism.* 2 vols. New York, 1931.

BEATRICE (POTTER) WEBB: *My Apprenticeship.* London, 1926. *Our Partnership.* London, 1948. *Diaries 1912–1924.* London, 1952.

WLADIMIR WEIDLÉ: *Les Abeilles d'Aristée: Essai sur le Destin Actuel des Lettres et des Arts.* Paris, 1955.

EDITH WHARTON: *A Backward Glance.* London and New York, 1934.

JAMES WHITALL: *English Years.* New York, 1935.

WHITALL FAMILY: *The Whitall Family of Red Bank.* Bulletin of the Gloucester County Historical Society, Vol. 4, No. 3, March 1954.

ALAN WOOD: *Bertrand Russell: The Passionate Skeptic.* New York, 1958.

Zu unserem Oktoberheft, Bernard Berenson. Zurich: *Du: schweizerische Monatsschrift.* October, 1954 (tributes and photographs).

Index

ABOUT THE AUTHOR

For ten years or more ROBERT ALLERTON PARKER was a regular contributor to such periodicals as *Current Opinion, Arts and Decoration, The Arts* and *International Studio.* He served also as drama critic for the weekly *Independent.* In 1935 he published the first full-length biography of John Humphrey Noyes, founder of the controversial Oneida Community. This was followed by an "anthropological study" of the Father Divine movement.

In pursuit of his studies of popular religious movements, Mr. Parker became a friend and student of the late Ananda K. Coomaraswamy, of the Boston Museum of Fine Arts, and introduced a volume of the latter's essays under the title of *Am I My Brother's Keeper?* It was during his research for his first volume that Mr. Parker discovered the amazing Smith family.

Born in Alameda, Calif., Mr. Parker is a graduate of the University of California at Berkeley. He lives in New York City, where his wife, professionally known as Jessica Daves, is editor-in-chief of *Vogue.*